MW00356450

Queer Embodiment

**Expanding Frontiers: Interdisciplinary Approaches
to Studies of Women, Gender, and Sexuality**

SERIES EDITORS:
Karen J. Leong
Andrea Smith

Queer Embodiment

Monstrosity, Medical Violence,
and Intersex Experience

HILARY MALATINO

University of Nebraska Press | Lincoln

Portions of chapter 1 originally appeared as "Queer Monsters: Foucault, 'Hermaphroditism,' and Disability Studies" in *The Imperfect Historian: Disability Histories in Europe*, edited by Sebastian Barsch, Anne Klein, and Pieter Verstraete (Frankfurt am Main: Peter Lang, 2013): 113–32.

Portions of chapter 4 originally appeared as "Gone, Missing: Queering and Racializing Absence in Trans and Intersex Archives" in *Queer Feminist Science Studies Reader*, edited by Cyd Cippola, Kristina Gupta, David Rubin, and Angela Willey (Seattle: University of Washington Press, 2017): 157–72.

Portions of chapter 6 originally appeared as "Nomad Science" in TSQ: *Transgender Studies Quarterly* 1, nos. 1–2 (2014): 138–41. © Duke University Press. Republished by permission of the publisher.

Library of Congress Cataloging-in-Publication Data
Names: Malatino, Hilary, author.
Title: Queer embodiment: monstrosity, medical violence, and intersex experience/ Hilary Malatino.
Description: Lincoln: University of Nebraska Press, [2019] | Series: Expanding frontiers: interdisciplinary approaches to studies of women, gender, and sexuality | Includes bibliographical references and index.
Identifiers: LCCN 2018023932
ISBN 9780803295933 (cloth: alk. paper)
ISBN 9781496213716 (epub)
ISBN 9781496213723 (mobi)
ISBN 9781496213730 (pdf)
Subjects: LCSH: Intersex people—Identity. | Human body—Social aspects. | Queer theory.
Classification: LCC HQ78 M35 2019 | DDC 306.7601—dc23
LC record available at https://lccn.loc.gov/2018023932

Designed and set in Arno Pro by L. Auten.

For Libby and Tobias, without whom most everything would be much less possible and much less magical.

CONTENTS

ILLUSTRATIONS

ACKNOWLEDGMENTS

The completion of this book is due to an extensive network of folks who kept me buoyant, inspired, and engaged in the midst of turbulent political times. My advisor, María Lugones, has taught me everything I know about infrapolitics, agency, and the hard work of building deep, resistant coalition. This book would have been impossible to conceive of without her friendship, support, and invaluable criticism. The community of radical intersectional intellectuals that emerged out of the crucible of the Philosophy, Interpretation, and Culture program at Binghamton University, where I completed my PhD, fostered collaborations, connections, and conversations that have informed this work in ways too numerous to count. Among them are Pedro DiPietro, Shireen Roshanravan, James K. Stanescu, Ovidiu Tichindeleanu, Xhercis Méndez, Nikolay Karkov, Carol Tushabe, Maria Chaves, Jen-Feng Kuo, Gabriela Veronelli, Gabriel Piser, and Josh Franco; their brilliance and generosity of spirit is a constant source of inspiration, and I'm incredibly lucky to count them among my friends and interlocutors. The other members of my committee, John Tagg and William Haver, greatly enriched the readings of theory and visual culture extant in this manuscript, and their rigor and humor enlivened my time in graduate school. Conversations and courses with Tom McDonough, Josh Price, and Deborah Elliston transformed my thinking about embodiment, representation, and possible forms of political resistance. My earliest engagements with thinking through intersex experience were supported by my undergraduate mentors at Florida Atlantic University—Jane Caputi, Ayşe Papatya Bucak, and Deborah Covino. They taught this first-generation student so much about committing to a life of writing, teaching, and research and demystified academia in ways that remain deeply significant.

Acknowledgments

The faculty, graduate, and undergraduate students in the Department of Gender Studies at Indiana University provided invaluable intellectual, queer, and feminist community during my time there as a postdoctoral fellow. Special thanks goes to Karma Lochrie, Jen Maher, Claudia Berger, Colin Johnson, Brenda Weber, Lindsey Breitwieser, Jocelyne Bartram, Jessica Hille, Nick Clarkson, Josie Leimbach, and Jae Basiliere. Shawn Wilson, associate director of collections at the Kinsey Institute at Indiana University, continues to be a great help.

I had the great pleasure of spending four years in the Blue Ridge Mountains as the assistant director of the Women's Studies program at East Tennessee State University. The time I spent in those mountains has deepened my love of the wild and my commitment to advocating for rural and southern trans, queer, and intersex folks. The program director at ETSU, Phyllis Thompson, was not only a wonderful interlocutor, co-conspirator, and colleague during my time there but has become one of my closest friends. I am inspired by, and aspire to, her intensity of commitment, humility, generosity, and institutional savvy. Jamie Branam Kridler, Stacey Williams, Katherine Weiss, Martha Copp, Rebekah Byrd, and many others provided community, support, and friendship during my time in the Appalachian South. I worked with too many inspiring students to name here (but they know who they are).

My colleagues in the Department of Women's, Gender, and Sexuality Studies and the Rock Ethics Institute at Penn State have been incredible, welcoming me graciously, sparking new dialogues, and demonstrating a deep and significant commitment to the flourishing of interdisciplinary, intersectional queer, trans, intersex, and nonbinary scholarship. Among those who have been, and continue to be, wonderful colleagues, mentors, and interlocutors are Melissa Wright, Alicia Decker, Terri Vescio, Jennifer Wagner-Lawlor, Rosemary Jolly, Lori Ginzberg, Carolyn Sachs, Lise Nelson, Jes Matsick, Nancy Tuana, Erin Heidt-Forsythe, Jill Wood, Laurie Spielvogel, Bénédicte Monicat, Ariane Cruz, Tracy Rutler, Ted Toadvine, Eduardo Mendieta, Ben Jones, Caitlin Grady, Jonathan Marks, and Francisco Javier López Frías.

I want to thank Susan Stryker, Paisley Currah, and all of the folks involved with the founding and operation of TSQ for giving some of my recent work a home and for contributing invaluably to the support and transformation of trans scholarship. Thanks to Morgan Holmes, editor of the foundational intersex studies reader *Critical Intersex*, for allowing my work to dwell in that volume. Her empathic and experientially grounded scholarship on intersex issues continues to inform and transform my thinking. Thanks to Eliza Steinbock for chasing me down at the National Women's Studies Association Conference to talk over intersections of trans studies, post-humanism, and intersex issues, for suggesting my work for a special issue of *Angelaki*, and for being brilliant and driven to produce a critical trans scholarly community. Thanks to all the folks on the executive board of the Southeastern Women's Studies Association—Jennifer Purvis, Kim Hall, Sushmita Chatterjee, Kelly Finley, Coral Wayland, Laura Tamberelli, Sydney Richardson, and Heather Brown—for being a joy to work with and for providing such incredibly supportive, motivating spaces to advance feminist thought in the South.

Much gratitude to Amos Mac, Ginger Brooks Takahashi, and Del LaGrace Volcano for their inspiring and provocative art practice and for their willingness to let me share images of their work in this volume.

Alicia Christensen, my editor at University of Nebraska Press, has been excellent. Her vision for the Expanding Frontiers book series has ensured that this book is in wonderful intellectual company. Thanks also to the series editors and advisory board. My gratitude extends to the anonymous readers of this manuscript for their invaluable rounds of commentary. This book is much better because of them. Thanks also to my undergraduate research assistant Arianna Hall, who provided useful commentary and assistance on the manuscript in its final stages.

I'd be lost without my magnificent and extensive family, chosen and otherwise. Thank you for all the backyard fires, camping adventures, long meals, porch hangs, dance parties, road trips, dive bar sojourns, game nights, and laughter. Thanks to Homoclimbtastic, and the co-organizers of our annual climbing convention, for carving space for queer and trans folks in adventure sports and for providing a much-needed reprieve where every June I can be surrounded by dozens of strong, sexy, whip-smart, and hilarious queer and trans athletes in the wilds of West Virginia. Deep gratitude to my mother, Laurie Garion, for making my life possible and for continuing to be a constant source of support, wisdom, really good food, and even better debate. My father, James Malatino, provided a whole lot of levity, dad jokes, pizza, and jam sessions while I worked on this manuscript, and for that I am extraordinarily grateful. Infinite love to my lifelong best friend, Tobias Packer, for showing up on my doorstep at the age of five and asking if the new kid could come out to play and for sticking by my side ever since. The earliest beginnings of this manuscript can be found in our late-night conversations behind the neighborhood 7-Eleven over coffee and stolen cigarettes.

Finally, the most enormous thank you to my partner, C. M. Libby: for crisscrossing the country with me (with our ever-growing family of non-human kin in tow), for the many hours spent reading and rereading this manuscript, for how hard she makes me laugh, for her endless and indefatigable patience, and for her transformative practice of loving. Her genius, generosity, grace, and good humor are indelibly imprinted on each of these pages, and I am so enormously privileged to have lucked into meeting her one quiet, late summer night many years ago in the Midwest.

Queer Embodiment

Introduction

Queer Embodiment: Monstrosity, Medical Violence, and Intersex Experience is a book about intersex experience written by an intersex person. It is not, like most books about intersex experience written by intersex people—of which there are very few to begin with—an autobiography, at least not in any straightforward sense. It draws on work in critical theory, queer theory, feminist philosophy, and science and technology studies. It does so because these fields have helped me more adequately understand and theorize the fraught experience that is being an intersex person in this contemporary moment in North America. In other words, the intellectual work done by this book is also work that felt personally necessary in order begin to grasp *who* and *what* I am. This means that *Queer Embodiment* is centrally preoccupied with the question of intersex ontology: what is it to be intersex? This is no easy question to answer, at least not for me: I have found that being intersex is complicatedly comprised of how modern and contemporary medical and scientific epistemologies have interpreted and diagnosed intersex conditions; how intersex activists have contested those definitions; how certain intellectuals have interrogated intersexuality to make broader points about contemporary understandings of pathology, queerness, sexed embodiment, and technoscientific methods of somatic normalization; and how actually existing intersex people have fought for and theorized ways of being in the world. Because of this, the book is an amalgam of genres and methods: part autobiography, part theory, part medical genealogy. I think of it as a monstrous assemblage, a hybrid project that has had to reject concepts of disciplinary purity and propriety to explore phenomena that trouble some of our most basic taxonomic and classificatory distinctions:

male and female, the pathological and the healthy, the normal and the abnormal, the biological and the technological.

I was at a conference in September 2017 where a presenter with an intersex condition responded to an audience question about the genetic inheritability of such conditions with the quip that *intersex* "is just a word." I understood them to mean that intersex is a deliberate human invention that expeditiously unites a large variety of congenital quirks of sexed being under a big tent (so if you want to know about genetic inheritability, you should just ask about a specific condition). While I was sympathetic to their call for specificity, I bristled at their claim. *Intersex* is a word, yes, but it is not "just a word." No word is. One of the things this book does is trace the work that certain words (like *intersex, hermaphrodite, male, female*) do: their material impacts, the ways they function in the translation of embodied experience, and the integral role they play in shifting, transforming, generating, and dismantling technoscientific knowledges and practices, as well as communities and consortiums of people negotiating these knowledges and practices.

This book examines what I call queer corporealities: bodies that don't cohere according to cis-centric, sexually dimorphic, ableist conceptions of somatic normalcy. I focus in particular on intersex bodies and examine their interarticulation with biomedical technologies and medicoscientific understandings of gender pathology. My focus throughout is on the ways in which the ontology of gender difference developed by the architects of modern sexology is consistently in tension with the embodied experience of intersex, trans, nonbinary, and gender-nonconforming subjects.

Queer Embodiment has two substantive components. The first part of the book deploys a genealogical methodology drawn from the work of Michel Foucault to track the divergent and often piecemeal biographies of intersex subjects found in biomedical archives, natural histories, and philosophical accounts (ranging from the early modern to the contemporary), developing a deep, variegated, and textured tale of the epistemological shifts that have informed how queerly built bodies are construed within current biomedical practice. The second part asks what this genealogy might mean, in existential terms, for contemporary subjects diagnosed with one of the many conditions that fall beneath the umbrella of intersexuality (which is also referred to as "disorders of sex development" or "differences of sex development," and commonly abbreviated as DSD), as well as those whose lives are shaped by and through grappling with other, closely related corporeal or psychosomatic queernesses, with varied trans subjectivities figuring chief among these.

This work is situated within the field of critical intersex studies, which has cohered only recently as a discrete academic specialization, has points of overlap with the realms of medical ethics and medical humanities, gender studies, and science and technology studies, and has been shaped by two fundamental, often interwoven, foci: the construction of medical histories of intersexuality and the generation of activist interventions in the field of contemporary intersex diagnosis and treatment. The foundational works in the field of intersex studies—Anne Fausto-Sterling's *Sexing the Body*, Alice Dreger's *Hermaphrodites and the Medical Invention of Sex*, Morgan Holmes's *Intersex: A Perilous Difference*, Elizabeth Reis's *Bodies in Doubt: An American History of Intersex*, and Katrina Karkazis's *Fixing Sex: Intersex, Medical Authority, and Lived Experience*—are compelling examples of the intellectual provocation and political effectivity of such interweavings. While my work is deeply influenced by, dialogues with, and critically examines these works, it charts different connections and is concerned less with intersexuality as an epistemological object of study (i.e., what intersexuality *is and has been*) and more with the ideological, political, and conceptual work that intersexuality *does*, in both its material and its figural and tropological dimensions. Put differently, I trace the itinerancies of intersexuality: I follow intersexuality in order to see where it goes, how it works, what arguments, assertions, and understandings of gender, sex, and sexuality it enables and disables. In doing so I construe intersexuality as something other than the product of a positivist pathology whose roots must be discovered and clarified in order for treatment to be reconsidered and reformed. Rather, I posit it as a philosophical and scientific concept that powerfully constructs our notions of subjective legibility, gendered realness, and sexed materiality.

The generative insight for the work is this: what it means and has meant to have a legible body in the West—at least since the early modern period—has relied, in ways both straightforward and subtle, on the utilization of intersex bodies as impossible objects, as limit-figures that become interred in the ground upon which legitimate, recognizable, and acceptable sexed bodies are built. Intersex bodies thus become a figure whose specter is called forth periodically in order to be disavowed, derealized, and delegitimated once more. I focus on the movement of intersex bodies from the realm of the monstrous to the realm of the abnormal—an uneven process spanning a few hundred years, beginning with the development of teratological med-icine in the sixteenth century and culminating in the recent consolidation of intersex conditions under the diagnostic umbrella of disorders of sex development—with a particular emphasis on early to mid-twentieth-century U.S. and western European sexology. I focus on this period because it is the historical moment wherein intersex conditions began to be figured as "pseudohermaphroditic"—that is, not "truly" mixed-sex conditions—as well as the moment wherein what we now consider homosexual identities were termed manifestations of "psychic hermaphroditism." Reading these two transformations in medical terminology allows me to consider the ways in which sexed mixity was relegated to the realm of the psychic at the same moment that it was construed as a biological impossibility. In other words, one could be born not hermaphroditic but only an "unfinished" man or woman, yet one *could* manifest a psychological disorder characterized by understanding—contra supposed biological fact—one's experience of embodied desire as merging elements of male and female. Sexed mixity becomes a mental rather than material phenomena.

This development presages the rift between biological sex and gen-der identity that was consolidated by U.S. sexologist John Money in the 1950s—a rift that became foundational for the fields of gender studies and queer theory. Mapping these complex interchanges between the realms of natural philosophy, medicoscientific research on gender deviance and congenital abnormality, and the development of contemporary theoriza-tions of queer embodiment and the ontology of gender is one of the central aims of the genealogical portion of this book. While the so-called linguistic turn taken by feminist and queer theory throughout the 1980s and 1990s sometimes reified and further entrenched this split between the psychic and the material, the recent turn toward a materialist approach enacted by theorists often grouped together as feminist new materialists—Donna Haraway, Elizabeth Grosz, and Karen Barad, in particular—proves a rich site of inquiry that I draw upon to make sense of queer corporealities beyond the limited, often reductive meanings assigned to them within the epistemes of modern medical science. The latter part of the manuscript takes up these theorists, in conjunction with the work of Gilles Deleuze and Félix Guattari, in order to develop a queerer ontology of gendered being that is both affectively oriented and posthumanist.

The theoretical labor of this project is informed by a desire to articulate the connections between trans studies and intersex studies through reconsidering the ontology of gendered being that posits gender as a processual, intra-active becoming. This foregrounding of ontological questions is also structured by another desire—a yearning to develop a deeper coalitional politic between trans and intersex subjects that can clearly articulate and amplify the conflicts between reductive pathological understandings of queer corporealities and the ulterior, alternative logics of embodiment developed in trans, nonbinary, genderqueer, genderfluid, and gender-inclusive political and infrapolitical spaces.

While working on this book, I had the privilege of spending significant time at the Kinsey Institute for Research in Sex, Gender, and Reproduction, which contains the largest archive of sexological scholarship in the United States. The Kinsey Institute houses the papers of multiple figures integral to the development of contemporary institutional understandings of intersex and trans identity, John Money and Harry Benjamin among them. In examining this material, particularly the case studies and patient-physician correspondence I've discovered therein, my focus shifted from mapping out the epistemologies of gender and gender nonconformance developed by these practitioners to teasing out the resistance that was coincident with the development of medical intelligibilities of intersex, trans, and gender-nonconforming subjects. There is manifest contestation throughout this archive, ranging from outright anger at the medical practitioners regarding the gatekeeping practices that barred access to technologies of gender transition for certain trans subjects, to intense disagreement with the proposal of gender reassignment and genital reconstruction recommended for certain intersex patients, some of whom went AWOL and refused any further contact with the gender clinics operated by these sexological luminaries.

I think of my approach as a way of encountering these archives from below, as one of the minoritized subjects whose body and life story has been integral to the generation of institutionally hegemonic understandings of queer corporealities but whose significant contestation to these hegemonic understandings has been placed under erasure. To ameliorate this erasure, *Queer Embodiment* amplifies the resistant traces I encounter amid historical accounts of intersex and trans embodiment. I want to demonstrate that intersex and trans folks often understand the experience of queer embodiment in a much more radically destabilizing manner than the boiled-down etiologies of deviance developed by twentieth-century sexologists. Approaching the archive from below and in conversation with my own experience of intersex embodiment allows me to develop a counternarrative that runs parallel to institutional accounts of intersex and trans embodiment.

Queer Embodiment seeks to do something other than aid in medical reform and further flesh out the historical account of intersexuality, noble though these aims are. Rather, I aim to establish the centrality of intersexuality to modern medicoscientific accounts of human embodiment and materiality and to chart the historical and contemporary links between the genealogy of intersexuality and the development of other ostensible pathologies of gender, sex, and sexuality. Through careful archival examination and close literary and philosophical analysis, I argue that intersexuality is a major conceptual center of queerness, the figure that nonnormative genders and desires are, and have been historically, understood through and in relation to. Simply put, I claim that medical, scientific, and philosophical discourse on intersexuality is at the very root of contemporary understandings of sexed selfhood. My greatest hopes for the book are that it performs an intervention in queer and gender studies that ameliorates the frequent sidelining of intersex and trans concerns; that it maps out some ground for potential political and intellectual collaboration between trans studies and intersex studies; that it encourages the development of interdisciplinary scientific literacies within gender and sexuality studies through making a case for the centrality and profound effects of medicoscientific discourses in the everyday lives of intersex, trans, and queer folks; and that it renders intersex issues more legible to audiences within and beyond the academy through exploring the wide-ranging implications of the concepts of corporeal sexual normality and abnormality.

By way of organization, this book is animated by two linked questions: How did intersexuality sediment as an anomalous type of bodily composition that needed to be corrected? How can we contest that understanding of intersexuality as we develop ways of thinking and enacting gendered embodiment otherwise? The first portion of the book is concerned with the former question and builds a critical genealogy of gender nonconformance and corporeal queerness. The second portion dwells on the construction of ways out, on emergent possibilities of gendered becoming beyond the redundancies of taxonomic identities. I begin the book with a prologue that meditates on the intellectual resources that were germinative for the project, detailing how my long engagement with the work of Anne Fausto-Sterling, Judith Butler, and Michel Foucault informs the ways I've come to terms with the phenomenon of being intersex.

The first chapter, "Queer Monsters: Michel Foucault and Herculine Barbin," marks the beginning of an effort to read intersex archives—the heteroclite, loosely agglomerated, and relatively scant discursive trails left by intersex lives—from below, as a queer feminist intellectual and as intersex myself. I perform an intensive and empathic close reading of the memoir of Herculine Barbin, the now-infamous nineteenth-century French hermaphrodite whose journals and medical dossiers Michel Foucault culled from the annals of French medicine and popularized as an intimate document attesting to a watershed moment in the formation and authoritative rise of biological explanations of sex and sexuality. In a sense, I am seeking a way to come to terms with the suicide that concludes this memoir, inquiring after the forces at work that rendered Barbin's life so tragically unlivable. This means attempting to reconstruct the intellectual, scientific, and political milieus that gave such conflicting senses to Herculine's queer corporeality. In mapping this epistemological-cum-cultural topos, I emphasize the radicality of the nineteenth-century invention of biological sexual dimorphism and situate the ascendancy of this concept as key to understanding Herculine Barbin's repeated lament of ontological impossibility—that is, the sense that she belonged nowhere on earth. I understand Herculine as a being who sought a way to understand herself beyond notions of bad mimesis, dissimulation, bodily entrapment, or teleological modes of gendered becoming.

I also propose two methods for reading Foucault's interest in hermaphroditism. The first focuses on the function of hermaphroditism in his formulation of the interwoven concepts of governmentality and biopolitics; the second analyzes hermaphroditism insofar as it informs his work on ascesis, self-constitution, and political resistance. On the first reading, the discursive traces of hermaphroditic subjects that Foucault exhumes from the French medical and juridical archives work illustratively, dramatizing the transformation of a discourse on the legitimacy of sexed mixity wherein "authentic" hermaphroditism is possible to one concerned with discerning the "true"—that is, dimorphic—sex of a body. The intersex body works, in this type of analysis, as a dense node wherein techniques of governmentality become interwoven with reproductive futurism, a burgeoning modern biopolitics of sexual dimorphism, and a proliferation of technologies of corporeal modification created for morphological normalization. The second mode of analysis reads Foucault as interested in these piecemeal biographies of hermaphroditic subjects because they offer traces of lives shaped, at least in part, by pleasures experienced by a subject shaped within a "happy limbo of non-identity" wherein one can "be without a definite sex" without being "deprived of the delights . . . experienced in not having one."[1] With this second approach the hermaphroditic body is reconceived as a line of flight, a repository of alternative sexual-social possibilities for ascetic self-construction within and against the structures of heteronormative sexual dimorphism. I argue for reading these two interpretive impulses as interwoven with one another and use this strategy throughout the rest of the book to consider the complicated coincidence of the biopolitical regulation of queer corporealities and trans and intersex logics of embodiment that definitively exceed these regulative processes.

The second chapter, "Impossible Existences: Intersex and 'Disorders of Sex Development,'" transports us from an engagement with the violence inherent in the invention of sexual dimorphism into more contemporary terrain while still keeping central the question of violence and the desirable difficulty of inhabiting nonbinary understandings of embodiment. I examine an apparent conflict between feminist and queer theory's use of the phenomenon of intersexuality and the newly reworked medical protocol for a more ethical treatment of intersex patients. While intersex conditions have been consistently used to encourage dialogue on the constructed nature of not only gender but also biological sex and as a means of furthering queer and feminist calls for the reworking of epistemologies of sex and gender, those nonprofits and activists most publicly involved in intersex medical reform increasingly cite the gendered normalcy of intersex folks as a way of sanctioning a return to the language of disorder within the diagnostic nomenclature used to identify intersex conditions. Laying out the history of U.S.-based intersex activism, primarily its turn from building allegiances with queer movements to focusing on a more limited interface with the medical world, I then chart the terms of contemporary debates over the recent embrace of *disorders of sex development* as the standard diagnostic term for intersex conditions as taken up by queer theorists, medical historians, feminist philosophers, and disability rights activists. I conclude with an argument for the political importance of refusing the language of disorder in instances of corporeal queerness, emphasizing the idea that this shift in nomenclature indexes a tendency to circumscribe the field of important political and cultural gender trouble intersex bodies are able to make.

The following chapter, "Gone, Missing: Queering and Racializing Absence in Trans and Intersex Archives," is a substantive engagement with the archival research I've undertaken at the Kinsey Institute. Based on a reading of case studies, patient testimony, and patient-doctor correspondence from both intersex and trans subjects, spanning from the early 1950s—when significant, clinic-based, quantitative sexological research on intersexuality and what came to be known as gender identity disorders gained steam in the United States—to the early 1980s, I focus on the tensions and conflicts evident in the articulation of medical etiologies of gender pathology and the self-understandings and experiential knowledges of trans and intersex subjects. I tease out two dominant tropes that emerge from this literature. The first is the repeated characterization of the medical practitioners able to green-light gender reassignment technologies as saviors, beings capable of bestowing life to people in dire existential circumstances, often shaped by grappling with suicide, poverty, social disenfranchisement, and significant quotidian violence. The second is the phenomenon of patient disappearance, often following a significant epistemological clash over the operations of medicalized gender reassignment or otherwise prompted by substantial disappointment upon realizing the financial and geographical limitations that have shaped access to technologies of gender transition. I pose three speculative questions to initiate analysis of these tropes: can we read these tropes as connected through a secularized loss of faith in the capacities of medicoscientific gender alteration? If so, what motivates this loss of faith? Finally, what happens after these research subjects become lost to the sexological establishment, and what are the consequences of this loss for the development of contemporary understandings of gender pathology, deviance, and nonconformance? I posit these questions to examine the deep historical exclusivity upon which current etiologies of transsexuality and current recommendations for intersex treatment are built. If the U.S. sexological archive is marked by the disappearance of beings unable to access or in disagreement with the gatekeeping protocols of gender assignation and reassignment, then contemporary hegemonic understandings of intersex and trans subjects are haunted by these minoritized queer specters. Parsing the ramifications of this haunting allows contemporary scholars in trans and intersex studies to develop a prehistory that helps cognize the contemporary exclusion of poor, genderqueer, and otherwise nonnormative trans and intersex folks from healthcare access and gender-confirming medicoscientific procedures.

At this point, the book takes a turn toward the aesthetic while continuing to hew closely to the Kinsey archival materials. In "Black Bar, Queer Gaze: Medical Photography and the Re-visioning of Queer Corporealities," I examine practices of medical visuality, particularly anatomical and histological photography, in the establishment of the corporeal facts of intersexuality. In this practice, the notions of transparency, objectivity, and pure denotation that govern hegemonic conceptions of photographic practice dovetail with the vested medicoscientific mission to establish the facts of ontological sex, but this mission is decidedly complicated by the sheer undecidability of certain images of intersex bodies. I chart tropic shifts in the medical photodocumentation of intersexuality that testify both to the frantic search for an absolute, material determinant of true sex in the early to mid-twentieth century as well as a later shift to a teleological notion of sexed development, precipitated by new discoveries in hormonal and surgical technologies that allowed for increasing refinement and technical control in the building of proper—that is, heteronormative and sexually dimorphic—men and women. Central to this chapter is an applied analysis of the Deleuzo-Guattarian concept of faciality that examines the function of the black bar utilized so often to block the faces of intersex folks undergoing medical photodocumentation. I argue that this black bar desubjectifies the intersex person, working as a visual trope that figures the ontological caesura intersex beings inhabit while undergoing gender assignment. I also address the ways in which these imaging practices shore up the authority of the doctor as a scientific modest witness, that figure Haraway has theorized as the arbiter of the universal fact, a position secured by possessing a corporeality that, contra Butler, *doesn't matter*, that doesn't impede or compromise processes of transparent truth-production.[2] Finally, I turn to contemporary queer and trans artistic practice—in particular, the mixed-media work of the queer collective LTTR (Lesbians to the Rescue) and the photographs of Amos Mac and Del LaGrace Volcano—in order to chart an alternative trajectory of witnessing queer corporealities that counters the mythification, clinical detachment, and social and scientific abhorrence that has shaped typical perceptions of queer corporealities. This counter-archive of intersex and trans imaging practices is shaped by a passionate attachment to these nonnormative embodiments. I read these art objects as indicative of a queer embrace of the interstitial, a refusal of sexed and gendered discourses of lack, passivity, and genital and psychosexual imma-turity in favor of an embrace of bodies in their complex, textured, malleable, and mutating surfaces. They mark a double distancing—not only from normative popular and biomedical readings of intersex bodies but from certain historic strands of feminist and lesbian artistic praxis, particularly what art historians Faith Wilding and Miriam Schapiro have termed cunt art, a generic convention best represented by Tee Corinne's early drawings and Judy Chicago's deployment of what she termed central core imagery.[3] I trace a feedback loop between the articulation of intersex and trans logics of embodiment and transformations in feminist art practice that has the potential to profoundly shift the politics of corporeal perception, gendered legibility, and queer communal imaginaries.

The final two chapters of the book, "State Science: Biopolitics and the Medicalization of Gender Nonconformance" and "Toward Coalition: Becoming, Monstrosity, and Sexed Embodiment," sketch out a concept of *queer becoming* as a form of radical political coalition. In these chapters, I explore the ontological and political ramifications of Gilles Deleuze and Félix Guattari's theorization of becoming in *A Thousand Plateaus*. Becoming is counterposed to taxonomic conceptions of being that operate through the establishment of integral, ostensibly essential traits that are then used for categorization—the dominant logic of scientific classifi-cation but also, importantly, the dominant logic of certain iterations of identity politics.

As a way into this exploration of Deleuzo-Guattarian becoming, I pro-vide a close analysis of their paired concepts of minor (which they also call "nomad") science and state science, exploring their amenability to cognizing the different ways in which gender nonconformance has been understood. These terms offer two distinct, incommensurable ways of thinking about bodily matter and embodied form. Minor science empha-sizes the malleable, fluid, and metamorphic nature of being, while state science conceptualizes being as solid, essential, and unchanging. Given the anti-essentialist focus of minor science, it is a particularly helpful concept in thinking transgender, transsexual, and gender-nonconforming modes of embodiment, particularly those that exceed or actively contest medical understandings of trans identity. Conversely, state science is a useful heu-ristic for considering the medical and psychiatric pathologization of trans and gender-nonconforming subjects.

Although the medicalization of gender nonconformance has developed guidelines and protocol for transition and would thus seem to be linked to a more fluid conception of gender, these practical protocols are nevertheless built upon conservative typologies of maleness and femaleness. They are not concerned with transition as a (potentially always unfinished) process but rather with the creation and suturing of firmly delimited, discrete, and binary-gendered entities. A nomad science of transition, however, would focus on the specific, resistant, and creative ways in which trans, intersex, and gender-nonconforming subjects reinvent and reconstruct themselves in manners irreducible to the medical logic of transition.

In the final chapter of the book, I explore the resonance between Deleuzo-Guattarian becoming and Karen Barad's theory of agential intra-action,[4] which draws on the ways in which feminist science studies has disrupted the dyads of nature/culture and subject/object in order to develop a deeply situational and relational understanding of matter. In Barad's compelling account, matter—including but not limited to human corporealities—is figured as an agent in deep intra-action (what we can also call co-constitutive becoming) with other phenomena. Pairing these insights with Deleuze and Guattari's thinking on the rhizomatic organization of the body and the ways that this informs their nonbinary, anti-essential theorization of *n-sexes*, I articulate the ways in which commonsense understandings of biological sex may be thought of as examples of incorporeal transformation: that is, the fabrication of a dimorphic understanding of corporeality through a set of order-words that are not at all commensurable with the lived realities of the body. I read becoming as a way to valorize monstrosity, a means of affirming gendered embodiment as always already made, mutable, nonsovereign, intra-active, and in excess of the regulatory logics of the human.

Between each chapter is a short, autobiographical vignette meant to encourage the reader to think through the connections between queer, trans, and otherwise critical theories and the lived experience of intersex embodiment. The work done in this book is intimately interwoven with the two decades of my life that I've spent coming to terms with being intersex, investigating what that means in everyday life and how that resonates in the communities in which I am embedded and transformed by. As heady as some of the theoretical work may seem, it has emerged from a set of quotidian traumas and difficult translations of intersex experience; it is grounded in my own partial perspective and an attempt to respond to, and make sense of, a long history of erasure of intersex experience. I seek a world wherein intersex embodiment isn't understood as being in need of correction, where gender is dignified as the complex, variegated, and diverse phenomenon that it actually is, where the medical establishment works to affirm and support intersex, trans, and gender-nonconforming folks, and respects the complexities of our identities.

Prologue

Neither/Nor (Notes on Theory and Livability)

There is nothing radical about common sense.

—Judith Butler, *Gender Trouble*

In the midst of the self-overcoming movement of
genealogy, I no longer felt compelled to know, once
and for all, the essence of anything. And in the dissipa-
tion of that all-encompassing organizing compulsion,
other concerns gained strength.

—Ladelle McWhorter, *Bodies and Pleasures*

I was sixteen when I first received an intersex diagnosis, though that wasn't
the terminology used. I had gone to a general practitioner—I hesitate to say
"my" general practitioner, as regular physician visits were an irregularity in
the hovering-around-the-poverty-line world of my adolescence—to find
out why I hadn't begun to menstruate. After multiple visits, bloodwork,
and trips to specialists, I was told that I wouldn't be able to have children,
that my body needed a bit of a push if it were going to more adequately
"feminize." When I requested my medical files years later while in graduate
school, I noticed that the formal diagnosis used in those files was "testicular
feminization"—an anachronistic term even then, in the late 1990s, when
the contemporary diagnostic terminology was androgen insensitivity syndrome, or AIS.

What being androgen insensitive means is this: I have XY chromosomes,
but my body is unable to respond to "masculinizing" hormones, resulting
in a more female-typical appearance but without reproductive ability or
the capacity to menstruate. Androgen insensitivity comes in both complete
and partial varieties; folks with partial androgen insensitivity syndrome

(PAIS) tend to have more mixed-sex traits than those who are completely androgen insensitive. I have PAIS.

I was told that I had gonads sunk deep in my lower abdomen that would need to be removed because they were, quite evidently, useless on account of their indecision—they seemed to have no idea what they wanted to be when they grew up. Testes? Ovaries? Meh. They were content to make a little nest in my viscera and crouch there until a urological surgeon removed them, following a consult with a pediatric endocrinologist. The stated reason was that there was a high risk of them becoming cancerous—a risk difficult to argue with. A side benefit, I was told, was that the removal would decrease the levels of masculinizing hormones in my body. Supplemented with estrogen pills, I'd develop larger breasts, my fat distribution would alter, I'd develop a more conventionally feminine figure. On estrogen I would inhabit a corporeality different from the athletic, rather railish one I dwelt in at sixteen.

These are things a teenage tomboy doesn't necessarily want to hear or to experience. After being on Premarin (one of the major mass-market hormone replacement therapy pills) for a handful of months, I simply stopped taking it. I'd gained something close to twenty pounds, felt like an emotional wreck (probably on account of altering my body chemistry while I was grappling existentially with the shock of an intersex diagnosis), and was self-medicating with many other substances to cope (or, rather, not cope) with these substantial shifts in my body schema and, by extension, my most basic modes of being in the world.

When my mother asked me why I stopped taking hormones, I told her I was vegan and that the thought of taking a pill derived from mare's urine clashed significantly with the ethics and politics of my dietary practices. (What I actually said was more along the lines of "I don't wear leather or eat dairy, so why would I swallow horse piss every day?") That was the last time we mentioned it. The pills were sunk in the garbage, covered over with coffee grinds, and taken to the landfill.

What was actually happening was much more complicated than a rigid dietary choice. I was tacitly refusing the idea that my body needed hormonal modification, that the advice of the medical establishment to ameliorate my failure to present as hyperbolically feminine was something other than sage, something less than useful for a masculine-of-center queer kid who didn't want to inhabit that kind of body to begin with.

There is a way in which receiving a diagnosis of this sort whittles down the complexity of subjective realities. I experienced that diagnosis, despite the softened rhetoric utilized by the medical professionals I interfaced with, as a declaration that I was neither male nor female on the "realest" level possible, that of the biological. This is, in part, why many intersex folks—myself included—are hesitant to mention their status as intersex unless rather necessary (in the context of sexual disclosure, for instance). Your congenital quirks often become the scrim or filter through which all other subjective aspects are read. You date women, men, and nonbinary folks, both cis and trans? Probably because you're intersex. You were a gender transgressive young thing, one who skateboarded and played in punk bands? Probably because you're intersex. This reductive game could proceed interminably.

Philosopher Ladelle McWhorter writes of this phenomenon in a different, though resonant, register, dilating on the ways in which she experienced coming out as a lesbian in the U.S. South in the 1970s. She describes the process as an emptying out of subjective interiority and identitarian complexity. After struggling for years against inhabiting an identity that didn't seem chosen but rather "steadily and progressively constituted and enforced at both micro- and macro-political levels for over a dozen years," she "'willingly'— whatever that can possibly mean here—affirmed it." She writes:

> Once I conceded the struggle and acknowledged (to myself at least) "what I am," the issue that confronted me was how to be it. According to everybody around me, homosexuals didn't have an inner life, didn't think or feel anything. Queers were surfaces merely, across which gender transgressions were written. It was as though to "be queer" was to be some sort of puppet whose strings were pulled by sexuality alone. Queers did nothing but perform-gaily, of course. Real feelings, thoughts, analyses, assessments, decisions, dreams, hopes, and ideas were only for straight people; only straight people actually had a point

of view. Homosexuals could be seen, but their eyes stared blankly back. There was no real person in there. So, once I'd acknowledged that I was a homosexual, what then? How could I *be* that? How could *that* have an I?[1]

Similar to what McWhorter describes, the notion that I was intersex was something that arrived from without, something that was "steadily constituted at micro- and macro-political levels"—through developments in medical imaging technology, mutations in Western epistemologies of gender, medicoscientific congresses, case study interviews, bloodwork, and transformations in genetic research, among other phenomena—long before *I* ever began the slow process of trying to make sense of myself in relationship to it. The question of consent or choice was as fuzzy for me as it was for McWhorter. When a verdict on what sort of being you are is delivered from without, particularly if that verdict bears the locutionary force of a medical professional, it is not a label you can choose or willingly assume. Rather, an authoritative judgment has been made regarding what sort of subspecies you are. The truth has been delivered, and your choices seem limited to acceptance or denial (which can, of course, take many forms). I accepted the diagnosis; I did not attempt to evade or deny the knowledge that was connoted by it—essentially, that I was neither male nor female. This knowledge, however, seemed to relegate me to an impossible subject position. It placed me squarely in the midst of a set of quandaries that echo, in part, those McWhorter faced. I was forced, once I'd acknowledged that I was intersex, to ask, "How could I *be* that? How could *that* have an I?"

That was precisely the sort of thing I wasn't supposed to be asking. I was supposed to heed the rhetoric of the medical professionals who focused on the notion that I was an "unfinished" woman, one who needed a bit of help along the path to full-blown ladyhood. I was meant to construe the diagnosis as a congenital disorder that *didn't* trouble me at the most basic ontological level. The performative linguistic protocols utilized by medical professionals in intersex diagnosis guard against this set of existential dilemmas regarding what one *is*. They are trained—though unevenly, given the relative infrequency of patients with intersex conditions crossing their paths—to emphasize the rightness of a sexually dimorphic understanding of corporeality and to posit the intersex patient as already well on their way toward one or the other of two incontrovertible sexes.

This set of protocols springs from an entrenched perception of intersex bodies as natural errors. Nature, whatever that is, had a set of intentions for a body, but somehow some other agencies intervened, and these intentions were forced off track, thrown awry. It is the job of medical professionals to fulfill the goals that nature, that strange entity, had all along. Voila! Within this schema, one can of course not be "mixed-sex" or, perhaps, something other than male or female, but not only that: within this schema, sex is nothing more complex than a strictly dimorphic conception of bodies allows. Within this schema, intersex bodies are inevitably failures, falling short of the dyadic natural forms of maleness and femaleness. But failures can be corrected; bodies can be placed in remediation. Enter hormonal treatment, genital surgery, electrolysis, postsurgical vaginal dilation, and the injunction delivered by many medical professionals that one must not speak of one's intersex condition.

I wasn't buying the narrative that was offered me, the notion that nature had an intention that my body was somehow disobeying or belying, that I was a failed but remediable woman. It didn't resonate with me; it seemed that I failed to meet the constitutive criteria for womanhood at what I had been taught was the most basic level—the biological—and that no amount of gender-appropriate dressage would change that.

That was when I began to ask myself I could inhabit a specifically inter-sex identity. I was preoccupied, above all, with the question of what I was, now that I considered myself neither male nor female. Some big questions concerning me, in no particular order: what was wrong with conventional understandings of biological sex, if a being like me could be produced? What did being intersex mean in terms of my sexuality? Could I still be heterosexual? Homosexual? Bisexual? Did any of these sexual identities pertain? Did this mean that my long history of gender transgression—which I'd staunchly claimed as avowedly feminist from the moment I was aware of suffragists and women's culottes—was somehow genetically encoded? Was there a way of being a person that didn't rely on also being either male or female? Was I human? What was *human*? What were these biological entities called *men* and *women*? What was this phenomenon termed *biological sex*? On what grounds was it distinguished from this other phenomena termed *gender*? If I was intersex, could I also be a woman or a man? If so, how? Through what understandings of gender, sex, the natural, the socially constructed, was this rendered either possible or impossible?

These are enormous, unwieldy questions for a sixteen year old to grapple with.

I would be dishonest if I said I wasn't sometimes miserable. I felt specifically marked as aberrant and constantly wondered whether or not strangers—casual passersby, folks in the grocery store line with me, other kids at school—*knew*. By "know," I mean I wondered whether they specifically registered that there was something corporeally abnormal about me; that I was something *beyond* merely tomboyish, dykey, butch; that I was different in a manner that strayed beyond the realm of (ostensibly "social") gender transgression and into a territory wherein I violated the natural order of things—what Foucault has so convincingly discussed as the realm of the monstrous. I often felt as if there were no space in the world wherein I could make sense, no space in the world where I could be known as something other than this breach of natural order, this wretched being, this monster. I felt—in brief—as if I were ontologically homeless, a being with no space to dwell legibly in this world.

But I also, often simultaneously, felt like I'd gotten off the hook big-time. I couldn't get pregnant! This seemed like permission to sleep around without deep worries about messing up my future plans, none of which included children. Since I was beyond all that boy/girl business, I was also beyond all those thorny dilemmas about whether I was gay or straight—dilemmas that had definitely occupied me in the years leading up to the delivery of this diagnosis. Thus, being told I was intersex felt like tacit permission to become erotically involved with whomever I desired. I could stop self-policing my behaviors in terms of their coincidence with a properly female identity because it turned out that I wasn't a girl anyhow. If I was neither/nor, or both/and, then the strictures, rules, expectations, modes of comportment, and ways of relating that so forcefully shape the inhabitation of proper masculinities and femininities didn't apply. If I was indeed dwelling in that beyond-space of the monstrous, then maybe that space beyond could be something like a queer utopia.

But I also wanted a way to be authentically intersex; I wanted there to be some content to that particular identification. I wanted an intersex identity, not an identity as a failed man or woman, some sort of natural error. How I longed to be something that was! But when all that "is" is male or female, and I had decided I wasn't either of those things on account of being atypically sexed, what was I to do?

There didn't seem to be a community that cohered around a conception of intersex as identity. At that point in time, the only real source of useful information on intersex issues was the Intersex Society of North America. While the ISNA did important work around issues of medical reform, it did not seem to be concerned with the possible valorization of intersexuality within the realm of identity politics. Rather, the conventional line—the line that has carried over into the newer instantiation of the ISNA as the Accord Alliance, a stakeholder consortium composed of doctors, bioethicists, and parents of intersex children working to institute best-practice guidelines within the medical profession—was that most all intersex folks identified unproblematically as male or female. While I've done nothing resembling a scientific survey of the responses of folks who have the experience of a diagnosis of this sort in their biography (such a study would be relatively impossible, for many reasons, and besides, if I were that kind of scholar, I would have become a quantitative sociologist), the scant experiential narratives I've been able to locate in sexological archives and university libraries and through engagement with minority queer and trans literatures seems to suggest otherwise, as does my own experience. And because I've intimately learned the lessons offered by feminist theorizations of the devalorization of traditionally "feminine" knowledge sources, I know that trusting experience is integral to the formation of a resistant political subject.

It was clear to me that if this rendering of an intersex subjectivity was going to be feasibly actualized, it would not be a matter of stepping into a ready-made political formation comprised of like-minded folks with similar, sometimes overlapping sets of experiences, shared logics of sense, and common engagements and aims. While I was fully on board with the efforts at medical reform that were the most—if not the only—visible face of intersex activism, I felt as though it were rather meager, thin-blooded, though essential nevertheless. The difficulties faced by intersex folks seemed to stem not only, and perhaps not even primarily, from maltreatment at the hands of medical professionals. Rather—and this is a hypothesis that I explore in-depth throughout this book—they seem to stem from the more entrenched epistemological underpinnings that shape the sense bodies are able to make both within and far beyond the boundaries of the medical establishment, boundaries that are of course fuzzy, permeable, and not hermetically sealed to begin with.

I credit Anne Fausto-Sterling's *Sexing the Body* as my first encounter with a discourse on intersexuality that was actually *critical* of the conception of intersex conditions as disorders in need of remediation. Her work placed the phenomenon of contemporary protocols of intersex diagnosis and treatment within the *longue durée* of shifting Western conceptions of sexed, gendered, and sexualized corporealities. These ranged from the ancient Greco-Roman conceptions of legitimate sexual mixity through to the Victorian consolidation of notions of strictly dimorphic "true sex," which essentially eradicated the notion of sexual mixity and formed the groundwork for contemporary protocols of intersex treatment that hinge on assigning the patient to one of two specific sexes (usually female) and subsequently "fixing" these bodies so that they more properly match an idealized conception of sexed morphology. Fausto-Sterling, after providing this account, goes on to examine the phenomenon of contemporary intersex diagnosis, the regulation of gender transition, the development of bioscientific discourse on "brain sex" and the construction of those strange entities misleadingly named "sex hormones" (they do a whole lot more, and a whole lot less, than determine sex). Throughout, she keeps her analytic lens trained on the complex interplay of the regulation of homosexual subjects with that of trans and intersex folks, attempting to think through their shifting coarticulations rather than treating them as discrete and separable subspecies of being, highlighting the ways in which, for instance, trans activists' successes "winning the right to surgical and legal sex changes" resulted in the "reinforcement of a two-gender system"[2] that poorly serves the aims of intersex folks seeking to ameliorate the damages inflicted by a medical establishment deeply invested in this two-gender system; or the ways in which sex reassignment in instances of both trans and intersexuality were caught up within a juridical apparatus that sought to prevent any semblance of a homosexual marriage.

Sexing the Body was published in 2000, only a year after I had received an intersex diagnosis; it was easily available, appearing in multiple big-box bookstores and written decisively for a lay audience. Her work suggested immediately a number of rather radical concepts: her assertion, following Donna Haraway's reassemblage of that infamous statement by Clausewitz, that biology is the continuation of politics by other means; her argument that, "while the state and legal system has an interest in maintaining only two sexes, our collective biological bodies do not"; and her overall intellectual framework, which modeled a kind of scholarship able to move well beyond biological essentialist–social constructivist debates that seemed to posit the "natural" and the "social" as thoroughly incommunicable realms. She executed this move by asserting that the relationship between biological material, behavior, and identity is more akin to that of a Möbius strip that leads "back toward, and beyond, the body's exterior," or like a series of nesting dolls we can utilize to envision "the various layers of human sexuality, from the cellular to the social to the historical." These metaphorical nesting dolls cohere around a hollow center rather than an essence, and their system cannot withstand modification at any one level—be it that of bioscientific research, activist contestation, popular narrative, or medical protocol—without altering the entirety of the structure. In other words, "change can happen in any of the layers, but since the entire assembly has to fit together, altering one of the component dolls requires the interlinked system—from the cellular to the institutional—to change."[3]

The idea that biological entities have political histories was revelatory. I began wondering about the political histories of bodies, about how specific biological material comes to signify. What was the political history of this body, my body? Fausto-Sterling's work forced a realization that to answer such a question would necessarily involve examining the historical links between intersexuality and the discourses enveloping other messily biologized, confounding, and hotly contested entities—women, inverts, homosexuals, transsexuals, gynomimetics, andromimetics, uranians, the list goes on. I needed to investigate the consolidation of modern Western sexology, the history of scientific debates regarding the constitution and classification of abnormal bodies, and the ways in which both of these inquiries have been indissolubly and unpredictably linked to forms of political contestation developed by gender and sexual minorities.

Perhaps more importantly, however, her work forced me to realize there could be no resistance that would ameliorate the maltreatment of intersex individuals without coalition made with trans and queer folks, particularly those that have been deeply affected by the administrative violence that attends processes of gender regulation. If the histories of the bodies we've come to inhabit are co-constituted and interlinked, then our possible futures must be as well. We can no longer afford to police lines of amity and enmity between us, marking off separate spaces and subcultures for gays, lesbians, trans folks, and genderqueers and sometimes rigorously, sometimes tacitly regulating lines of inclusion and exclusion. In other words, any effort to foment political resistance capable of engaging administrative violence at the same time that it invents new modes of being in the world needs to take seriously the disjunct between the sexually dimorphic imaginaries we've inherited and the queer productivities of our collective biological bodies. In order to think this disjunct, we need to seriously reconsider the patterns of relation between the ostensibly natural phenomena of biological sex, the ostensibly social phenomena of gendering, and the consolidation of sexual identities that sometimes claim to be natural or biological and, at other times, in other milieus, to be radically socially constructed. If our collective biological bodies are constitutively queer, infinitely more complex than a dimorphic conception of corporeality allows, then it seems all of the common sense that has been made of the links between sex, gender, and sexuality are split at the root, fucked up (desirably, I think) from jump.

It is this set of political intuitions regarding the necessity of rethinking the status of the natural and the continuities between sex, gender, and sexuality in the service of developing more effective queer coalitional politics that made my encounter with Judith Butler's comments on gender, grammaticality, and sense-making so resonant. She writes that

> neither grammar nor style are politically neutral. Learning the rules that
> govern intelligible speech is an inculcation into normalized language,
> where the price of not conforming is the loss of intelligibility itself.
> As Drucilla Cornell, in the tradition of Adorno, reminds me: there is
> nothing radical about common sense. It would be a mistake to think
> that received grammar is the best vehicle for expressing radical views,
> given the constraints that grammar imposes upon thought, indeed,
> upon the thinkable itself. But formulations that twist grammar or that
> implicitly call into question the subject-verb requirements of propo-
> sitional sense are clearly irritating for some. They produce more work
> for their readers, and sometimes their readers are offended by such
> demands. Are those who are offended making a legitimate request
> for "plain speaking" or does their complaint emerge from a consumer
> expectation of intellectual life? Is there, perhaps, a value to be derived
> from such experiences of linguistic difficulty? If gender itself is natu-
> ralized through grammatical norms, as Monique Wittig has argued,
> then the alteration of gender at the most fundamental epistemic level
> will be conducted, in part, through contesting the grammar in which
> gender is given.[4]

There are two central components to this assertion of Butler's. The first—
that there is nothing liberating, radical, or forward-thinking about common sense—has prompted me to consider conventionally accepted and
routinely inherited modes of speech with extreme criticism. The demand
that folks "make sense" carries a force that inevitably reduces the complexity of the entities attempting to express themselves. There is a reductive
violence implicit in the demand that one speak plainly, that one become
fully intelligible to an interlocutor. The second component of Butler's
assertion—that there are explicitly gendered implications to this demand
that one make sense commonly—is perhaps more imperative than the
first, for it intimately links this demand that one make sense to issues of
gendered intelligibility and subjective becoming that range well beyond

the bounds of "common"—which Butler seems to understand as an alibi for hegemonic—sense.

I collude with both Wittig and Butler when it comes cognizing the necessity to "[alter] gender at the most fundamental epistemic level"; when I write of the sense of ontological homelessness I and many other intersex, trans, nonbinary, and gender-nonconforming folks experience, it is intimately interwoven with the sense that one's being is epistemologically impossible to *make sense of* given the linguistic constraints we are forced to submit to in order to become intelligible subjects. This is, of course, why we have invented alternative linguistic genders. But these are counter-languages, not linguistic common sense, and moreover, they are counter-languages that are definitively short-range, not even shared or intelligible when one is among many cisgender gay- or lesbian-identified folks. I have repeatedly had the discomfiting experience of discoursing with cisgender gay and lesbian folks who absolutely, stubbornly, and perhaps half-unconsciously refuse to utilize the correct pronouns for intersex, trans, nonbinary, and gender-nonconforming folks even after being *repeatedly reminded* of them by other folks present, often to the extreme chagrin of the person being misrecognized.

So there is this need for a counter-language, a different way to speak of gender, but also a need to disarticulate assumptions about corporeality from gender identification, to deliberately insert a breach in this naturalized continuity between bodies and gender so that the experiential narratives of intersex, trans, and genderqueer folks become epistemically and linguistically possible to articulate. How are we forming this language? What are the limitations, obstacles, and impasses that we run up against in this process? How does thinking the development of this alternative sense translate to the development of efforts to eliminate administrative violence, transphobic and homophobic modes of relation, and the force of institutionally sedimented hetero- and homonormativities? In order to parse these questions I've turned, throughout this book, to narratives wherein this struggle to articulate intersex, trans, and gender-nonconforming forms of being is vividly at work, attempting to read for acts of resistance that may not appear as such if one is reading without an attentiveness to these issues of *epistemological impossibility* (not being understood) and *ontological homelessness* (lacking space for being in the world).

Butler's work has been an invaluable resource as I develop responses, however partial, to these questions. The very articulation of the heterosexual matrix—that term Butler uses to index the naturalization of a continuity between dimorphic biological sex, dyadic gender identity, and reproductive heterosexual desire—makes it possible to think about the production of credible and intelligible subjects of sex, gender, and desire but also—more importantly for me—the production of *in-credible* subjects as well. I began to consider a queer politics that would cohere not through the claiming of a positive, substantive identity but rather one that developed coalition in relation to this estrangement from the heterosexual matrix, a shared disruptive and disarticulative capacity produced through failing to cohere in and through these naturalized, phantasmic continuities.

I puzzled over certain sentences in *Gender Trouble* as if they were Zen koans. Lacking a familiarity with the field of reference Butler relied upon when I first encountered her work, I accessed the import of many of the central concepts through intuition. I'd keep a statement on mental repeat for days—for instance, "gender is an identity tenuously constituted in time, instituted in an exterior space through a *stylized repetition of acts*"—until its meaning gradually became clear.[5] I'd be at work behind the coffee shop counter, making an Americano and thinking "Okay, gender is about repeating certain acts. So you do it. It's not something you are; it's something you do." Grind, tamp, lock the group in the group head, commence espresso pour, repeat. "Alright, but what about this weird shit about it being 'constituted in time, instituted in exterior space'? I mean, of course all acts are temporal, unfold over a series of moments, a lifetime. That's clear enough. But 'exterior space'? That must mean that gender, again, is not something I am, something felt in a purely interior way. So, I'm doing gender, I'm acting it out. But if it's 'instituted in exterior space,' then I'm not the sole or sovereign author of these acts. So, gender's doing me, too? Yes, yes—I'm doing gender; gender is doing me. We're switch. Okay."

Gradually, my desire for an intersex identity was mutating; in grappling with the work of Fausto-Sterling and Butler, I began to realize that I had been conceptualizing identity as a substantive possession that I could somehow seek and claim, when what was actually happening—despite my best efforts to signify in ways consistently in excess of binary understandings of gender, call it deliberate androgyny or something else—was that I was being claimed by exterior readings of my identity, readings that were wildly contradictory. I was moving, in the space of a few hours, between classrooms where I was recognized consistently as female to a workplace where most patrons read me as male—as a gay teenage boy, usually—to spaces of friendship and romance where I felt a bit more complexly known, where partial knowledges of my complex sexed and sexual biography were understood and dignified. Slowly, I became able to think about these different interpellations in a way that ranged beyond anger at being misrecognized. Thinking with *Gender Trouble,* I began to consider identity as something constantly negotiated within and across different milieus, as something that *feels* extraordinarily intimate but is in fact transindividual, in some respects radically impersonal. Moreover, I realized that the inhabitation of this liminal gender—sometimes read boy, sometimes read girl, nearly always read queer—was perhaps precisely what I desired when I yearned to claim a substantive intersex identity. This meant that, in the years immediately following diagnosis, I often conflated gender transgression and queer sexuality with intersex, at least insofar as my own person was concerned. Being what I still think of as corporeally queer, I began to think of gender transgression as intimately linked to this bodily queerness. It was difficult to invest in the performance of more conventional masculinities or femininities, given that I felt they were part of the same oppressive machinery as the dimorphic demands of the medical establishment. A dual refusal of both, by way of resisting these apparatuses of corporeal-cum-subjective sense-making processes, was intuitive to me, a response so visceral and subtly inferential that I rarely stopped to consider performing my gender otherwise. Moreover, being difficult to read or eliciting vastly disparate readings on the level of gender identification was not a phenomenon divorced from my bodily reality. In refusing medical normalization through hormonal and surgical treatment, my body itself—to heuristically isolate it for the moment, no matter how inseparable it is from all sorts of other phenomena in actuality—signified queerness, regardless of whether one had access to my naked flesh or not. Intersex conditions, though often discussed only at the level of genital anomaly, often effect a far more holistic set of corporeal queernesses. As for myself, I have quite broad shoulders, narrow hips, small breasts, and more body and facial hair than is normatively typical for a woman. What this means is that, even if I'm performing something like a normatively feminine gender—garbed in lady-typical clothing, a slip dress and ballet flats, for instance—I am read as performing a femininity I wasn't "born into"—a transwoman, a queer man in drag, or an andro-butch dyke being forced to wear an outfit they don't particularly feel comfortable in.

There is a way in which I've grown quite accustomed to all of these points of identification delivered from without, and I began a practice in my early twenties that runs as such: when asked about what I am (an interrogation that happens fairly often, sometimes initiated by children on the street, sometimes in queer spaces, sometimes, more tacitly, by students in courses I teach), I respond with the counterquestion, "What do you think I am?" I don't deliver this response in a hostile manner; I *am* actually infinitely curious about the different ways in which my gender is perceived. This question is sometimes met with irritation or confusion, but often—particularly when I've been engaged by children—what follows is a laundry list of isolated factors that are then evaluated with reference to a dimorphic ideality. My voice is taken into account, the configuration of different body parts, the clothing I'm wearing, the way I walk. It is, in a sense, a submission to the always already operating interrogative, taxonomizing process of gendering in routine perception. I find this submission easy to activate and think that perhaps it follows from my earlier submissions to the much more forceful taxonomizing practices I encountered during diagnosis. The logics, in both sets of practices, are similar: my being is broken down into specific elements or signs, and a process of investigation commences that seeks to adjudicate the relative masculinity or femininity of each component; a tally sheet is kept in the mind of the observer, and a more holistic perception is cobbled together from these evaluated parts; a verdict is then delivered, one that may even be inconclusive.

This *perceptive fragmentation* is a phenomenon common to not only gender-nonnormative queers but also those included more or less problematically in the category of woman. It is part and parcel of much feminist discourse on practices of sexual objectification to critique the phenomenon of perceptive fragmentation that operates through isolation and eroticization of particularly sexualized body parts at the expense of perceiving a woman as a whole being, that disregards the particularities of personhood in favor of a traveling perceptive fixation on hips, breasts, and buttocks. The main feminist objection to this process of fragmentation is that it effects, first, a separation of a woman's body from her mind and, second, reduces a woman to nothing but the body.[6] It is crucial to think the differences between this experience of perceptive fragmentation and the one I and many other gender-nonnormative folks experience. Sexualization is often a part of our experience, but it is not nearly as neat a process as that glossed by the term *sexual objectification*. What is instead happening is often prior to a process of sexual objectification; "what we are" must be adjudicated prior to sexualization or erotic interest, so that the boundaries of the perceiver's sexual identity are not broached; our bodies are disarticulated from a corporeal whole not *because* we are women, *but because the perceiver doesn't know what we are*. In order for routine social interaction to proceed, the perceiver must know the incipient (and insipid) scripts to follow; the performance of a legible gender is thus essential if one is to have a none-too-slippery footing in their perambulations through the everyday. When the process of gender verification, proceeding by way of perceptive disarticulation, results—as it often does—in an inconclusive verdict, these scripts—sometimes erotic, sometimes not—are quickly abandoned or forced to stammer ("Sir . . . I mean, ma'am, I mean . . .").

While this process of perceptive disarticulation in the reading of gender is something those who fail to cohere according to dichotomous logics are uniquely and especially attuned to (this is one of the multiple epistemic privileges that attend experiences of gender nonnormativity), it is actually the process through which *all* beings who are subject to regimes in which subjective intelligibilities are built within the heterosexual matrix assume an intelligible mode of being in the world. As Butler reminds us, "gender is a complexity whose totality is permanently deferred, never fully what it is at any given juncture in time."[7] What this means is that the experience of feeling oneself a whole—unified, coherent, complete—woman (or man) is an experience that may in fact stem from certain privileges, for instance, cis privilege, able-bodied privilege, the many forms of privilege that accrue to those who live without experiencing significant corporeal trauma.

There are, of course, differences between *experiencing* oneself as a whole person and *longing to be* a whole person, but both felt disingenuous to me. For what was a whole person to begin with? A body-mind unity, one with definitive boundaries, one whose mind was capable of executing sovereign control over their soma? If that was what being whole meant, I wasn't sure I could sign on for that particular desire. I listened to my body and to other people far too much; I was fully aware that whatever meaning my being had in the world was not up to me but was instead trans-individual and historically contingent. Had I been born only two hundred years earlier or in a different geopolitical location or both, the meanings ascribed to my corporeality would have been vastly different. I could have, for instance, been negotiating a Boston marriage with a woman who, knowing of my anomalous corporeality, encouraged me to petition for a legal change in what was then understood as "sex," not gender, so that we might become legitimately wed. I could have lived anonymously, negotiating my intersex condition without the interference of medical practitioners, coming under investigation only posthumously, my body brought into a surgical theater for dissection to discover the mysteries of sex difference and the development of hermaphroditic conditions. There are many of these alternative narratives of intersex experience that I'll address by way of constructing a genealogy of intersex treatment; each of them attests, when considered as an ensemble, to the radical contingency of corporeal meaning and by extension the given-over-ness of the body to shifting regimes of meaning-making. Given this, it would be foolish of me to cling to or long for a subjective holism, wherein my self would be a closed system that ends at the skin.

Much feminist discourse on the fragmented perception of bodies in the service of sexual objectification is underwritten by a Kantian conception of personhood that insists objectification is a means of reducing a person—

ideally, a being that is an end in itself, a free, rational, and autonomous agent—to a mere instrument, valued only for its use. It is also underwritten by a Cartesian understanding of body-mind that posits a division between *res cogitans* (a thinking thing, a mental substance) and *res extensa* (a material thing, a corporeal substance). My engagement with Butler's work made it increasingly difficult to intellectually or politically invest in understandings of gender and sexual politics underwritten by either of these philosophical shibboleths. I knew I was not in sovereign control of my being, and I knew that, no matter how I tried to become nothing but pure intellect, one cold stream of logic, no matter how I tried to negate, ignore, or detach from my body, it insisted on being listened to, on having its desires, affects, percepts, and potentials engaged. And I had begun to ask whether attempting to establish sovereign, autonomous control was desirable in the first place, on intellectual as well as interpersonal registers.

The multiple violences engendered by this Kantian understanding of subjectivity are well documented: it works to atomize the social, to produce persons who consider their incapacity to, for instance, make a living wage, obtain a college education, not get arrested, hold a steady job, save enough for retirement, adequately support children, or resist emotionally and phys-ically abusive relationships, as personal failures rather than as systemically produced oppressions in a late-capitalist, sexist, and racist situation that unevenly distributes life chances. We have extremely minimal agency in relation to what Dean Spade calls this "maldistribution of life chances," but the only way we can exercise it at all is if we can actually realize it in the first place.[8] The widely disseminated myth of autonomous, self-contained individualism radically blocks this realization.

Butler, in the face of this myth, offers an account of gender identity and subjectivity that remains focused on the conditions of possibility that enable both the production of normatively intelligible bodies, genders, and sexual-ities and those alternative networks—those "emergent matrices of cultural intelligibility"—that enable transgression, subversion, all manner of queer difference.[9] She remains committed to thinking these nonnormativities as spaces of possibility rather than alternative lifestyles fixed within a pre-given taxon of sexual intelligibility. She writes, in an essay preceding the publication of *Gender Trouble*, of her difficulty claiming a lesbian identity because it seemed to substantiate and render artifactual and sensible an experience of desire that remained infinitely opaque, beyond pat definition. While not deriding identity politics, she asks after what criteria might be used to establish a sexual identity, be it lesbian, gay, bi, or hetero, writing, "if a sexuality is to be disclosed, what will be taken as the true determinant of its meaning: the phantasy structure, the act, the orifice, the gender, the anatomy? And if the practice engages a complex interplay of all of those, which one of these erotic dimensions will come to stand for the sexuality that requires them all?"[10] She goes on to worry the emphasis on gay and lesbian visibility as political strategy and the concomitant identity policing and foreclosure of possibilities for queer being that seems to come with it:

> There is no question that gays and lesbians are threatened by the violence of public erasure, but the decision to counter that violence must be careful not to reinstall another in its place. Which version of lesbian or gay ought to be rendered visible, and which internal exclusions will that rendering visible institute? Can the visibility of identity *suffice* as a political strategy, or can it only be the starting point for a strategic intervention which calls for a transformation of policy? Is it not a sign of despair over public politics when identity becomes its own policy, bringing with it those who would "police" it from various sides?[11]

I had already asked similar questions regarding the constitution of sexual identity, as it seemed that I was estranged irrevocably from any of the conventional offerings—hetero, homo, bi—on account of their linkages to certain anatomies, certain acts involving certain orifices, certain criteria of biomorphic constitution that I, being intersex, didn't fulfill. I figured, then, that if I were to have a sexuality, it would be one that didn't cohere neatly with any of the sexual identity categories on offer—in other words, I sensed such a messy set of discontinuities between phantasy structures, acts, orifices, genders, and anatomies that parsing them so that they might appear sexually legible seemed first boring and second impossible.

I found myself, in my early twenties, having essentially given up on conventional understandings of what it meant to have a gender identity as well as a sexual identity. I did not think that the search for an identity—no matter how complex, how intersectional—was a viable endeavor, and I had moreover decided that a queer politics based on identity and visibility was not nearly radical enough to address some of the more pressing political concerns forcibly molding the lives of minoritarian queer and trans subjects. It may have been, as Butler suggests, a starting point for strategic intervention, but it fell radically short of an adequate political end in itself. It was in this moment that I turned to the work of Michel Foucault.

I had been meaning to read *The History of Sexuality*, Volume 1: *An Introduction* for quite a while, given its oft-citedness in nineties-era queer theory. My initial forays into the library stacks to pull work by folks like Diana Fuss, Lillian Faderman, Laura Doan, Gayle Rubin, Pat Califia, and others turned up countless references to this one book, so I knew that it was profoundly influential, but I wasn't quite sure why. I had a working knowledge of the repressive hypothesis and his formulation of *scientia sexualis*, derived inferentially from essays committed to putting these concepts to work. I knew, given my growing realization that I needed to write about intersexuality in-depth, that Foucault's effort to examine the flourishing of modern Western scientific and psychoanalytic discourses on sexuality, deviance, and perversion were going to be necessary to grapple with. I wasn't quite prepared for how deeply the text would shift my approach to considering the constitution of queer subjectivity, however; nor could I have predicted the ways in which my lasting preoccupation with his oeuvre would not only enable a critique of sexual speciation and its aftereffects in contemporary identitarian political formations but would also elicit considerable thought on ways out of these modes of subjectivation, how it would aid in thinking through how resistant queer and trans communities are cobbled together through ascesis, friendship, and affective intensities.

Foucault lays out his central doubts regarding the repressive hypothesis as follows:

First doubt: Is sexual repression truly an established historical fact? Is what first comes into view—and consequently permits one to advance an initial hypothesis—really the accentuation or even the establishment of a regime of sexual repression beginning in the seventeenth century? ... Second doubt: Do the workings of power, and in particular those mechanisms of power that are brought into play in societies such as ours, really belong primarily to the category of repression? Are prohibition, censorship, and denial truly the forms through which power is exercised in a general way, if not in every society, most certainly in our own? ... A third and final doubt: Did the critical discourse that addresses itself to repression come to act as a roadblock to a power mechanism that had operated unchallenged up to that point, or is it not in fact part of the same historical network as the thing it denounces (and doubtless misrepresents) by calling it "repression"?[12]

I knew, from my engagement with the careful historiographical work of Fausto-Sterling, that what Foucault is pinpointing as the ostensible Victorian-era birth of massive sexual repression was roughly contemporaneous with the burgeoning of large-scale medicoscientific research regarding the constitution of sexual difference; this field of knowledge production seemed to signify anything but a growing, gathering silence around sexuality. Foucault's work verifies this. The development of a modern Western science of sexuality is his central counterproof to the repressive hypothesis. The advent and sedimentation of a scientia sexualis signals a growing preoccupation with sexuality and the increasing reterritorialization of bodies in relation to these sexual knowledges. Was it not the case that early modern research into the etiology of intersex conditions invested heavily in preventing ostensibly "unnatural" and perverse couplings, was even governed—at certain times—by a eugenic impulse that sought to prevent such anomalous births? For this to be the case—that is, for the backstory of modern Western intersex diagnosis to cohere in a manner capable of explicating the diagnostic procedures I'd undergone—there needed to be a massive backlog of knowledge production regarding sex acts, sexual identities, and sex constitution. This is a long way of saying that I was, in short, in agreement with Foucault's first doubt—that sexual repression may not be an established historical fact.

But it was the second doubt, really, that forced my breath to catch a bit. The idea that power was productive, rather than restrictive, made enormous intuitive sense but had been up until that point an idea that had remained pre-articulate. I lived, then, in a political milieu molded by an anarcho-punk conviction in the importance of liberation, the processual freeing of oneself from the ostensible shackles of heterosexism, patriarchy, fundamentally racist modes of perception, and (of course) capital. But if there was some viability to Foucault's suspicion that mechanisms of power weren't wholly, or even primarily, repressive, then it was impossible to retain this vocabulary of liberation, impossible to keep hold of this emphasis on the business of getting free, one that often manifested in practices of attempted escape (in the form of dropping out, substance abuse, traveling, too-fragile living situations) that ultimately ended up producing blockages on the way to building radical alternative spaces rather than enabling their construction. If Foucault wasn't misled in his suspicions about the fundamental productivity of power, different questions need be asked, with new terminological sets that weren't sunk deep into notions of repression, constraint, and liberation. Critical emphasis need be placed on two interwoven questions. The first: how were the categories of gender and sexual identity I experienced as simultaneously compelling and coercive produced in such a way that they seemed to exhaust the realm of the possible? The second: how could a counter-power be developed that enabled different subjective productions that are resistant but not caught in purely negative, critical, and contestatory relations to the biopolitical regulation of sex, gender, and sexuality?

This second question anticipates Foucault's third doubt, that critical discourses on repression are indissolubly tied to the very historical networks that they denounce in the name of liberation and, furthermore, that these critical practices of denunciation fundamentally misrepresent the actual operations of the historical networks that produce the contested phenomena. This style of critique composes a redundant and endless feedback loop and, in this act of composition, also serves to block lines of flight, processes of deterritorialization that Deleuze and Guattari call *becomings*, which Elizabeth Grosz glosses as "the operation of self-differentiation, the elaboration of a difference within a thing, a quality, or system."[13] I understand the forms of gender transformation initiated by trans, intersex, and gender-nonconforming subjects as becomings, not mimetic repetitions of hegemonic forms of masculinity and femininity; the dyad of repression and liberation isn't the most helpful when considering these "elaborations of difference" that are actually intimately and intricately transforming systems of sex and gender legibility.

This book project began with my refusal to be medically normalized, corralled within dimorphic conceptions of sexed embodiment. I have tried to trace, here, how that refusal precipitated an intense engagement with the work Fausto-Sterling, Butler, and Foucault because they each in their own way offered important context and conceptual tools for understanding the emergence of modern Western understandings of intersex embodiment as a form of natural error in need of correction, as a form of disordered embodiment that posed such a threat to hegemonic conceptions of sex, sexuality, kinship, and the overall gendered logic of social order that it needed to be "corrected" at any cost. Fausto-Sterling documents the coercion implicit in efforts to medically normalize intersex individuals, highlighting the ways in which ostensibly objective forms of medical knowledge-practice act in the service of maintaining sexist, heterosexist, and essentialist conceptions of social order. Butler articulates the inability of "common sense" modes of understanding sex, gender, and sexuality to dignify the experiential complexities of gender and sexual minorities, and highlights the ways in which gender is always actually inessential, always a trans-individual negotiation with forms of discursive and administrative power. Foucault, too, highlights the regulation, administration, and governance that forcefully produces specific historical forms of gender and sexual legibility, emphasizing the productivity of power relations in the construction of both normative and deviant forms of subjectivity, arguing that sexuality in the modern West becomes a rich nexus of subjective modification in the service of population-level systems of control. Together, these thinkers helped me to develop a vivid image of the trauma, coercion, and violence that impacts modern Western subjects diagnosed with intersex conditions. They helped me think through the production of intersex existence as an epistemological impossibility that generates a felt sense of ontological homelessness among intersex subjects. They helped me understand how and why intersex bodies have been so frequently subject to forms of perceptive fragmentation that trouble and traumatize us while we are merely attempting to exist.

In the following, initial chapter of the book, I take an in-depth look at the memoir of Herculine Barbin, a person with an intersex condition born in France in the mid-1800s who left a memoir unpublished upon her suicide. Foucault had this memoir placed into broader circulation 1978. This edition of the memoir came replete with an enframing essay by Foucault himself, medical and news reports on Barbin's case, and a short story inspired by the memoir. While this edition documents the medical and administrative violence enacted upon subjects of "indeterminate sex" during a period of intensely consolidating medical and scientific authority on matters of abnormality, pathology, and "deviance," it is also an account of an early instance of contestation and resistance to these emergent protocols of intersex normalization. It is, thus, both a testimonial and a manifesto, both a detailed account of the intimate effects of trauma and a document that traces the contours of intersex rage and resistance. It offers readers a glimpse of a way of being in the world not fully underwritten by naturalized, institutionalized presumptions of dimorphic sexed embodiment at the same time as it documents the shunted possibility of enacting such a way of being.

1 Queer Monsters

Michel Foucault and Herculine Barbin

Not a living creature was to share in the immense
sorrow that seized me when I left my childhood,
at that age when everything is young and bright
with the future.

That age did not exist for me. As soon as I reached
that age, I instinctively drew apart from the world, as
if I had already come to understand that I was to live
in it as a stranger.

—Herculine Barbin

Herculine Barbin became famous among academics long after her death,
following French philosopher Michel Foucault's publication of her memoir.[1] His interest—as well as his lengthy introduction to her memoir—
authenticated the text for contemporary readers, marked it of interest,
somehow integral to unraveling modern Western methods of pathologizing nonnormative bodies and pleasures. Her words have been deployed
repeatedly since, by scholars as distinct (and distinguished) as Judith Butler,
Ladelle McWhorter, and Gayatri Chakravorty Spivak, on a diversity of
topics—subalterity, gender performativity, disciplinary power, the medicalization of gender, and identity politics.[2] The memoir has become a
touchstone in contemporary queer, trans, and intersex scholarship. Because
there are few autobiographical documents tracing the contours of intersex
existence, particularly documents predating the emergence of intersex
activism in the 1990s, Barbin's memoir is a work of great intellectual and
historical import. My goal in this chapter is to map the way this memoir has
been used in order to sketch a rough intellectual history of intersexuality.
I center Michel Foucault's account of Barbin's work as it sets the terms of

intellectual engagement, with later scholars elaborating upon, problematiz-
ing, and critiquing his analysis. I seek answers to the following questions:
what have we collectively learned from Barbin? What promise does her
text hold? Why have so many folks—myself included—been so intensely
interested in her life story?

But first the facts: in 1838 Alexina Herculine Barbin was born into poverty
in Saint-Jean-d'Angély, France. Upon birth, she was designated as female. She
received an Ursuline convent school education thanks to a charitable scholarship. In 1856 she left the convent to begin training to become a teacher.
Upon completion of this training in 1857, she received a post as an assistant
teacher at a girl's school. It was at this post that she fell in love with Sara, a
fellow teacher. She began experiencing sharp abdominal pains. A doctor
was sent to the school to examine Barbin, and upon this examination it was
discovered that she possessed a sex-atypical—that is, intersex—body. The
visiting doctor argued that Barbin should, on account of this atypicality, be
forced to leave the all-female realm of the school. She did not do so. In 1860,
however, Barbin confessed the details of her situation to the Catholic bishop
of the La Rochelle diocese, where the school was located. After hearing
Barbin's account, he advised her to flee the school and begin a nun's life.
He also ordered another medical examination, this time performed by one
Dr. Chesnet. This medical examination heralded a decisive verdict: Barbin
was not a woman but a malformed man, replete with partially descended
testicles in a divided (thus, labial-appearing) scrotum and supposedly
possessed of the capacity to produce sperm. Upon receipt of Chesnet's
report, the bishop rescinded his initial advice and set about creating the
circumstances that would enable a gender transition for Barbin, allowing
the newly ordained male Barbin to assume a properly male station in life.
This transition was also geographical—Barbin moved to Paris, embarking
upon a life of poverty due to his poor training in the prototypically male
professions, unable to fruitfully utilize his training as a teacher. In 1868 he
was found dead in his rooms in the rue de l'École-de-Medécine. He had
committed suicide by inhaling gas from his stove. His memoir was left near
his bed. This memoir was published in a French medical journal in 1874
under the title "La question médico-légale de l'identité dans les rapports

avec las vices de conformation des organes sexuels" ("The Medical/Legal Issue of Identity in Relation to Irregular Formation of the Sexual Organs"), enframed by and published at the behest of French medical doctor and forensic scientist Auguste Ambrose Tardieu. This journal was unearthed by Foucault in the mid-1970s, presumably while he was doing research for the proposed multivolume *History of Sexuality*. The first volume of *The History of Sexuality* appeared in 1976. Foucault's edition of Barbin's memoir appeared in 1978, with a preface by Foucault himself and a dossier including a timeline, newspaper reports on Barbin's case, the medical reports filed by both Dr. Chesnet and one E. Goujon, the doctor who performed Barbin's autopsy, as well as a short story inspired by Barbin's life entitled "Scandal at the Convent," written by German psychiatrist and author Oskar Panizza in 1893. All of this was collected under the title *Herculine Barbin: Being the Recently Discovered Memoirs of a Nineteenth Century French Hermaphrodite*.

It was a deceptively straightforward story. As is the case with all simple narratives, a significant amount of excision and reduction—of emotion, of ideological complexity, of historicity, of subjective specificity—has taken place in order to render this series of intellectually digestible, ostensibly factic pronouncements. In presenting this tight narrative, I am deliberately mimicking the logic enacted by the disciplinary agents—doctors, priests, judges—whose diagnoses and pronouncements forcibly shaped and constrained Herculine's life; I engage this mimicry in order to accentuate the difference between these official logics—those that decree everyone must have a true sex and that this sex must be either male or female—from those alternative, minoritarian logics at work in the autobiographical record left by Herculine, who consistently disidentified with binary schemes of gender, and the medical and juridical systems that supported and enforced such notions. Disidentification refers to the practice of utilizing the codes of dominant culture as "raw material for representing a disempowered politics or positionality that has been rendered unthinkable by the dominant culture," and thus fashioning a self that is situated both within and against those normative cultural discourses and modes of belonging.[3] It is a tactic Barbin deploys repeatedly, in relation to maleness and femaleness, and the dyad of hetero- and homosexuality built on those limited conceptions of embodiment.

What can we make of the pronounced narrative differences between the medical accounts of Barbin's case and her own account? Why is this narrative disjunct of note—historiographically, conceptually, and politically? On what grounds and for what reasons did Foucault grant such importance to this memoir and, more broadly, to the phenomenon, both discursive and material, of hermaphroditism?[4] How do we engage in a reparative reading practice that situates this interest in hermaphroditism in relationship to the rest of Foucault's oeuvre, specifically as pertaining to his figuration of governmentality, biopower, ascesis and technologies of the self?

The practice of reparative reading, as theorized by Eve Sedgwick, is motivated by a fear that the culture surrounding the object of analysis is "inadequate or inimical to its nature" but also by a desire to "assemble and confer plenitude on an object that will then have resources to offer to an inchoate self."[5] I read Foucault's interest in Barbin's memoir as motivated, in large part, by a reparative impulse. The text is useful not only insofar as it illustrates the disciplinary powers that install and regulate binary, univocal understandings of sex difference but also because it offers a glimmer of a possible world wherein embodied pleasure isn't entirely caught up in the stranglehold of heterocentric, dimorphic systems of sex, gender, and desire. It is this possibility that Foucault latches onto, this glint of a space wherein intersex and otherwise queer bodies might experience pleasures beyond the forms of embodied desire currently legible, beyond the categorical forms of gender and sexual identity currently on offer.

I, too, read this memoir reparatively. I have learned from Herculine what intersex resistance to the biopolitical regulation of sex, gender, and sexuality might look like; I have learned, devastatingly, that it sometimes takes the form of suicide. Her struggles with the various legal and medical apparatuses that regulate sexed and sexual identity resonate with my own, as does her trenchant critique of these apparatuses.

Two Foucaults? Disciplinary Power, Governmentality, and Technologies of the Self

There is a distinct discursive polyphony contained between the covers of *Herculine Barbin*, characterized by a fundamental tension between the minoritarian and resistant narrative voice of Barbin, who repeatedly and complexly disidentifies with the proclamations made on and about her person, and the discourse utilized by institutions fully invested in reducing and taming the affront to the logic of sex, gender, and social organization precipitated by Barbin.

To read Barbin's memoir as a document of resistance, however, entails relying on conceptual tools drawn from what has been called the "late" Foucault—the Foucault of volumes 2 and 3 of *The History of Sexuality*—*The Use of Pleasure* and *The Care of the Self*—the Foucault who, in an unlikely extension of his thought around disciplinary power, biopolitics, and governmentality, turned toward Greco-Roman antiquity to investigate what he called *technologies of the self*. These techniques are thought by Foucault as ascetic practices of self-fashioning that entail putting knowledge to work in the active negotiation and transformation of the self. Technologies of the self entail a relation to truth, knowledge, and the act of knowing that is radically different from the all-too-familiar Enlightenment-era epistemology that hinges on a *nonrelation* between truth and subjectivity. Foucault, in *The Hermeneutics of the Subject*, refers to the formation of this modern episteme as the "Cartesian moment"—though he's careful to make clear that it does not begin with nor is it solely attributable to Descartes—and goes on to describe it as such: "I think the modern age of the history of truth begins when knowledge itself and knowledge alone gives access to the truth. That is to say, it is when the philosopher (or the scientist, or simply someone who seeks the truth) can recognize the truth and have access to it in himself and solely through his activity of knowing, without anything else being demanded of him and without him having to change or alter his being as subject."[6] Within this epistemological formation, the task of knowledge is one of conquest, acquisition, possession, and accumulation, but these endeavors remain external to the constitution of the subject herself—they don't change her, they don't transform her, they are about uncovering truths *external* to the subject. There is a deep and unhealable rift between being and knowing here, a decisively modern, Western dyadic formulation of epistemology and ontology. Counterposed to this, for Foucault, is a set of practical knowledges that refuse the presupposition of a division between knowledge and subjectivity and are instead simultaneously ontological, epistemological, and ethical (or more succinctly, ethico-onto-epistemological). It is in his examination of Stoic, Epicurean, and Cynic knowledge-practices that Foucault finds a framework for thinking the profound interweaving of these registers so violently rent apart from the Cartesian moment forward.

For Foucault, ancient technologies of the self function as an ethics (understood as a deliberate style of life that one enacts in order to mold and mutate one's character) capable of "working as a very strong structure of existence, without any relation with the juridical per se, with an authoritarian system, with a disciplinary structure."[7] In what is perhaps the most well-known Foucauldian definition of these technologies of the self, he construes them as "techniques which permit individuals to effect, by their own means, a certain number of operations on their own bodies, on their own souls, on their own thoughts, on their own conduct, and this in a manner so as to transform themselves, modify themselves, and to attain a certain state of perfection, of happiness, of purity, of supernatural power, and so on."[8] Insofar as these technologies of the self work in a manner nondetermined (or, at least, not fully determined) by the institutions and apparatuses of disciplinary power, they become the site wherein one may act out possibilities of freedom, autonomy, and becoming in a sociohistorical milieu always already forcibly shaped by normalizing biopolitical forces. This is not to say that technologies of the self are necessarily or always liberatory or resistant. It is important to remember that these technologies may also take the form of instances of internalized oppression wherein one intentionally fabricates a style of life fully compatible with normativizing demands, a phenomenon easily witnessed in instances as diverse as the valorization of marriage among gays and lesbians, the extreme dieting of women and girls, and the generalization of conspicuous consumption. The central point is that these technologies of the self illuminate the productive (rather than repressive) function of power through illustrating its capillary, micro-level operations.

It is perhaps easier to think of the disciplinary, normativizing functions of certain technologies of self, particularly given Foucault's assertion that they are inextricably interwoven with technologies of domination in the formation of a complex he terms "governmentality." Governmentality is conceptualized by Foucault as a contact point "where the technologies of domination of individuals over one another have recourse to processes by which the individual acts upon himself. And conversely, he has to take into account the points where techniques of the self are integrated into structures of coercion or domination." The subject, in this formulation, is the site of an enfolding wherein forces of domination, conflict, normalization, and biopolitical regulation ferment unpredictably with autonomic processes through which we struggle to establish, as Gilles Deleuze writes in *Foucault*, "a relation of veracity with our being."[9] Our selves are constituted, in other words, through a terse and unpredictable interaction of technologies of domination and technologies of the self, forces of oppression, and more or less successful attempts at transformation and metamorphosis wherein we realize an always present potential to become something other than what technologies of domination attempt to make of us. While there is, of course, no sovereign subject here, there is a certain kind of autonomy, a certain practice by which one can exercise a conditional and conditioned freedom. This is where, in a Foucauldian framework, the capacity for resistance is located—in the same intimate folds where the capillary operations of domination also dwell.

An exclusive focus on operations of domination and normalization when utilizing a Foucauldian framework often results in a firmly social constructivist account of a given phenomenon, wherein the subjects so affected are figured as determined, done over, and at least temporarily fixed in terms of corporeal meaning and subjective intelligibility. The widespread use of this method of analysis is, of course, the precipitating factor for reductive readings of the political effectiveness of Foucault's central concepts. To gloss this sort of reading: Foucault's work is posited as less than useful for thinking about resistance, agency, and intentionality in the service of social and political transformation on account of his treatment of the subject as solely an effect of power, lacking autonomy and unable, even when thinking or acting self-reflexively, to counter, contest, or move beyond this determination.

This mode of analysis overdetermines Foucault's consideration of subjective construction. It is not that the subject radically lacks autonomy but that the conditional and contingent ground of autonomy lies in a tense and constantly mutating field of power relations rather than with the subject herself. What this means is that the subject, while fully capable of engaging in the work of self-constitution, is simultaneously receiving, navigating, and being molded by subjective determinations that come from without. So the subject is not the sovereign author of herself—this much is true. Rather, she is both produced and producer. It is not that agential autonomy is impossible in this framework, only that, as Amy Allen writes in *The Politics of Our Selves*, Foucault's conception of "autonomy—both in the sense of the capacity for critical reflection and in the sense of the capacity for deliberate self-transformation—[is] always bound up with power."[10]

With this understanding of subjective constitution—which hinges on an interwoven coupling of production of self through technologies of self that cohabits with the capillary experience of disciplinary, normativizing power—we can move beyond the illusory rift between understanding the subject as power effect and understanding the subject as capable of resistance and transformation. This means, however, encountering accounts of disciplinarization and normativization with an attunement to both extant and possible resistances, metamorphoses, and transformations. It also means encountering accounts of autonomy, agency, and resistance with an attunement to the ways in which technologies of domination both subtend and trouble efforts to enact technologies of the self. In other words, where there is domination, there is always resistant invention (and vice versa).

What this approach necessitates, then, is a refusal of the common division of Foucault's oeuvre into an "early" Foucault concerned with constructing a genealogy of the subject as power effect and a "late" Foucault concerned with radical politics, ascesis, subjective and social transformation, and *le souci de soi*. As Foucault's own account of what he means by *governmentality* makes clear, these two lines of inquiry are irrevocably yoked together, and each component runs the risk of languishing in philosophical and political ineffectiveness without the other.

Two Foucaults, then? No. A doubled, enfolded Foucault, committed to examining what we can think of as the exteriority that dwells within the subject alongside the inventive, novel interiority the subject projects outwards. I read Barbin's memoir (and Foucault's reading of Barbin's memoir) with this enfolding of the subject in mind.

Monstrosity or Disability? Situating Intersex Issues

This approach to Barbin's memoir allows me to examine how intersex conditions were transformed from monstrosities to disabilities in the late nineteenth century, how this transition was resisted, and the foundation of that resistance. This focus—simultaneously constructivist and attentive to resistant potentialities—is one way a Foucauldian framework merges the ostensible structuralist focus of an "early" Foucault with the radical political engagements of a "late" Foucault.

To begin I'd like to inquire after what Foucault means when he deploys the term *monstrosity*. If we look to the lecture series delivered in 1974–75 at the Collège de France, published under the title *Abnormal*, we see that first and foremost monstrosity is characterized by mixity. Foucault offers a veritable laundry list of modes of mixity by way of example, and it is instructive to examine this list to see both what forms of embodiment may have been included beneath the big tent of monstrosity and how he periodizes the tenure of this particular understanding of monstrosity:

> From the Middle Ages to the eighteenth century . . . the monster is essentially a mixture. It is the mixture of two realms, the animal and the human: the man with the head of an ox, the man with a bird's feet—monsters. It is the blending, the mixture of two species: the pig with a sheep's head is a monster. It is the mixture of two individuals: the person who has two heads and one body or two bodies and one head is a monster. It is the mixture of two sexes: the person who is both male and female is a monster. It is a mixture of life and death: the fetus born with a morphology that means it will not be able to live but that nonetheless survives for some minutes or days is a monster. Finally, it is a mixture of forms: the person who has neither arms nor legs, like a snake, is a monster.[11]

A mélange of figures appear in this list, some of which we recognize as disabled bodies (infants born with congenital quirks, like conjoined twins or intersex folks), and others that may refer to newly taxonomized animal life or beings present in myth alone. They are united by only one facet: mixity, an irreducible estrangement from the purity of composition meant to constitute and maintain the boundaries between sexes, species, life, and death. For it is not only that these beings are mixed; it is that they are mixed in such a way as to trouble and transgress the categories of being which give the law (conceived in various registers—civil, canon, divine) its meaning. They are seen as transgressions of nature, products of a divine playfulness or sometimes, more sinisterly, portents of divine wrath visited upon a community. Monstrous bodies are wondrous precisely because they confound the order of things.

Wonder is an expansive category that includes those beings understood as monstrous. Grasping intersex bodies as monstrous wonders is key to understanding the prehistory of positivist biological materialism—that is, the forms of knowledge that precede modern Western understandings of intersex bodies as disordered. Before the conceptual transformation they underwent in seventeenth- and eighteenth-century natural philosophy, wonders "hovered at the edges of scientific inquiry. Indeed, they defined those edges, both objectively and subjectively. Wonders as objects marked the outermost limits of the natural. [They] registered the line between the known and the unknown." As markers of this sort, wonders refuse ascription to the status of an epistemological object, a facticity about which knowledge may be produced. Rather, they defy categorical logics of the natural order and function not as a supplement to knowledge production about this order but as a rupture, a fissure, a break. Wonders are those beings that disrupt the possibility of continuing to make sense of an established natural order. They are preludes to "divine contemplation, a shaming admission of ignorance, a cowardly flight into fear of the unknown, or a plunge into energetic investigation."[12]

Relatedly, Foucault writes "there is monstrosity only when the confusion comes up against, overturns, or disturbs civil, canon, or religious law." Confronted with monstrosity, "law must either question its own foundations, or its practice, or fall silent, or abdicate, or appeal to another reference system, or again invent a casuistry."[13] In the case of Herculine Barbin, the invented casuistry entails denying that anything other than two discrete and dimorphic sexes exist and subsequently calling forth the medical establishment to determine the "true sex" of Barbin; the only other option available would entail a radical re-visioning of the operational understandings of sex that so thoroughly shape social organization and subjective intelligibility. In opting to eradicate the phenomenon of "true hermaphroditism" and placing in its stead two varieties of sexed mixity in the form of "male pseudohermaphroditism" and "female pseudohermaphroditism," intersex conditions are transformed from monstrosities to disabilities.[14]

This transition is detailed in medical historian Alice Dreger's *Hermaphrodites and the Medical Invention of Sex*, a rigorously researched history of the development of intersex diagnoses. Dreger situates Barbin's case in relation to two other historically contemporaneous cases to provide a picture of the hotly contested field on which struggles over theories that sought to provide definitive accounts of sex constitution took place. She writes that Barbin lived at a time when "it was not only the hermaphrodite's body that lay ensconced in ambiguity, but the medical and scientific concepts of the male and the female as well," a time when "sex itself was still open to doubt."[15] Barbin's memoir is in large part a document of how religious and medical professionals attempt to clarify this ambiguity.

See, for instance, this report written by Dr. Chesnet, the man charged with Herculine's examination before the reversal of her sexed civil status.

Is Alexina a woman? She has a vulva, labia majora, and a feminine urethra, independent of a sort of imperforate penis, which might be a monstrously developed clitoris. She has a vagina. True, it is very short, very narrow; but after all, what is it if it is not a vagina? These are completely feminine attributes. Yes, but Alexina has never menstruated; the whole outer part of her body is that of a man, and my explorations did not enable me to find a womb. Her tastes, her inclinations, draw her toward women. At night she has voluptuous sensations that are followed by a discharge of sperm; her linen is stained and starched with it. Finally, to sum up the matter, ovoid bodies and spermatic cords are found by touch in a divided scrotum. These are the real proofs of sex. We can now conclude and say: Alexina is a man, hermaphroditic, no doubt, but with an obvious predominance of masculine sexual characteristics.[16]

It is at the point where Chesnet writes "the whole outer body is that of a man" that his diagnosis takes a decisive turn toward ushering in evidence that will attest (incontrovertibly, it seems) to Herculine's "true sex." This evidence begins with a focus on Herculine's external bodily significations, is shored up by her sexual inclinations, and moves toward a final, damning, ostensibly irreproachable fact: the presence of testicles "in a divided scrotum." How is it that the presence or absence of testicles becomes the "real proof of sex," the explanatory principle that is framed as generating Herculine's "inclinations . . . toward women," particularly in light of the assertion Foucault makes in his introduction to Herculine's memoir that "it was a very long time before the postulate that a hermaphrodite must have a sex—a single, true sex—was formulated"? After all, Foucault writes, "for centuries, it was quite simply agreed that hermaphrodites had two."[17]

Barbin's memoir vividly depicts the replacement of one system of bodily intelligibility by another: the teratological classificatory system formulated by Isidore Geoffroy Saint-Hilaire that allowed for *multiple hermaphrodisms* was supplanted by the linked concepts of "true" and "pseudo-" hermaphroditism. Within Saint-Hilaire's teratological system, the study of hermaphroditism constituted one of his "four great teratological kingdoms," a special and privileged set of the categories he utilized in the scientific study of monsters (teratology is derived from the Greek word *tera*, meaning "monster" or "marvel"). Hilaire analyzed hermaphroditic bodies using a six-part segmentation of what he termed "human sexual anatomy" into distinct zones, articulated as such: "the profound portion, which included the ovaries or testicles and their anatomical dependents; the middle portion, which included the uterus or prostate and the seminal vesicles, and their anatomical dependents; and the external portion, which included the clitoris and vulva or penis and scrotum." Within this system, if all six zones of discernibility were "evidently" or "unambiguously" male, the object of investigation was classified as such, and vice versa. Any mixity or ambiguity in one or more of these zones engendered a hermaphroditic classification within a schematic composed of "first-class" and "second-class" hermaphrodisms, the former containing four "orders" and the latter three. Thus, this system produced *seven possible hermaphrodisms*. As Dreger writes, his "system of hermaphroditic variations did not rest upon a rigorous notion of, or obsession with, a 'true' gonadal sex of each hermaphroditic body [nor] the latter-day obsession with 'true' versus 'false' hermaphrodites."[18]

The discursive rise of the "true" and "pseudo-" hermaphrodite was actually the conceptual death of the true hermaphrodite. This new mode of sex intelligibility necessitated the eradication of the true hermaphrodite—that is, a conception of the hermaphrodite as possessing both sexes. When hermaphrodites were understood as having two sexes, sex assignation relied on what Anne Fausto-Sterling terms, citing early modern English jurist Sir Edward Coke, the doctrine of the "sex which prevaileth."[19] While the idea of a "prevailing" sex attests to the legal and juridical fixity of a two-sex system, it nevertheless acknowledges a certain sexed copresence in cases concerning hermaphrodites. It is precisely this conception of sexed copresence that is erased with the rise of the pseudohermaphrodite, which relegated hermaphroditic hybridity to the realm of the chimerical, claiming that behind the apparently mixed sexual attributes of hermaphrodites lay a "true" sex rather than a prevailing or dominant one.

What ensued was the development of a variety of methodologies and experiments that sought to find one *absolute* material determinant of sex and, thus, to discredit true hermaphroditism in order to reify and further congeal dominant cultural conceptions regarding the ostensible truth of univocal sex. The pinnacle of this search for the one absolute material determinant of sex is the distinction made in the late nineteenth century by German physician Theodor Albrecht Edwin Klebs between true and false hermaphrodites. The criteria he set up revolved around the kind of tissue found in the gonads of hermaphrodites—if ovarian tissue, the hermaphrodite would be reclassified as a female pseudohermaphrodite and have their gender reassigned accordingly; if testicular tissue, then the obverse. Klebs's taxonomy effectively abolished the true hermaphrodite, rendering the criteria for that categorization so narrow that very, very few ever fit.

Klebs's taxonomy was both accepted and elaborated upon in the medical realm around the turn of the twentieth century. Two British physicians, George F. Blacker and Thomas William Pelham Lawrence, published an article in the 1896 volume *Transactions of the Obstetrical Society of London* that aimed to "tighten the definition of true hermaphroditism and to clean the historical record of any alleged cases of true hermaphroditism that did not fit their refined, stricter definition."[20] This new, tightened criterion insisted upon the necessity of a microscopical examination of the gonads to determine the type of tissue present—ovarian, testicular, or, in extremely rare instances, a combination thereof. The paper was primarily dedicated to a close scrutiny of prior cases of "true hermaphroditism," reviewing twenty-seven of these cases and refuting all but three.

Given these historically contemporaneous developments, we can read Barbin's memoir as a parable of modern Western understandings of sex, a microcosmic repository of the struggle and eventual consolidation of contemporary truth-regimes of sex. Indeed, it's all there: the development of gonadal determinations of sex, the concomitant erasure of "true hermaphroditism," the evidentiary utilization of Barbin's desire for women as proof of maleness, the priestly struggle over whether to quarantine Barbin in the nunnery or facilitate the complicated and not-yet-codified realities of public gender transition. This has been the tendency in much of the literature in intersex studies, and in utilizing the story as a parable of this sort, scholars are taking a cue from Foucault himself, who writes in his preface to the volume that he would be "tempted to call the story banal were it not for two or three things that give it a particular intensity. The date, first of all. The years from around 1860 to 1870 were precisely one of those periods when investigations of sexual identity were carried out with the most intensity, in an attempt not only to establish the true sex of hermaphrodites but also to identify, classify, and characterize the different types of perversions."[21] We are invited, then, to conjecture this text as minor and unexceptional were it historically situated otherwise. It is the fact that Barbin, as well as the institutional interlocuters attempting to establish the truth of Barbin's sex, are located in a moment wherein the biopolitical regulation of sex and sexuality is flourishing that is of interest. We can trace the contours of these burgeoning regulations onto the texts presented and are invited by Foucault himself to do so.

This is, of course, a necessary starting point for the analysis, but a more robust engagement is essential if we are to move beyond understanding intersex diagnoses as mere evidence of the biopolitical regulation of sex or, perhaps concomitantly, as tragic byproducts of the consolidation of dimorphic understandings of "true sex." If we are to understand, in a full sense, the importance of this memoir, we must focus on the fact that in addition to being a parable of the ascendancy of sex dimorphism in cases of ambiguous or indeterminate sex, it is also one of the only documents from this period that charts the experience of intersex diagnosis from below. While I agree with Dreger's assertion that "the absence of documents like Barbin's memoirs cannot justify the far too sweeping conclusions—about scientific and social concepts of sex, gender, and sexuality—that have been drawn by some recent scholars simply from the singular case of Barbin," I think that focusing on the singularity of her words offers a way out of reading her experience as that of a mere power effect, one of the many casualties precipitated by the biopolitical regulation of sex.[22] We need to read the protestation, resistance, and alternative modes of being that are worked out in the text—the technologies of the self at work—alongside our tally of the effectivity of disciplinary technologies of normalization.

When intersex conditions come to be understood as disorders rather than monstrous wonders, they are no longer an affront, a transgression, or a confounding limit-instance. Instead they become invitations to diagnosis, and intersex people become experimental subjects on which the medical apparatus may machinate and elaborate its account of the constitution of sex difference in a way that all too often denies our autonomic capacities, exhorting us to, as Foucault writes, "wake up . . . from your illusory pleasures; strip off your disguises and recall that every one of you has a sex, a true sex."[23] This exhortation is familiar not only to intersex folks but to genderqueers, nonbinary and agender folks, trans folks, and gender-nonconforming queer folks. It is this demand to discover our "true sexes" that gives intersex an intelligible position within the law while relegating the enactment of something like intersex subjectivity to the status of impossibility. One can be intersex but only if it's a trait or disorder; one is always, despite being intersex, also irrevocably male or female—and it's the job of modern Western medical science to discern which of those one is.

Foucault writes that "disability may well be something that upsets the natural order, but disability is not monstrosity because it has a place in civil or canon law. The disabled person may not conform to nature, but the law in some way provides for him."[24] For intersex persons, the providence of law works to offer a choice that feels more like a conscription or a sentence: Here is your diagnosis. You may choose one of two paths; each will entail extensive surgical and chemical reconfiguration. A choice is necessary if you want to access the rights and privileges of sexed and sexual normalcy.

It is precisely this choice that Barbin resents and resists. In so doing she refuses a system of bodily intelligibility that is radically intolerant of mixity and abnormality. She refuses to be understood as disabled and in her own way insists on a right to monstrosity, a right to transgression, a right to determine her selfhood, a right to difference, opacity, and singularity. In this insistence, she enacts a prefigurative politics that resonates deeply with contemporary intersex, disability, queer, and trans activisms that seek to disrupt, transgress, and unfix the politically loaded epistemes that divide bodies and behaviors into dyads of normal and abnormal in order to more effectively invent casuistries that allow technologies of normalization to be inflicted upon beings of difference.

Re-membering Herculine:
Toward a Queer History of the Present

To parse the resistant moments of this memoir, it is important to bear in mind its position in relation to Foucault's proposed genealogy of modern Western power-knowledge networks at work in the regulation of sex, sexuality, and embodiment. In his brief prefatory notes to the dossier, Foucault writes that he intends to keep the published subsidiary documentation of the case to a minimum, as "the question of strange destinies like her own, which have raised so many problems for medicine and law, especially since the sixteenth century, will be dealt with in the volume of *The History of Sexuality* that will be devoted to hermaphrodites."[25] This volume—along with many of the other volumes Foucault initially proposed—never saw the light of day, as the initial plans for the series took a significant turn with his decision to return to the Greeks in the second and third completed volumes. However, Foucault's biographer Didier Eribon provides commentary on the relation of this memoir to that initial proposition, discussing the fact that at the moment of publication Foucault intended this volume as a companion text to *The History of Sexuality*, forming part of a series entitled Parallel Lives. These texts would be selected precisely for what Foucault understood as the "infamous" nature of the authors. What he sought to expose through the Parallel Lives series (which was, like the original proposal for *The History of Sexuality*, later abandoned) was, as Françoise Proust puts it, not "figures of revolt (heroic or otherwise) against injustice or figures of combat against oppression" but instead "figures of originary and anonymous resistance which are brought, despite themselves, to a visible or non-visible confrontation with power."[26] Through the republication and dissemination of this memoir, Foucault hoped to illuminate the lives of everyday folks, familiar in their mundanity, who—in unwilled confrontations with power-knowledge regimes—nevertheless manifested resistance in situations wherein their agentic capacities were extraordinarily minimal, forcibly and violently curtailed. Barbin is one of these figures.

She is thought by Foucault as something other than a spectacular subject of heroic resistance or a bleakly victimized persona; rather, her life is molded by a set of continuous quotidian confrontations with institutional apparatuses whose logic she (sometimes subtly, sometimes vociferously) contests. Much of this contestation occurs in and through the writing of this memoir. This act of writing resistance to disciplinary regimes can be thought of as an instance of countermemory, one plugged immediately into what Foucault understood as integral to the construction of what he called *histories of the present*.

To write a history of the present is to work with a past that is not merely artifactual, unified, or sedimented and thus not objectively knowable and explainable in terms of a fully given, understood, and transparent present. Rather, as Michael Roth summarizes pithily in his important essay on the concept, one writes a history of the present "in order to make that present into a past"; this occurs through uncovering ignored or devalorized pasts that work to "rupture the present into a future that will leave the very function of history behind it."[27] Thus, histories of the present undo the tendency to understand history as a narrative to which a person clings tightly in order to provide coherent, legible, and reductively sensible understandings of the present. A history of the present works to rupture that present in order to make metamorphosis and change (rather than linearized understandings of "progress") possible. Histories of the present interrogate the relationship between the historical a priori and lines of flight—that is, the relationship between the power-knowledge regimes that give forceful shape, structure, and legibility to a given historical moment and those parallel lives shaped by efforts to rework and exceed those regimes, by efforts to make sense otherwise. To uncover those traces is to undertake a genealogical endeavor concerned with producing countermemories that rupture the sutures of hegemonic historical accounts.

When Barbin's memoir is put to work in the service of illustrating the historical a priori of sex intelligibility, we're only getting part of the story. What's missing is an account of Herculine's resistance, ineffective though it may have been; what's missing is an account of what made Herculine's life truly parallel to, and not consanguineous with, the power-knowledge regimes she found herself subject to.

The following passage (probably the most oft-cited portion of Foucault's introduction to the memoir) documents Foucault's investment in Barbin as a resistant figure:

[Herculine] wrote her memoirs . . . once her new identity had been discovered and established. Her "true" and "definitive" identity. But it is clear she did not write them from the point of view of the sex which had at least been brought to light. It is not a man who is speaking, trying to recall his sensations and his life as they were at the time when he was not yet "himself." When Alexina [Herculine's given name] composed her memoirs, she was not far from her suicide; for herself, she was still without a definite sex, but she was deprived of the delights she experienced in not having one, or in not entirely having the same sex as the girls among whom she lived and whom she loved and desired so much. And what she evokes in her past is the happy limbo of a non-identity, which was paradoxically protected by the life of those closed, narrow, and intimate societies where one has the strange happiness, which is at the same time obligatory and forbidden, of being acquainted with only one sex.[28]

He understands Barbin as someone who refuses to accept the assignation of a sex-based identity—someone who was "without a definite sex," someone who disidentifies with their newly assigned male identity because it had been utilized to corral and misidentify her desire as heterosexual and force her out of a sphere insulated, to some extent, from male contact and patriarchal and masculinist values.

His assertion that Barbin's life pre–gender reassignment was replete with the "delights" of not having a definite sex, shaped by the "happy limbo of non-identity," has become the occasion for much academic debate. Judith Butler, in particular, has taken issue with this reading, arguing that his understanding of Herculine's relationship to sex identity is a "sentimental indulgence" shaped by the problematic idea that an "overthrow of 'sex' results in the release of a primary sexual multiplicity." In other words, Butler believes Foucault is embracing an emancipatory sexual politics rooted an understanding of sexuality as repressed by hegemonic gender and sexual orders and thus in need of liberation. This is, of course, the very understanding of sexual liberation that Foucault so roundly critiques in the first volume of *The History of Sexuality*, where he argues that that there is no concept of sexuality prior to or outside of matrices of power. Butler works what she calls the "official Foucault" of *The History of Sexuality* against the Foucault of the memoir introduction: "on the one hand, Foucault wants to argue that there is no 'sex' in itself which is not produced by complex interactions of discourse and power, and yet there does seem to be a 'multiplicity of pleasures' *in itself* which is not the effect of any specific discourse/power exchange. . . . On the other hand, Foucault officially insists that sexuality and power are coextensive and that we must not think that by saying yes to sex we say no to power." Butler goes on to identify Herculine's sexuality as "ambivalent"—not a "happy limbo of non-identity" as per Foucault but a sexuality that "recapitulates the ambivalent structure of its production, construed in part as the institutional injunction to pursue the love of various 'sisters' and 'mothers' of the extended convent family and the absolute prohibition against carrying that love too far." In Butler's account, Herculine's sexual identity is ambivalent because it is produced by a structuring prohibition—what she calls an "eroticized taboo" against same-sex intimacies in female homosocial spaces.[29] These spaces encourage sisterly love, as long as it remains chaste. Herculine comes to understand sexual desire, in Butler's reading, through engaging the varieties of female homosexual identification present in her homosocial milieu—not a nonidentity, then, but a disidentification with female homosexuality. The issue Barbin encountered—whether in relation to male heterosexual identity or female homosexual identity—is that her body exceeds the biological dimorphism that both of these sexual identities are predicated upon. Thus, there is no legible sexual identity available to her, nothing for her to identify with. Disidentification is her only option.

Butler senses this, I think, in her gloss on the manner in which Herculine conceives of the relation between her embodiment, her gender, and her sexuality. She writes, "Perhaps because Herculine's body is hermaphroditic, the struggle to separate conceptually the description of her primary sexual characteristics from her gender identity (her sense of her own gender which, by the way, is ever-shifting and far from clear) and the directionality and objects of her desire is especially difficult. She herself presumes at various points that her body is the *cause* of her gender confusion and her transgressive pleasures, as if they were both result and manifestation of an essence which somehow falls outside the natural/metaphysical order of things." Butler suggests that the problem lies with Barbin's conjecture of an essence "outside" the order of things; rather, she understands Herculine's life as structured by a "fatal ambivalence" that, "for all its effects of happy dispersal nevertheless culminates in Herculine's suicide."[30] I imagine it would have been very hard for Barbin to imagine her life as structured by fatal ambivalence. Rather, she is reasonably happy, even as she senses her embodied difference from the girls and women around her until she is forced into a "true sex," a male sex. In other words, Herculine's ambivalence wasn't always fatal; it became fatal when the space for the everyday enactment of ambivalence is foreclosed—when Herculine is forced by religious, legal, and medical authorities to become a man. It is the foreclosure of lived ambivalence that produces fatality, not the ambivalence as such. Indeed, for much of the memoir, Herculine's ambivalence with respect to sexed and sexual identity is a source of pleasure.

Herculine never (either intentionally or unwittingly) posits herself as a being before or outside the laws that constitute sexed and sexual identity but consistently performs a critique of the law itself through recapitulating the terms of the utter impossibility of her inhabiting a subjective position within it—not because she is over the law nor has never been under it, put precisely because she knows better than to let it stick, than to let it mold and thoroughly constitute her desire, her subjectivity. Rather, she lives the impossibility of sexual subjectification and lives this impossibility intimately, in every breath, in every moment of self-reflexivity, in every desirous becoming. She is neither duped nor misled. Rather, she inhabits her desire through the deliberate rejection of sexed and sexual identity—not because she yearns to become a hero, a rebel, a criminal, or a pervert, but because she seems to understand that none of those subjective positions, female or male, hetero- or homosexual, can legitimately constitute nor totalize her. All of these forms of identity seem to ring false. Her rejection, her disidentification, takes place firmly within and against the law (whether scientific, juridical, or religious), not from some phantasmic position before or beyond it. This is precisely why Herculine is a resister, a saboteur, though one with woefully inadequate language for the modes in which she enacts her subversion. I wonder, sometimes, what she would have written had the conceptual toolbox of queer theory—and contemporary forms of nonbinary gender identification—been available to her.

The memoir is fragmented; the portion of the narrative that falls between Barbin's account of her upbringing and the final pages articulating her contemporary existential difficulties is missing, ostensibly lost as it was shuttled from one doctor to another following Herculine's death. On account of this gap in narrative, the text that Foucault had published seems to fall neatly into two narrative modalities—the first, more lengthy portion of the text reads as a nostalgic account of Barbin's upbringing in the female milieus of convent and boarding schools and includes a rather veiled account of her passionately engaged, secretive relationship with her lover Sara. The latter portion of the memoir, occurring after this long, detailed account of Barbin's life up to and including gender reassignment and movement to Paris, reads as a text that hovers undecidedly between castigation and lament. For this reason, as Foucault recounts, the doctor who performed the autopsy on Herculine's body—who initially had possession of the memoir—considered them problematically tainted by intense emotion and published, alongside the autopsy report, only the more straightforwardly autobiographical material.[31]

Foucault's restoration of the latter portion of the memoir works against the wholesale elision of Herculine's critique of the institutional powers that force her into a male role. It is in this portion of the memoir that Barbin most vociferously resists the ideological and material impositions made on her person in the service of gender assignation. While she castigates medical and juridical authority as well as the logics of sexual difference undergirding and consolidated through the treatment she received, her lament emanates from her at least partially consensual agreement to place herself squarely in the hands of authorities—religious and lay—who would ostensibly work in her best interests to discern a path of action that would relieve her guilty conscience regarding her illicit relationship with Sara and perhaps resolve some of her sense of existential misplacement. In other words, she initially believes these authorities seek only to help her, but upon realizing the cost of such help—exile from her community and her loved ones, loss of employment, and conscription to a male gender role that she abhors—she retaliates. As Geertje Mak attests in her masterful rereading of Barbin's memoir, "sex reassignments lead to a radical shift of positions in society, often including work, social relations and love life or marriage. The embarrassment it invoked made a lot of hermaphrodites decide to escape their home town. Such was also the case with Barbin. His memoirs show how crushing the practical consequences of such a dislocation were."[32]

Guilt regarding her affair with Sara and a sense of existential misplacement are the motivations that precede Herculine's offering of her story to, first, a prelate and then, at the suggestion of the prelate, a doctor. Just before these dual confessions, Herculine had been visited by a doctor at the girl's school where she worked, following intense abdominal pain (more than likely a result of complications elicited by Barbin's partially descended gonads); this visiting doctor, while not forthcoming regarding the details of his investigation to anyone but the school's director, Madame P., recommended that Barbin be sent away from the school at once. This recommendation was summarily refused by the director of the school, who was fond of Barbin and wanted to quash scandal before it had the chance to arise. Dismissing Barbin would raise suspicion, so Barbin was kept on in the capacity of instructor—though this solution was short-lived.

Although Barbin was not, at this point, familiar with the medical details of her case, she was able to intuit that there were a series of abnormalities that troubled her relationship to dyadic sex difference. A quick reference to her account of this medical investigation renders clear the probability that Barbin conjectured herself a misfit with regard to sex typicality:

> He wanted to examine me. As it is known, a doctor enjoys certain privileges with a sick person that nobody dreams of contesting. During this operation, I heard him sighing, as if he were not satisfied with what he had found. Madame P. was there, waiting for a word.
>
> I too was waiting, but in an entirely different frame of mind.
>
> Standing near my bed, the doctor considered me attentively, full of interest, while giving vent to muffled exclamations of this sort: "My God! Is it possible?"
>
> I understood by his gestures that he would have liked to prolong this examination until the truth sprang to light!!![33]

Deprived of a consultation regarding these apparently shocking medical discoveries, Barbin knew only that her body was a near-impossible object on the cusp of medical credulity; moreover, she came to find out that that this aberrant corporeality was somehow considered necessary and sufficient grounds for her dismissal from her post in an all-female milieu. Somehow, then, her bodily atypicality was linked to a hovering threat of sexual impropriety. This was a common linkage in Renaissance-era European thinking on hermaphroditism. Ann Jones and Peter Stallybrass attest to this phenomenon in their article "Fetishizing Gender: Constructing the Hermaphrodite in Renaissance Europe," asserting that "In France, there was certainly an increasing tendency to absorb the hermaphrodite into the figure of the deviant woman, a conflation which was made more plausible by the medical rediscovery of the clitoris in the mid-sixteenth century. Henceforth, in France, at least, the hermaphrodite could be categorized as a woman with an enlarged clitoris, and was thus prosecutable for committing sodomy with other women."[34] The conflation of tribadism and hermaphroditism engaged by Barbin's examiner attests to the shaky diagnostic status of hermaphroditic "true sex" at this particular historical moment. The Barbin case, as discussed above, is located on the cusp of a shift in the medical perception of atypically sexed bodies. The ascendancy of "true" and "pseudo" forms of hermaphroditism coexisted with understandings of hermaphroditism as a form of female deviance. So it's perhaps not surprising that, as Barbin begins the castigation of the medicoscientific establishment that ends the memoir, she couples it with a deep critique of what we would now call *heteronormativity*. If tribadism and hermaphroditism were conflated, then a critical response must address both medicoscientific protocol as well as sociosexual normativity. In particular, she finds herself disgusted with what we might now label *hegemonic masculinity*. She excoriates this form of masculinity, in particular the conventions of the uncontrollable male libido and the sexual duplicity rife within the marriage contract: "Men! I have not soiled my lips with your false oaths, nor my body with your hideous copulations. I have not seen my name dragged in the mud by a faithless wife. I have been spared all the filthy sores that you display in broad daylight." Though she writes that the "family's hearth is shut" to her, her outsiderhood is something she relishes, for it means she's dodged the bullet of heteronormativity.[35] While she may not ever be able to—nor want to—embody hegemonic forms of masculinity, she has also avoided becoming some man's wife or mistress, avoided being subject to their "hideous copulations." Herculine Barbin: original misandrist.

Given the competing scripts of intelligibility regarding hermaphroditism, it's also perhaps not surprising that Barbin relies on another trope of queer corporeality to frame her critique: the virile woman. She posits herself, just prior to suicide (and contra Catholic belief that one cannot enter the kingdom of heaven after suicide) as "partaking of the nature of the angels," as a being divinely marked for suffering on account of her ontological homelessness. She writes that while "others have the earth," she has "boundless space"; while others are "enchained here below by the thousand bonds of your gross, material senses," she claims that, through her saintly apprenticeship in suffering elicited by this existential placelessness, she has a spirit able to "plunge into that limpid ocean of the infinite" and a knowledge of "surges of pure ecstasy" of soul she is capable of only because her "earthly ties to humanity have been broken."[36]

Subjectivities shaped by conventional sexualities and embodiments are relegated to a position of base, material enslavement by the sensorium, while Herculine conjectures her dire circumstances as a Job-style trial of faith, a test of suffering that opens one up to great spiritualized ecstasies. Barbin, on account of her deeply religious education, was certainly familiar with understandings of female Christian devotees as virile women, as beings who, in leaving their carnal forms of sexuality behind and devoting themselves to spiritual ascesis, attain a masculinized mode of being in the world. Barbin believed that she, too, had undergone this cross-gender transition and had in the process abdicated her embodied sexual self. In grasping this alternative logic of gender transition, Barbin constructs a history of the present—she repurposes saintly cross-gender tropes in a way that ruptures the ascendant medicoscientific emphasis on sexual dimorphism. This reframing of her experience places her beyond the stranglehold of modern Western forms of bodily intelligibility and enables the following moment of vitriolic critique, one that resonates deeply with contemporary efforts to depathologize understandings of nonnormative bodies. Barbin presciently conjectures the fate of her body following her suicide, writing that "when that day comes a few doctors will make a little stir around my corpse; they will shatter all the extinct mechanisms of its impulses, will draw new information from it, will analyze all the mysterious sufferings that were heaped upon a single human being. O princes of science, enlightened chemists, whose names resound throughout the world, analyze then, if that is possible, all the sorrows that have burned, devoured this heart down to its last fibers; all the scalding tears that have drowned it, squeezed it dry in their savage grasp!"[37] Here, Barbin works the importance of phenomenological, affective, experiential modes of knowledge against the detached, investigative (and invasive!) empiricism of scientific modes of analysis that work through severing corporeality from experience. She insists on the inadequacy of this valorized, hegemonic mode of knowledge production and counters it with a call to consider the violence produced by the power-knowledge networks that construct intersex bodies as freakish, marginal, deformed, somehow imperfectly human.

My hope is that we allow this complex style of resistance to inform and complicate our understandings of abnormality, sex, and gender difference in the multiple contexts our current historicopolitical conjuncture affords. For this to happen, we must refuse positioning this memoir, as well as other traces of intersex and trans counterhistories, as medicoscientific artifacts that speak to us only of disciplinary power. Rather, we can connect with this particular text in a mode that focuses on Barbin's queer pleasures and her longing for a social world not so straitjacketed by the violent presumptions of modern positivist understandings of sex difference and corporeal normality. In other words, we can deploy Barbin's critiques in the context of developing a critical queer and trans politic. What we need today, to resist the violences entailed by late modern disavowals of corporeal and sexual difference, is a coalition of monsters—those beings that embrace corporeal nonnormativity, hybridity, and mixity as a source of strength and resilience capable of challenging understandings of extraordinary bodies as pathological, aberrant, and undesirable.[38]

This chapter draws out a way of thinking about the resistance of intersex subjects in the context of intense administrative regulation by examining an early instance of such resistance in a moment shaped by an intense consolidation of medical authority in diagnosing and treating ostensible abnormalities of sex. The following chapter traces a much more recent genealogy of contestation: the intense debates, beginning in the mid-2000s, regarding the nomenclatural shift in medical diagnostic practice from "intersex" to "disorders of sex development." While this shift has, to date, been only partial, the positions articulated in the context of these debates illuminate much about the function of the concept of "disorder" in the context of regulating sex and gender differences, as well as the deeply differential deployments of intersex bodies by, on the one hand, relatively gender-conservative medical practitioners and parents of intersex children and, on the other, feminist and queer theorists. I ultimately argue that a return to the language of disorder serves to retrench sex dimorphic schemas of corporeal intelligibility; as such, this nomenclatural shift runs the risk of reproducing much of the same trauma documented so vividly by both Barbin's memoir and the activist practice of adult intersex folks.

capacity

I clip the anchors at the top of a steep route in Kentucky's Red River Gorge and look out at the rhododendron-choked forest, the sandstone cliffs encircling the holler, the phlox and dwarf irises that bloom on the forest floor. I'm exhausted–"worked," I say to my friends below—but make sure to take in the view before I lower down. The Red, as climbers lovingly refer to it, is known for its sometimes brutally overhung rock formations. Folks flock from all corners of the earth to pull on the sandstone in this little pocket of southeastern Kentucky; it's not surprising to find professional climbers from Eastern Europe cragging next to a group of ribald spring-breakers from the University of Kentucky. Before my first trip out here, a buddy of mine told me that while climbing in the Red, he finds himself—dyed-in-the-wool atheist though he is—thinking there must be some kind of intelligent design. The rock there, he says, is just made for humans to scramble up. It's too good to have happened by chance.

Climbing is hard. The learning curve is steep, and the horizon of improvement—in terms of both strength and technique—is ever-receding. In the years since I started, I've built muscle in places I didn't know muscles existed. My arms have doubled in size. My upper body and core has broadened, thickened. I'm able to physically accomplish tasks my younger self would think near-impossible: I can do two-finger pull-ups, dangle my body off of dime-edge cracks, throw a heel up onto a ledge near my head and use it to leverage my body upwards.

The physical transformations have been rewarding but the metaphysical ones more so. For years, my body was something I abhorred—or perhaps more to the point, something I was taught to abhor. It was a tacit lesson, but I absorbed it nevertheless, learning it when my pediatric endocrinologist told me I shouldn't speak publicly about my intersex status, when I found out one of my high school boyfriends had a collection of intersex and trans fetish porn, whenever I tried to find clothing that fit my frame, which is not quite male-typical or female-typical: broad shoulders, narrow hips, small breasts. I hated the way I looked. Raised and socialized as female, I had internalized the idea that my self-worth was yoked tightly to my ability to approximate girl-beauty, and lord, was I bad at doing so. No one told me there were other ways to relate to your body.

Feminist philosopher Iris Marion Young, in her classic essay "Throwing Like a Girl," writes that female socialization too often produces an experience of the body as a "fragile encumbrance, rather than the medium for the enactment of our aims."[1] We are taught to treat the body as both an aesthetic object and a delicate husk in need of protection. Not only had I been subject to this socialization—the doctrine of girlhood as pretty and protected—I had a deeply adverse response to it that involved the wholesale rejection of sports culture. My teenage self, disgusted with gender norms while also deeply affected by them, thought sports was some bullshit normal boys and girls did—a highly gender dimorphic, heterosexist culture of jocks and cheerleaders, Friday night football games, and beneath-the-bleachers makeouts.

Like Herculine, I sensed my body was different from the girls around me long before I knew I was intersex. Because of this, I avoided locker rooms at all costs, taking my required high school PE course over the summer so I could roll up to school in my gym shorts and white t-shirt and leave in the same get-up, never having set foot in a single-sex space where I was required to undress. My best friend—a trans guy, not yet out—did the same. We spent most of that summer sharing a friend's contraband Percocet and playing ping-pong. At some point, we had to run a mile—an item on the instructor's tick-list imposed by the state to make sure we were somehow moving our bodies—but because it was summertime in south Florida, ninety-five degrees and 200 percent humidity, the instructor exhorted us to walk the track—no jogging, no running. That was as physically intense as it got.

High school ended; college was a whirlwind of balancing a full-time job with a full course load; then suddenly I was in graduate school, admitted with five years of funding—poverty-level funding but funding nonetheless. I felt, suddenly, as if I had all the time in the world. I gave up my car (poverty-level funding) and began biking everywhere—long jaunts to campus, shorter ones to the grocery store, the dilapidated Irish pub that all the grad students attended with the regularity of praying people. I began to understand what Iris Marion Young meant about relating to the body as if it were "the medium for the enactment of our aims." My legs carried me so many miles; they delivered me over and again into the rooms of friends and lovers, into seminars on decolonial philosophy, into the air-conditioned embrace of the produce aisle in midsummer.

I had begun to sing the body electric, begun to feel what that old queen Whitman felt: the "curious sympathy one feels when feeling with the hand the naked meat of the body, / The circling rivers the breath, and breathing it in and out."[2] The body is a goddamn miracle, I thought, capable of so much more than I had ever thought possible. With this realization came love for my own body, tortured vessel though it was, love for its potential, love for its capacities. I thought less and less about how it appeared, less and less of its sexed atypicality. Movement, physical challenge, was a way out of my lifelong body-hatred. The harder I pushed it, the more my possibilities expanded—the more terrain I could explore, the more landscape I could take in. I could take this body miles and miles through the wilderness. It could run a marathon. It could push its way up thousands of feet of vertical terrain.

Or rather, *I* could do all of that. That gap—between my self and my body—was closing, increasingly indistinguishable. My body had become me. I stopped having a body; I started being a body. Climbing, running, and cycling had helped me heal from the trauma of growing up intersex, had taught me that my body was something other than an object to be repaired, amended, corrected.

So when I began to learn about the long history of gender policing intersex athletes, I was incensed. Knowing that the International Association of Athletics Federations and the International Olympic Committee submitted athletes to the same humiliating practices—blood tests, ultrasounds, urinalysis—that I had been subjected to in the name of determining and regulating sex was terrible enough. To learn that they then adjudicated upon whether or not atypically sexed folks would be able to compete in the events they had dedicated their lives to training for was tantamount to learning that international athletics was governed by a eugenic impulse. Negative eugenics—the practice of eradicating populations deemed unfit or undesirable—was at work, albeit in a softened form. Careers were being destroyed; intersex folks were being told they could not participate in their chosen events unless they submitted to "normalizing" hormone therapy. These were soft eradications—intersex bodies can be included in athletics as long as they erased any physical manifestations of intersex traits.

Then I learned of other eradications. Certain doctors were treating pregnant folks with the steroid dexamethasone in order to prevent the birth of visibly intersex children. When a fetus is found to be at risk for congenital adrenal hyperplasia (CAH)—an intersex condition resulting in genital ambiguity and sex-atypical hormonal levels—dexamethasone can be utilized to remediate these perceived sex abnormalities—to prevent genital ambiguity and so-called "tomboyism."

It seemed, increasingly, like the ability to live in an intersex body—unmonitored, unharassed, with some modicum of joy or pleasure in one's embodied experience—was impossible. In some instances, that possibility is eradicated before birth or immediately thereafter; in others, it is robbed by athletic regulatory agencies. In all of these instances, though, intersex bodies are understood as disordered, in need of repair.

My body is a whole lot of things—strong, vulnerable, sensate, sometimes injured, sometimes ill—but when and if it needs repair has absolutely nothing to do with being intersex. The harms it has accrued—the bodily trauma I've lived—stems directly from the gender normalization efforts I've had coercively imposed upon me. I dream, daily, of a world wherein that ends. Where intersex bodies aren't regulated out of existence. Where we don't need to be fixed.

2 Impossible Existences
Intersex and "Disorders of Sex Development"

In 2009 South African runner Caster Semenya—after a sudden dramatic improvement in her sprint times—was subjected to sex-verification testing by the International Academy of Athletics Federations (IAAF). They suspected she was too fast for a woman, that she must have "abnormally" high levels of testosterone that altered her performance and surpassed the so-called "upper limit" on testosterone levels within female athletes that the IAAF enforced. She was prevented from competing until 2010 and ran, then, only under the condition that she undergo hormone therapy to bring her testosterone levels back within the female-typical range. In 2016, after years of continuous pressure from intersex and trans rights advocates, medical professionals, and bioethicists, officials revised their stance, effectively eliminating this upper limit on testosterone. In the 2016 Olympics in Rio, Semenya competed in the women's eight-hundred-meter. For the first time in years, she competed with the cocktail of hormones her body—her "hyperandrogenic," possibly intersex body—naturally produces. She won.

The Semenya case has been covered internationally, receiving hostile and not-so-hostile press that nevertheless nearly always remains sensational (if not with reference to Semenya herself, then at least regarding the implications of Semenya's genotypical and phenotypical affront to gendered common sense). The coverage crested in 2009, immediately following her subjection to gender verification and again during the lead-up to the 2016 Olympics, when she was able to go off of hormone therapy and thus shaved seconds off of her (already record-breaking) times. The public commentary surrounding Semenya is rife with mean-spirited, invalidating references to her gender identity (she is repeatedly referred to as "it," for example), and her case is consistently used as an exemplar of why intersex and trans women shouldn't be allowed in female-specific athletic competitions—or should be forced to compete with men.

There have been a handful of notable exceptions in this journalistic morass, one being Ariel Levy's well-researched article "Either/Or," which appeared in the *New Yorker* on November 30, 2009. Levy contacted prominent intersex studies scholars from multiple disciplines—among them, Alice Dreger, Vernon Rosario, and Anne Fausto-Sterling—as well as South African athletic professionals and human rights activists and adequately reiterates the contestations of intersex scholars and activists alike regarding the multiple gradations and infinitesimal differences that disprove strictly dichotomous understandings of the constitution of biological sex. She frames the dilemma surrounding Semenya's career in women's track as a highly contested field where numerous conceptions of intersex conditions are operative, ranging from the outright denial of intersex conditions evident in the statement issued by the African National Congress Youth League, a division of the African National Congress, claiming that it "will never accept the categorization of Caster Semenya as a hermaphrodite, because in South Africa and the entire world of sanity, such does not exist" to Winnie Madikizela-Mandela's statement of support that uses a theological discourse to testify to the naturalness of intersex conditions: "There is nothing wrong with being a hermaphrodite. It is God's creation. She is God's child."[1] At the center of this discursive whirlwind is Semenya herself, who is depicted within Levy's article as a reticent being who has been fundamentally wronged by the process of being deployed and redeployed within the media as the figure around which debates cohere regarding, minimally, the ethical rectitude of sex-testing in the sports world and, more broadly, the constitution of biological sex itself.

The legally intelligible wrong, however, is whether or not Semenya will be able to retain her medals and continue competing in women's athletics at both national and international levels. This wrong is the hinge of the rights discourse utilized by the law agency of Dewey and LeBoeuf, which represented Semenya pro bono in her contestation of the International Association of Athletics Federations, the organization responsible for both ordering and subsequently leaking the results of the sex-verification tests.

In the words of the firm's South African managing partner Greg Nott, the agency aims to "do everything possible to make certain that her civil and legal rights and dignity as a person are fully protected."[2] While Dewey and LeBoeuf has been at least partially successful in this limited endeavor, securing a restitution of Semenya's medal and prize money in November 2009, debates have continued to rage over whether or not Semenya's possible intersex condition should disqualify her for participation in the international arena permanently. What is being adjudicated upon, however, is much more than Semenya's career—it is the authenticity and legibility of womanhood itself and by extension, whether this legibility can be institutionally granted to Semenya. The notion that one's sex is up for institutional adjudication is perhaps the real human rights violation of the Semenya case, a violation that will remain undisputed regardless of the legal efforts of Dewey and LeBoeuf.

Levy, in recounting her one and only contact with Semenya on the training grounds of the University of Pretoria, plays up her gender ambiguity, harping on the sexed undecidability of Semenya's body and gender presentation.

> A figure in a black sweatshirt with the hood up walked along the path about thirty yards in front of me. There was something about this person's build and movements that drew my attention. I got up and followed along the path, until I caught up to the person where he or she was stopped behind the cafeteria, talking to a waiter and a cook, both of whom were much shorter than she was. It was Caster Semenya. She wore sandals and track pants and kept her hood up. When she shook my hand, I noticed that she had long nails. She didn't look like an eighteen-year-old girl, or an eighteen-year-old boy. She looked like something else, something magnificent.[3]

The deferral and suspense with which Levy imbues this scene heightens our sense of Semenya's appearance as a spectacle. Levy embraces the same problematic tropes of sex-skepticism omnipresent in Semenya's life (as well as the reportage on it). She has been forced to have her genitals inspected at track restrooms by women on competing teams. She has been subject to a makeover in the South African women's magazine *YOU* that attempts to corral her gender presentation back within the proper confines of the feminine. Her trainers received a payoff for this makeover. She has had her body discursively dissected by the news media over and over again.

Admittedly, Levy submits Semenya to a critique of sex that results in the conclusion that she is, although corporeally atypical and butch-presenting, "something magnificent" rather than abhorrent or in need of gendered normalization. This valorizing response, however, seems opposed to the subjective desires of Semenya herself, who wishes to be out of the spotlight, no longer a speculative object, no longer represented as a gender outlaw or as living proof of any theory—feminist, biomedical, psychosocial, or otherwise—about the nature of biological sex differentiation. The article concludes with a final word from Semenya, issued just before walking away from Levy: "'It sucks when I was running and they were writing those things. That sucked. That is when it sucks. Now I just have to walk away. That's all I can do.' She smiled a small, bemused smile. 'Walk away from all of this, maybe forever. Now I just walk away.' Then she took a few steps backward, turned around, and did."[4] Semenya's decision to walk away from the limelight in order to avoid further media contact and its attendant sensationalism is only a more exaggerated instance of one many intersex folks make: to live as normal and unscrutinized a life as possible. This often coincides with the embrace of medical understandings of intersex conditions as constituted by the phenomenon of being sexually unfinished—that is, well on the way toward the normative categories of male and female, with a few corporeal, hormonal, or genotypical hiccups along the way. This understanding of intersex embodiment has resulted in the current medical terminology of intersex conditions as "disorders of sex development," which conversely presumes typical cisgender embodiments of maleness and femaleness as the be-all and end-all of nonpathological forms of embodiment.

Embracing an understanding of intersex conditions as disorders leaves the internal coherency of biological sex unquestioned and supports the notion that intersex folks have a "true"–dimorphic—sex that needs to be uncovered by medical professionals. Accepting the discourse of disorder is an understandable response, given the shame and secrecy that too often attends intersex conditions, as well as the years of medical scrutiny most North American and European intersex folks have undergone. The idea that one just needs a little assistance in order to become the fully gender-typical being their body is already leaning toward is comforting. One can leave the gender binary in place and merely take their rightful place within it. This strategy might, indeed, ameliorate the difficulty reliving one's years as a lab rat, a biomedical case of intense interest.

The problem is, it's a fiction. The notion of intersex bodies as "sexually unfinished" is, as explored in earlier chapters, a deliberate strategy deployed by medical professionals to sugarcoat intersex diagnoses. It's reassuring. One need not be banished to the outskirts of gendered legibility; one can live as a "normal" man or woman if one submits to the regimen of hormonal and surgical treatment prescribed. It's no wonder many intersex folks ascribe to this understanding. Georgiann Davis, in her excellent sociological investigation of intersex advocacy groups (in particular, the U.S.-based Androgen Insensitivity Syndrome–Disorders of Sex Development Support Group), confirms that most support group "participants presented as men or women rather than, say, genderqueer." Additionally, she comments that the majority of the doctors she interviewed over the course of her research "hold narrow beliefs about gender: they believe that gender is biologically determined, and their descriptions of it evoked Western, white, middle-class understandings of femininity and masculinity."[5] Intersex patients are interpellated by medical professionals in extraordinarily gender-conservative ways and seem to a considerable extent to accept and embody these gender norms. Alternately, within the field of feminist and queer theory, intersex conditions have been repeatedly utilized to illustrate the social construction of biological sex and to argue for a radical reconfiguration of the ways we understand both biological sex and gender diversity. In the former instance, intersex folks are ordinary men and women in need of medical assistance to bring their bodies in line with the cultural expectations that accrue to their gender. In the latter instance, intersex folks are living proof of a natural order of sex that proliferates far beyond binary understandings. It seems, on the face of it, that these two understandings are incommensurable.

But does respecting the decision of many intersex folks to live within one or another socially intelligible gender necessarily entail a refusal to deploy intersex conditions in order to undo conventional understandings of sex? To establish an ethically empathic relationship with intersex folks, is it necessary to accept wholesale the language of "disorders of sex development" or, put another way, accept understanding intersex as a "disorder"? Are the two movements—on the one hand, to deploy intersex as a form of gender trouble and thus a prompt to radicalize understandings of sex, gender, and sexuality and on the other, to embrace the biomedical understanding of intersex as "disorder"—actually incompatible? Or can we admit that while most intersex folks seem to lead relatively gender-normative lives, there is still a necessity to understand intersex conditions as radically disruptive of binary understandings of sex and gender? Moreover, can we imagine that in a world more accepting of a wide range of gendered embodiments, in a world where intersex conditions aren't stigmatized and shrouded in shame and secrecy, fewer intersex folks would identify in gender-normative ways?

Intersex to DSD, Gender Radicalism to Gender Conservatism

The historical narrative of U.S. intersex activism begins in the 1990s with the Intersex Society of North America (ISNA). The ISNA focused on denouncing the routine practice of performing damaging clitoridectomies on nonconsenting intersex infant bodies, encouraged intersex individuals to come to voice and speak out about medical and social maltreatment, and embrace themselves *as intersexuals*. The organization made strong connections to both LGBT and disability rights movements. This period, spanning roughly from the formation of the ISNA as a nonprofit advocacy group by Bo Laurent (a.k.a. Cheryl Chase) in 1993 until the early 2000s, witnessed the publication of the newsletter "Hermaphrodites with Attitude," the compilation of a documentary entitled *Hermaphrodites Speak!*, and extensive contact with the mainstream news media and the academic world, which resulted in a series of books, among them works on intersexuality by Alice Dreger, Anne Fausto-Sterling, and Suzanne Kessler, that tackled head-on the challenges and potential lessons proffered by intersex folks to the medical establishment and to understandings of gender more generally. The merger of intersex concerns with poststructuralist and anti-essentialist strains of feminist theory resulted in a series of arguments pertaining to what can be loosely termed as the *social construction of biological sex*. Against the prevailing medical claim that had emphasized the psychosocial necessity of genital alignment with social gender—an assumption that had dictated, up until the early 1990s, medical protocol concerning genital surgery and sex reassignment in intersex cases—an argument was launched that explicitly tied the interests of genderqueers, transsexual and transgender folks to intersex folks. This argument is neatly articulated by Kessler in her conclusion to *Lessons from the Intersexed*:

> In the acceptance of genital variability and gender variability lays the subversion of both genitals and gender. Dichotomized, idealized, and created by surgeons [in the case of intersex folks], *genitals mean gender.* . . . Accepting more genital variation will maintain, at least temporarily, the two-gender system, but it will begin to unlock gender and genitals. Ultimately, the power of genitals to mark gender will be weakened, and the power of gender will be blunted. . . . We rightfully complain about gender oppression in all its social and political manifestations, but we have not seriously grappled with the fact that we afflict ourselves with a need to locate a bodily basis for assertions about gender. We must use whatever means we have to give up on gender. The problems of intersexuality will vanish and we will, in this way, compensate intersexuals for all the lessons they have provided.[6]

Kessler begins with the notion of a variable spectrum that pertains not only in cases of gender and sexuality but also at the level of primary sex characteristics and deploys this genital variability in conjunction with the gender variability enacted by trans and genderqueer folks, forcefully arguing for an initial wresting of genital appearance from gender determination, a thorough delinking of genitals and gender. This, in Kessler's imagined schematic, is only a pivotal first step, the basis for undoing all efforts to locate a bodily basis for gender expression. For her, this is the route to a queer liberation of sorts, but moreover it is also seen as a form of reparations, a means to "compensate intersexuals for all the lessons they have provided"—to medicine, to feminist and queer theory, to any field engaged in researching human variability. Thus, "giving up on gender" is both a political strategy and an apologia, a proposed quid pro quo between poststructural feminist theory and intersex lives.

I agree with Kessler. In fact, I find myself making a similar argument time and again regarding the critical necessity of developing, at minimum, a postbinary schematic of gender if we are to ever fully do justice to intersex folks. It is necessary for feminists, in their deployment of intersex case studies and scholarship, to bear in mind that the ultimate goal is not an abstract proof of the messiness and undecidability of sexed corporeal constitution but a political praxis that creates and sustains the possibilities for living beyond simple cognizance of this proof. Setting these complexified understandings of sex and gender into motion in community and alliance with other movements seeking to reinvent the social is a praxical engagement that continues to lack broad-based support outside of queer urban enclaves—spaces that are not, by any means, sites where most intersex folks live. This lack of sociocultural support or engagement with reformulating sexed intelligibility elicits a tension in the space between Kessler's call to give up on gender and the caveats made frequently within the contemporary intersex movement regarding the necessity of rearing intersex folks in one of two gender categories, coincident with an emphasis on the psychosocial necessity of doing so. This call is as old as the inception of the ISNA, which advocated for both an end to surgery and to medical and parental determination of a gender until the child is of cognizant age to determine his or her own gender. While practically speaking this move within intersex advocacy makes absolute sense, it also sets intersex medical advocacy apart from the deployment of intersex bodies and lives within feminist and queer theory, with the former advocating a much more conservative approach to understanding the social ramifications of intersex conditions than the latter.

Morgan Holmes, intersex scholar and activist, writes in response to the misapprehensions intersex activists face when dialoguing with medical professionals that

Intersex activists are not suggesting that children be raised without a gender identity. The approach many now advocate neither subverts the notion of individual identity nor questions the limits of free will. Rather, by extending those ideas, the most active groups propose to reorient treatment to focus on the consumer demands of individual intersexuals. The potential for intersexed persons to express their own desires and needs is at the center of activist discourse and hinges on the notion of individual choice/will. Suggesting that early cosmetic surgery should be postponed is not equal to arguing that children should be raised as radical gender experiments.[7]

Holmes's reiteration of the ISNA's long-held stance against infant and adolescent genital surgery comes with a disavowal of the ostensible radicalism potentially associated with this strain of advocacy. In this way, it is quite dissimilar from Kessler's hopes regarding a large-scale retooling of gender itself, a collective and active "giving up on gender." The difference hinges on the primary stakes of these writers—Kessler looks to intersex experience to learn certain lessons regarding the nonbinary nature of biological sex that may then be deployed elsewhere, to the benefit of the intersexed and the non-intersexed alike, while Holmes foregrounds the experience of the intersex patient, asking what can be done in terms of the interface of biomedical apparatuses and intersex bodies to ameliorate the violences inflicted upon these bodies. Thus, while Holmes grants that, at bottom, "'intersexuality' is nothing more than a perpetually shifting phantasm in the collective psyche of medicine and culture" and that "when we appreciate that the difference between intersexed and non-intersexed can be a few millimeters [referring to the size of one's phallo-clitoral structure], it seems that no one is truly intersexed, but we are all, in our infinite differences from each other, intersexed," she also temporalizes the failure of intersex activism to radicalize understandings of sex and gender. Despite the initial promise of intersex activism to undo binary schematics of sex/gender, she writes, "the deployment of intersexed monsters as culture jammers par excellence has stalled, resulting not in substantive interference ... but in the reification of the proper place of traditional visions and modes of masculinity in opposition to femininity. In short: the promise has been stolen and reappropriated, and the intersexed body rendered as a neuter is thus neutralized, repositioned not as a disruptive agent but beyond and outside the realm of gender altogether."[8] For Holmes the rebels have lost. While in the giddy early days of intersex activism, the goal may have been far-reaching social disruption in the realms of sexed and sexual intelligibility, that promise and those efforts have lost steam. Conventional, conservative gender ideologies have prevailed, and intersex activism has responded in kind, winnowing its field of intervention down to an almost exclusively medical interface.

This temporalization of intersex activism—from gender radicalism to a primary engagement with the medical-industrial complex that leaves binary sex and gender systems intact—can be indexed by the transmutation of the ISNA into the Accord Alliance. While the ISNA placed a high priority on creating dialogue with surgeons, endocrinologists, and psychiatrists, their model of activism rhymed with that of early 1990s queer organizations like ACT UP and Queer Nation, emphasizing a politics of confrontation and subversion over a politics of assimilation and inclusion. It was presumed in the early days of the ISNA that in order to garner the attention of the medical establishment, a politics of confrontation and contradiction were necessary.

This approach was based in a definite political reality. The prevailing model of intersex treatment sanctioned nonconsensual infant genital surgery, advocated use of misleading diagnostic discourse in the dealings of medical professionals with the parents of intersex infants, and exaggeratedly emphasized the potential horrors of nondimorphic forms of embodiment in order to persuade parents to comply with prevailing medical protocol. This model of treatment relies on fundamentally patriarchal and heterosexist assumptions not only concerning the necessary alignment of genitals with gender but moving beyond the cosmetic to emphasize the importance of vaginal penetrability and proper—that is, heterosexual—male or female psychosocial identity formation, governed entirely by an attempt to ensure the likelihood of more or less successful hetero marital partnerships. The medical establishment was certainly not ready or willing to question these sacrosanct precepts that were nearly forty years in the making, dating back to the early research of Dr. John Money in the mid- to late 1950s. Confrontation by former patients physically and psychically victimized by this model of treatment was seen as a necessary antidote to medical arrogance, an effective parrhesiastic maneuver with the potential to cut through dense layers of institutional authority to secure at least an audience with the medical practitioners working to normalize intersex bodies.

In the years between the foundation of the ISNA in 1993 and its mutation into the Accord Alliance in 2008, this audience was indeed granted. Rather than crashing medical conferences, as the members of ISNA had in the early days, Accord Alliance members became legitimate participants, becoming a force in patient advocacy primarily through providing an informed critique of intersex genital surgery in tandem with developing a new model of patient-centered care guidelines based on the actual testimony of intersex folks rather than on a version of intersex narrative mediated through a medical apparatus highly invested in a politics of sexed and sexual normalization. The inclusion of both ISNA members and concerns in the medical realm resulted in an apotheosis of sorts in 2006, a year that witnessed the publication of a revised "Consensus Statement on the Management of Intersex Disorders" in *Pediatrics*, the official journal for the American Academy of Pediatrics. Based on dialogue undertaken at an interdisciplinary consortium of medical professionals specializing in the treatment of intersex conditions and intersex activists and scholars, this consensus statement has become a milestone of sorts, marking the considerable successes of the ISNA in reformulating medical protocol while illuminating what points of tension persist.

In a goodbye letter posted on the ISNA's website in 2008, the society summarized the central advances evinced by this consensus statement: "Progress in patient-centered care: The CS states that psychosocial support is integral to care, that ongoing open communication with patients and families is essential and that it helps with well-being; that genital exams and medical photography should be limited; and that care should be more focused on addressing stigma, not solely gender assignment and genital appearance."[9] This set of interventions regarding patient-centered care is perhaps the most revolutionary aspect of the improved guidelines, as it radically undermines a set of prior medical claims that emphasized secrecy or euphemizing of case details when delivering information to both patients and parents; sanctioned the all-too-common treatment of intersex patients as lab rats, valued and sought after for documentation and circulation as case studies; and falsely testified to the satisfactory social adjustment and psychosocial health of intersex patients following nonconsensual subjection to surgical and hormonal treatments. These claims were deployed to shore up the ostensible rectitude of medical procedures of gender normalization.

Each of these aspects of medical maltreatment have been contested by intersex folks, who have emphasized both the need for transparency in parent-patient-doctor communication and the avoidance of potentially shaming medical practices such as repeated genital examinations and photodocumentation of bodily atypicalities. The new suggestion of psychosocial support regarding the potential stigma engendered by intersex conditions attempts a limited address of the sociocultural difficulties encountered by intersex folks. What goes unmentioned here, however, is that the experience of stigma that psychosocial treatment is meant to militate against is, in fact, engendered by prior dealings with the medical apparatus responsible for "treating" intersex conditions. That is, intersex folks need psychosocial support in large part *because of* medical trauma.

The consensus statement also recommends a more cautious approach to surgery, declaring "no vaginoplasty in children; clitoroplasty only in more 'severe' cases"; and no vaginal dilation before puberty. It also states that the functional outcome of genital surgeries should be emphasized, not just cosmetic appearance. Perhaps most importantly it acknowledges there is no evidence that early surgery relieves parental distress."[10] This represents another pronounced victory for the ISNA, as it documents a nearly complete reversal of the medical protocol on practices of infant and child genital reconstruction. *Nearly* complete because, of course, one wonders what the qualification for severity is and whether or not it will be a revised version of what intersex activists of the late 1990s termed *phallometrics*. This denotes the practice of deciding gender assignment and genital surgery based on the size of an infant's phallo-clitoral structure (phalloclit, for short). The details of this metrics dictate, essentially, that a medically acceptable clitoris must measure less than 0.85 centimeters in length, and that a medically acceptable penis must measure at birth at more than 2.5 centimeters. This schematic of measurement leaves a large gray area encompassing, quantitatively, what counts as ambiguous genitalia—that is, genitalia subject to clitoridectomy (removal of the clitoris) or clitoroplasty (surgical reduction of the clitoris). The female assignation of those born with ambiguous genitalia is attributable to concerns only partially technical and thoroughly related to the grand old positing of woman as lack: "surgeons aren't very good at creating the big, strong penis they require men to have. If making a boy is hard, making a girl, the medical literature implies, is easy. Females don't need anything built; they just need excess maleness subtracted."[11] Given this history of phallometrics, the appearance of any terminology regarding "severity" or lack thereof with reference to intersex genitals is disturbing. However, the shift in medical assumptions regarding parental distress at the sight of ambiguous genitalia is a marked improvement in keeping with a pronounced shift to patient (rather than parent) centered care of those with intersex conditions.

As it draws to a close, the statement "recommends as best practice getting rid of misleading language: By getting rid of a nomenclature based on 'hermaphroditism,' our hope is that this shift will help clinicians move away from the almost exclusive focus on gender and genitals to the real medical problems people with DSD face. Improving care can now be framed as healthcare quality improvement, something medical professionals understand and find compelling."[12] Perhaps most controversially, this document codifies the shift in medical nomenclature from intersex to disorders of sex development. The language of disorder as applied to intersex conditions has a long history hearkening back to the assignation to the term *disorders of sexual differentiation* coined by John Money in the late 1950s and popularized by the publication of a text for medical professionals and laypeople alike in the 1968 volume *Sex Errors of the Body*. This history of the construal of intersex bodies as disordered implies immediate reference to a normative corporeal ideality, a dimorphically sexed model of bodily normalcy that, in its deployment as standard reference, has been enormously stigmatizing. The imposition of this standard has sanctioned routine violence in the name of treatment and has become a concept that intersex activists have struggled to critique and refuse as a barometer of corporeal and social intelligibility and belonging.

This movement away from a dyad of the normal and the disordered was indexed by the reclamation of the term *intersex* as more than a descriptor of a disorder but a positively subversive tactical subject position that provided a means of understanding oneself as gender variant or corporeally queer rather than abnormal. Folks inhabiting this subject position launched medical and social critique shaped by the refusal of both pathologization and hormonally and surgically aided corporeal assimilation. They found their strongest allies in queer and trans communities. Activist Emi Koyama attests to this in her response to the shift in nomenclature, writing that these reclaimed and subversive deployments were "obviously influenced by queer identity politics of the 1980s and 90s that were embodied by such groups as Queer Nation and Lesbian Avengers." Koyama goes on to argue that "intersex activists quickly discovered that the intersex movement could not succeed under this model" as it became clear that "intersex individuals were not interested in building intersex communities or culture; what they sought was professional psychological support to live ordinary lives as ordinary men and women."[13]

Any amount of time spent engaging in the virtual community constituted by intersex folks verifies Koyama's interventions.[14] It has been extremely difficult to cohere a sustained public mode of activist confrontation given both the geographic dispersion and institutionally encouraged reticence of intersex folks. The absence of this community, coupled with the problematic terms according to which intersex concerns have been taken up within queer and feminist activism as a theorematic proof regarding both social constructivist and biologically essentialist arguments on gender identity and the constitution of sexuality, renders Koyama's assertion that most intersex folks seek "psychological support to live ordinary lives as ordinary men and women" wholly unsurprising. The experience of ordinariness is hard to come by, however, given the traumas that many intersex folks wear in the form of scarification, destruction or curtailment of capacity for orgasm, decreased genital sensitivity, and hormonal supplementation.

Koyama ends her piece calling for a renewed coalition between intersex folks—or those diagnosed with a DSD—and the disability rights movement, a coalition resultant in the "queer disability politics of gender" she refers to in the title of her piece. The primary task of this coalitional politics would be to conceptualize the shift (back) to a language of disorder "not as the embrace of the medical model, but a commitment to the political strategy that seeks to radically redefine and re-read it." That is, to view the reversion as a way to establish a firm link with the history and accomplishments of the disability rights movement, particularly around its efforts to "de-pathologize pathology itself," and to minimize and attempt to ameliorate the stigma attached to the concept of disorder coincident with a reframing of medical practice as a set of available tools and resources to enhance the quality of life of those diagnosed *as* disordered.[15]

This move to reframe the interface of intersex and the medical establishment is reiterated in Ellen K. Feder's writing around the shift in nomenclature from intersex to DSD, albeit absented from the coalitional concerns Koyama is interested in. Feder argues that this shift makes possible a consideration of intersex as a "disorder like many others" rather than a "disorder like no other."[16] The status of intersex as a brand of disorder beyond the pale, so to speak, so desperately in need of correction that breaches of medical ethical standards have been practically routinized, is potentially corrected by the shift in nomenclature. Utilizing an argument derived from both a Foucauldian conception of power and the unintended or unpredictable productivities of even the most seemingly regressive or draconian biopolitical processes, Feder likens the potential medical normalization of intersex as a "disorder like many others" to the inclusion of gay and lesbian folks within the purview of the normal, a development which Feder, following Foucault, posits as an inextricably related if unintended product of the prior historical medicalization of homosexuality. The inclusion of gays and lesbians within the realm of the normal, the unremarkable, the quotidian hinges on *a recasting of normalcy* rather than a *refusal to be normalized.*

Writing of her hopes for the productivities of the rechristening of intersex as a disorder of sex development, Feder states, "if the change in nomenclature can promote the important development of attention to the genuine health issues associated with many intersex conditions, and so displace the concerns with sexual identity, then intersex can be counted among the many disorders for which the terms *normal* and *abnormal* are taken to mark differences—some consequential and others less so—in the functioning of human bodies." In Feder's purview, *normal* and *abnormal* are terms that seem to bear no mark of either corporeal ideality or stigmatization but rather index an indisputable malfunction or blockage to physical health. The categories of normal and abnormal are, in Feder's reimaginings, no longer value-laden, somehow absented from recent histories of medical violence inflicted upon intersex bodies, and instead merely medically helpful characterizations, terms for correctable deviations. To Feder's mind, "disorders of sex development" may enable intersex conditions to signify similar to, say, cancer, which "we do not question the characterization of... as an abnormal division of cells," or "thyroid disorders like Hashimoto's," as people affected by such disorders "are grateful for the normalization of thyroid hormone levels treatment can bring." She concludes this line of argument by emphasizing that "the operation of normalization in producing the distinctions between the normal and the abnormal in these cases [cancer, Hashimoto's thyroiditis] forcefully illustrates how this power must be recognized not only to promote docility but to enhance a subject's capacities as well." Essentially, Feder argues that it is possible to normalize intersex alternatively in a manner that does not reinscribe the supposed necessity of surgical correction but does enable access for both intersex folks and the parents of intersex folks to medical procedures that would rectify *aspects* of particular DSDs that "curtail one's capacities and so impede one's projects."[17]

In order for this to actually be the case, though, in order for this sort of subjectively contingent and agentic treatment protocol to be realized, *medical practice must be queered*. To my mind, the language of normality and abnormality and the attendant concepts of corporeal order and disorder must be deeply rethought (and perhaps even scrapped altogether) if medical practice is to avoid treating intersex folks as if a nondimorphic corporeal constitution is in need of treatment by virtue of the fact that it happens to be nondimorphic but instead is in need of medical care in only a small number of circumstances that have nothing to do with genital reconstruction nor any other sort of corporeal modification but rather with the correction of, for instance, a severe case of salt-wasting syndrome, which is found in a number of folks with congenital adrenal hyperplasia and can be effectively treated with cortisone. There is no medical necessity demanding the recommendation of lifelong feminizing hormonal treatments to counteract the ostensible overproduction of masculinizing hormones produced by the adrenal glands. To both avoid the cajoling of CAH folks into medically unnecessary treatment regimens and simultaneously enable them to access such treatments without such punishments as sensed medical stigmatization or refusal of insurance coverage would be to revolutionize the gendered politics of medicine. Feder concludes her article with a similar hope, arguing that

> if the effects of a DSD are benign or might be understood to provoke concerns that would be understood as social rather than medical, then psychosocial support should be offered. . . . As we know from the experience of parents of children diagnosed with any number and variety of congenital disorders, parents frequently need support when, in Dreger's words, they "have the child they weren't expecting" and also because, as we know from adults with DSDs, it is not the medical condition or even the social stigma associated with having atypical anatomy that causes psychic pain, but the projection of the stigma onto them by their parents and physicians.[18]

Given this, it is understandable that parents of intersex folks and intersex folks themselves may desire access to therapy to explore attendant social difficulties and to work through the emotional hardships this may prompt. I'm a firm believer in the necessity of training therapists of many stripes to deal carefully and in as informed a manner as possible with intersex youth and adults and to have a refined and subtle understanding of sexed and sexual subjectivity that sidesteps the shoehorning of an intersex child into any category, be that male, female, hetero, homo. What I have difficulty with—particularly given what seems to be Feder's shared understanding that in most cases, intersex is primarily a social dilemma—is how the utilization of a mutated understanding of intersex as a "disorder of sex development" moves anyone—parents or intersex folks alike—to depathologize their understandings of intersex conditions, to understand both the sociohistorical contingency of the intersex diagnosis itself, but also, and more importantly, the fact that there is nothing *wrong* with the body in question, nothing disordered about it, and in most (though not all) cases, no imminent medical issue on the horizon. The option for intersex folks to seek out technologies of corporeal modification later, whether these modifications would more firmly align their bodies with a gendered corporeal ideal or not, should be understood as a subjective matter of desire, with no entailed relationship to medicalized conceptions of normality or abnormality. These desires for modification could perhaps be understood on a singular basis, in concordance with the importance of medical access to ameliorate whatever is sensed by patients as an impediment. If Feder's desire is to recast normalcy in more expansive terms that ameliorate conceptions of intersex as aberrant, then the most helpful move would be to demedicalize intersex and to do theoretical and activist work on intersex in nonmedical realms. Feder ends her article by recapitulating her Foucauldian argument on the potential of redeploying concepts of the normal, asserting that "We should, in other words, seek to recast what it means to 'normalize intersex conditions': we need no longer understand normalization to entail the surgical correction of so-called ambiguous genitalia but the treatment of intersex conditions as disorders like any other."[19] Feder, then, hopes to normalize intersex *through* the language of disorder. Years of activism have sought to restructure understandings of intersex claiming that the primary problem facing intersex folks, the problem that undergirds all the gritty specificities of medical maltreatment, is the notion that intersex is necessarily *an explicitly medical concern.* If the mission is to socially normalize intersex conditions, I believe it would be more useful to frame them, echoing Kessler, as a *social rather than a medical dilemma.* Insofar as intersex interfaces with the medical apparatus, this fact should be made exceedingly clear, and the so-called solutions to the dilemmas posed by intersex bodies should be outsourced to other realms of the social, rather than placed squarely on the shoulders of intersex folks. Of course, folks need to learn survival skills and coping mechanisms to deal with numerous attendant life issues complicated by intersex conditions: to think carefully about the politics of sexual disclosure, to move past self-loathing and the internalization of social oppression. Perhaps psychosocial therapeutics may aid these processes. But I fear that this shift in nomenclature retrenches the tendency to render intersex an explicitly medical problematic, and to this end, I fear that it may herald a return to social secrecy regarding intersex conditions and thus a curtailing of the politically desirable trouble intersex makes in myriad situations and institutions well beyond those of the medical-industrial complex.

Alice Dreger has written and presented on the implications of this shift in nomenclature and has tended to err on the pragmatic side when considering the potential work this shift is capable of. She has been instrumental in implementing this shift both in her writing and her presence in numerous dialogues wherein the adoption of the new terminology was on the agenda. She is also one of the key authors responsible for the production, under the onus of the ISNA, of two handbooks concerning the treatment of DSDs: *Clinical Guidelines for the Management of Disorders of Sex Development* (cited extensively above) and a *Handbook for Parents*. She argues that the primary motivation for this shift is the need for a new umbrella term that would allow medical professionals an opportunity to establish a revised consensus on treatment protocol. Too often in the past, argumentation over what precisely counts as an intersex condition had derailed potentially productive conversations. Dreger explains that she was "spending so much energy playing the 'is CAH intersex? is AIS intersex? is hypospadias intersex? is Klinefelter Syndrome intersex?' name game" that she "couldn't get people to talk about the (problematic) clinical practices that all these conditions had in common." She goes on to cite, as a secondary reason for moving with the new term, that "a few of the docs helping with the handbooks, a lot of the parents, and a small number of the affected adults made it clear that they found the term 'intersex' shaming and stigmatizing. They didn't want to talk about care for 'intersex' people because they felt about the term the way we felt about the term 'hermaphrodite'—that it was a pathologizing misnomer." *Intersex* is *of course* a misnomer in a discourse that presumes intersex bodies as dedicated to eventual inhabitation of a dimorphic schema of sexed intelligibility—in this schema, reiterated within the medical establishment in discourses of intersex bodies as sexually unfinished, *intersex* marks the phantasmic site of an impossible subjectivity. There is no way for an inhabited interval to legitimately exist in a binary sex and gender system. It is for this reason that a group predominately composed of non-intersex adults finds the term *intersex* difficult, unwieldy, perhaps thorny to employ. Gender radicals they are not. Their unitary aim is the treatment of these bodies, which may or may not in this revised protocol, involve extensive surgical and hormonal treatment but which is nonetheless not estranged from the aim of providing intersex bodies with a passable (workable, legible) sexed corporeality. Dreger acknowledges this, granting that the revised DSD guidelines aim solely at medical reform and that to that end they have been moderately successful. Framing intersex as a disorder has resulted, in Dreger's informed account, in markedly *less* medical intervention. She writes that, for some parents, intersex "had a way of feeling totalizing, because it had come to represent an identity (thanks to the intersex rights movement) . . . if their children just had a DSD, well, then they just had something that went funny in development, but it didn't mean their whole bodies and identities were taken over by this thing."[20]

In this mode of cognition, intersex is something one *is*, DSDs are something one *has*. Thus, if one *is* intersex, one *cannot* be a man or a woman; if one *has* a DSD, one *is still* either a man or a woman and has just hit a bump in the road on their way to a finally and firmly sexed designation. Never is the radical suggestion made that gender identity may very well have no causal relation to one's corporeal configuration upon birth or even at adolescence. This is, however, more than *just* a radical suggestion—it is a material reality for scores of people: trans folks, genderqueers, and intersex folks alike.

From Intersex to Quantum Sex

There is a historical specificity to the constitution of those conditions labeled intersex, but as Dreger attests, it has never been firmly fixed. In fact, the only period of broad-based consensus regarding both what intersex is and what is to be done with it is one we've only recently phased out of, largely as a result of the contestations of the intersex rights movement. This period of consensus began in the late 1950s, a small handful of years after a then-unknown researcher by the name of John Money finished his PhD in psychology at Harvard University, his dissertation entitled *Hermaphroditism: An Inquiry into the Nature of a Human Paradox*. Developing his initial interventions regarding gender formation from a series of case studies, Money went on to work primarily with living intersex folks, treating roughly two hundred intersex patients over the course of his fifty-year stint at Johns Hopkins. I explore the resistant strategies of these subjects in the following chapter; for now, I want to focus on the ideology and protocol that emerges from his research.

Money developed what was, in some ways, a more subtle and decidedly less shoehorned approach to gender assignation than that which had emerged in Barbin's time, definitively arguing against doctrines of a physiognomically isolatable determinant of "true sex" and for a process of gender designation that doesn't rely on notions of biological hardwiring. Often credited as a pioneer of social constructivist understandings of gender, Money was in all actuality much more syncretic in his approach. Early in his career, he formulated a table containing six variables of sex, with a contingent seventh variable that opened the terrain onto what we now understand as gender identity/role (truncated often within Money's work to G-I/R). Importantly, gender variability was not taken into account unless the preceding six variables witnessed some degree of deviation from a deeply heteronormative understanding of maleness and femaleness—only then, in supposedly pathological instances, was the specter of gender variability introduced. This sex variable system was constituted as such: assigned sex and sex of rearing, external genital morphology, internal accessory reproductive structures, hormonal sex and secondary sexual characteristics, gonadal sex, and chromosomal sex. Money then added a caveat, deeming that "patients showing various combinations and permutations of these six sexual variables may be appraised with respect to a seventh variable: gender role and orientation as male or female, established while growing up."[21]

Money, in his early work, granted precedence to contemporary understandings of the biology of sex in determining gender. It was only in instances of mixity and nondimorphic alignment that a psychosocial take on gender constitution came to matter. The now-hoary assumption of the irrevocable rift between the biological sex of the body and social gender receives one of its fundamental articulations here. This early schematic for gender assignment is thus indispensable to understanding the later deployment of the split within feminist political projects, insofar as many of the political successes that have hinged on an argumentative coup de grâce against biological essentialism stem from this schematic and are on that count genealogically linked to the ultimately gender-conservative, deeply binary, and heterosexist agenda of John Money. There is, thus, nothing *inherently* progressive about social constructivist understandings of sex, gender, and sexuality, but rather differential articulations of the concept of gender role and orientation become caught up in complex discursive fields concerned with questions of embodiment, social role, and sexuality. The notion of "gender role and orientation as male or female, established while growing up" indeed expands our concept of the development of gendered subjectivity, positing gender as gradated and at least partially mutable. To what projects we harness more subtle and performative understandings of gender is another question entirely—Money himself utilized gender to tame unruly corporealities in line with heterosexist dictates.

To garner a more thorough sense of this newly subtle understanding of the production of gendered subjectivity, we can look to Money's footnote on this final, contingent variable, which opens onto the realm of the performative, examining quotidian practices and modes and manners of presentation on a microphysical level:

> By the term, gender role, we mean all those things that a person says or does to disclose himself or herself as having the status of boy or man, girl or woman, respectively. It includes, but is not restricted to sexuality in the sense of eroticism. Gender role is appraised in relation to the following: general mannerisms, deportment and demeanor, play preferences and recreational interests; spontaneous topics of talk in unprompted conversation and casual comment; content of dreams, daydreams and fantasies; replies to oblique inquiries and projective

tests; evidence of erotic practices and, finally, the person's own replies to direct inquiry.[22]

This increasingly refined taxon of *gender identity*, rather than biological sex, uses dimorphism and heterosexist conceptions of subjective normalcy as an ideality, a barometer, not as an immutable factic truth. This barometer is the gauge that guides a gendered reterritorialization of the body, where signs of gender disobedience are sought after in the service of medical rectification. It is in the service of proper gendered alignment that Money placed his lengthy interrogations of patients, advocating not for the discovery of a true sex but a careful weighing of all of the aforementioned variables to determine a "best sex." Money's construction of a microphysics of gender, wherein seemingly insignificant and heretofore nonmedicalized behavioral patterns are coded as evidentiary testaments to one's most workable—that is, most normative—gender, while laying the groundwork for feminist arguments against biological essentialism, also aided the expansion of medical authority in situations of intersex intervention and gender transition, widening the terrain of judgment and active behavioral and corporeal regulation.

The notion of gender malleability developed by Money and his numerous clinical cohorts never functioned as separable from one's physiognomic and hormonal constitution. Rather, the notion of gender malleability rendered the decision-making process in instances of intersex bodies infinitely more fraught, as it concatenated with the prior sex variables in all their muta-bility over the lifespan of the patient. In order to arrive at an assignment, Money and his team utilized their knowledge of the patients' biological constitution to predict the likelihood of future pubertal masculinization or feminization, then proscribed a treatment regimen in order to stave off a potential misalignment of corporeal constitution and recommended gender of rearing. Moreover, for Money, while gender was seen as malleable, this malleability carried with it an expiration date—selection of a "best sex" must take place before eighteen months, and the earlier, the better.

Why this cutoff point? Money contends that this early designation, if fully supported by those present in the child's intimate sphere, results in maximal success in normative gendering. He repeatedly metaphorizes gender acquisition as language acquisition, claiming that "one may liken the establishment of a gender role through encounters and transactions to the establishment of a native language. Once imprinted, a person's native language may fall into disuse and be supplanted by another, but is never entirely eradicated. So also a gender role may be changed or, resembling native bilingualism, may be ambiguous, but it may also become so indelibly engraved that not even flagrant contradictions of body functioning and morphology may displace it."[23] Gender, while not biologically hardwired, is nevertheless more or less indelibly imprinted through duration and repetition. This notion of limited gender fluidity, a concept of gender as a process of temporally capped flows and sediments, is at the crux of what we can call Money's *heteronormative morphological pragmatism*. While he grants that gender is malleable, this knowledge is deployed exclusively in the service of normalizing both somatic and psychosocial deviance, with the aim of ensuring the likelihood of a normatively gendered heterosexual body. Malleability is construed as liberatory only insofar as it releases subjects from the bonds of perversion, from the threat of falling into queer netherworlds comprised of subcultural sexual practices and nonfamilial orchestrations of intimacy and sociality. The professed aim with intersex patients is to "reinstate the case into a framework of overall normality," which necessarily means guarding against the conflation of intersex conditions with queerness and moreover ensuring the production of intersex bodies that, if assigned female, are adequately penetrable.[24] The emphasis on penetrability works to ensure the ascendancy of heterosex over all other sex acts, further girding the heteronormativity of Money's diagnostic framework.

The protocols regarding intersex treatment—early gender assignment and execution of surgery so that genitals correspond to gender assignment in order to avoid suspected psychosocial difficulties, both in the patient and in familial intimates—held for quite a while, on account of wide diffusion prompted by a near immediate incorporation of Money's findings in the treatment recommendations of the 1957 volume *The Diagnosis and Treatment of Endocrine Disorders in Childhood and Adolescence*, authored by Lawson Wilkins, a pediatric endocrinologist who worked closely with Money at Johns Hopkins, and the 1958 *Hermaphroditism, Genital Anom-*

alies, and Related Endocrine Disorders (authored by gynecologist Howard Jones and urologist William Scott), the first medical text in the United States devoted to the treatment of hermaphroditism since Hugh Hampton Young, head of genitourinary surgery at Johns Hopkins and pioneer in genital surgery, published his 1937 book *Abnormalities, Hermaphroditism, and Related Adrenal Diseases.*[25] This early text laid the groundwork for later genital reconstructive procedures used on intersex bodies.[26] Money, in concert with his colleagues Jones and Wilkins, built on the work of Young and developed Johns Hopkins's reputation in the mid- to late twentieth century as the central and authoritative node of research on and treatment of otherwise under-researched intersex conditions.

This authoritative position held until quite recently. We are now, in the early twenty-first century, in the midst of a revision of intersex treatment protocol prompted by intersex activist movement, which has facilitated the implementation of a less harmful approach to medical treatment, primarily in that the medical establishment no longer recommends infant and childhood genital reconstruction. There is, however, another aspect to the revision of intersex treatment protocol that is decidedly estranged from activist trajectories—this is the reemergence of a discourse of genetic essentialism working in tension with contemporary research on brain sex, or the influence of prenatal hormone levels on the development of gender identity. This is a potent cocktail of simplistic truisms in tension with one another but resulting in various determinisms that speak to a desire for a neat, linear, causal determinant of sex—in other words, the reemergence of a discourse on "true sex." In one manifestation, it takes the form of assigning intersex infants according to karyotype, above all other determinants. This is a marked difference from the protocol devised by Money, which often resulted in those with forty-six XY chromosomes (for instance, those with complete or partial androgen insensitivity syndrome) being assigned female, on account of the body's insensitivity to androgen production by internal testes in conjunction with the already more or less feminized appearance of the genitalia. In another manifestation, it involves gauging the infants' prenatal exposure to androgen through a variety of faulty means, ranging from inferring it from the degree of genital masculinization to ordering tests on androgen levels shortly after birth. The logic of this assignation works in line with a belief in the capacity of prenatal androgen influxes to indelibly and irreparably "virilize" the brain of an intersex infant—a virilization that, ostensibly, no amount of surgical or hormonal reconstruction can undo. In accordance with this, there is a growing skepticism among physicians working with intersex infants to assign gender in contradistinction to androgen production in, for instance, folks with congenital adrenal hyperplasia who, unlike CAIS and PAIS folks, *are* receptive to androgen production. Both of these methods of gender assignment are motivated by a desire to simplify diagnosis—one prefers karyotype as the designator of true sex, the other androgen receptivity.

There is an irony to this rebirth of the doctrine of true sex, in that the further biomedicine delves into this series of corporeal explorations, the further it gets from a neat or causal determination. Recent neurogenetic research into the molecular genetics of sex presages an increasingly necessary shift in biomedical templates for understanding sex, from the binary to what historian of science and psychiatrist Vernon A. Rosario has termed "quantum sex." Rosario predicts that "the complex new molecular genetics of sex—along with widespread genetic testing—will widen the sphere of or, at least, further blur the boundaries of what is intersex" insofar as it is already producing results that attest to the existence and interaction of "a dozen or more genes each conferring a small percentage likelihood of male or female sex that is still further dependent on micro- and macroenvironmental interactions." These findings, rather than shoring up and reinscribing an endlessly reiterated binary, are instead establishing a neurological and genetic basis for the singularity of sex or, if not (yet) a conception of *singular sex*, at least a "more complex understanding of sex/gender/sexuality as a biological, psychological, and cultural phenomenon that is rich, diverse, and indefinitely complex, resistant to all simplistic reductionism, whether biological or discursive."[27]

If it is becoming increasingly clear that most bodies are (to some minor degree) intersex, and if we consider this in addition to the decades-old argument that intersex is a primarily social difficulty, is it beyond the realm of possibility that medical professionals would relinquish the concept of sex disorder? Long after medicalized understandings of homosexuality have been thrown on the biomedical ash heap, these disciplines still hold fast to the notion of biological sex abnormality, and in fact *need* it to reach consensus on intersex conditions. Dreger suggests that folks concerned with the political potentiality of intersex see the terminological shift pragmatically, given its positive impact on the medical treatment of intersex folks. She implores us to sidestep perceiving the terms *intersex* and DSD as mutually exclusive and instead to strategically and differentially deploy them according to their situational or institutional weight and purchase, arguing that each one has limited relevancy in one of two unfortunately disparate systems that interpellate intersex bodies. She posits that there is "one system for intersex in minors, and that is a medical system virtually devoid of political consciousness, and that there is a separate system for intersex adults, and that is a politically-conscious activist system nearly devoid (tragically) of specialist medical care."[28] What Dreger neglects to comment upon is that for intersex folks, these two systems are experienced as inseparable and irrevocably linked. A large part of what Dreger views as a sad lack of specialist medical care for intersex adults is at least in part a refutation of the so-called need for specialist care prompted by the simultaneous education on and politicization around intersex issues initiated and undergone as adults. This political education is also a way to heal from the consistent psychic and somatic reminders of medical maltreatment that intersex folks live with. The notion that the trauma of an intersex youth becomes an embodied memory schizzes the heuristic division imposed by Dreger.

For all that, it is true that these two systems, *as systems*, are currently incommensurable, that the latter realm is shaped by a deep distrust of the medical establishment resultant in an extremely limited engagement and an overwhelming desire to depathologize the meanings of intersex while the former seems, as signaled by this return to a concept of sex disorders and the current revised reascendance of doctrines of "true sex," to be fully invested in continuing to pathologize intersex bodies. Accepting the language of disorder depoliticizes the medical establishment's long-standing investments in normalizing the gendered embodiment of intersex folks.

This manifests in what is essentially a kinder, gentler institutionalization of sex dimorphism, a medicalization that mediates the supposed crisis of intersex bodies without immediate recourse to the knife but nevertheless leaves the perception of crisis itself wholly intact.

Disordered bodies, it seems obvious to state, are bodies that need fixing, not bodies holistically intact and nonpathological as they are. The diagnosis of DSD, rather than offering an exit from cycles of pathologization and treatment as a medical oddity for intersex folks, an exit integral to preventing further harm, instead provides something far more meager—an exoneration, in the form of diagnosis, that allows parents and medical professionals alike a more comfortable way out of addressing institutional heterosexism and the entrenched demand for a neat, univocally gendered soma. This is a means of deflecting the social and political problematics posed by intersex bodies, a corralling of their unruliness back within the domain of disorder rather than attempting to build a world where intersex bodies, in all their diversity, are embraced as nonpathological variations. While this shift in diagnostic nomenclature may partially ameliorate the coercion entailed in the medical garnering of parental agreement to dangerously desensitizing genital surgeries (insofar as they seem to panic less when the DSD diagnosis is utilized), it doesn't address the prior, more fundamental issue: that existing—visibly, publicly, and unapologetically—in a non–dimorphically sexed body is still, for far too many people, an impossible reality.

So far, I have focused primarily on the trauma of grappling with intersex diagnoses and manifestations of resistance to those diagnoses, truncated or curtailed as they may have been. The next chapter sustains this attention to resistance by focusing on moments within the medical archives of mid-twentieth-century U.S. sexologists where intersex subjects are quite obviously contesting medical treatment protocol. I couple my analysis of these traces of resistance with a long meditation on the structuring absences of mid-twentieth-century Western sexological practice, focusing on the ways in which, in the interwoven archives of trans and intersex diagnosis and treatment, nontransnormative subjects—be they queer, nonwhite, poor, rural, or located subjectively at any or all of these intersections—are actively regulated out of medical treatment (and, therefore, medical record-keeping and medical archives). Focusing on these structuring absences allows me to center questions of racialization and colonization vis-à-vis the development of modern Western sexological knowledge about intersex and trans people and to investigate the role medical sexology has played—and continues to play—in the necropolitical regulation of nonnormative trans and intersex lives.

repair

In *Sexing the Body* Anne Fausto-Sterling presents the contemporary Western ur-narrative of intersexuality:

> A child is born in a large metropolitan hospital in the United States or Western Europe. The attending physician, realizing that the newborn's genitalia are either/or, neither/both, consults a pediatric endocrinologist (children's hormone specialist) and a surgeon. They declare a state of medical emergency. According to current treatment standards, there is no time to waste in quiet reflection or open-ended consultations with the parents. No time for the new parents to consult those who have previously given birth to mixed-sex babies or to talk with adult intersexuals. Before twenty-four hours pass, the child must leave the hospital "as a sex," and the parents must feel certain of the decision.[1]

The narrative focuses on the loaded decision-making process in the first days of an infant's life, when arrogant physicians and intentionally uninformed parents take on the grave responsibility of determining and assigning a sex, with a side dish of surgical and hormonal treatments meant to shoehorn the child's body into garden-variety forms of masculine and feminine corporeality.

I want to tell a different story. It starts like this: a child is born in a small-town hospital in a desiccated postindustrial county in the foothills of upstate New York. They have no idea how the medical professionals responded to their birth or whether they appeared *of indeterminate sex* at the moment of birth. Their parents both deny having any knowledge of an intersex condition before their teenage years. They know that there is a mysterious scar on their lower belly, just above where the pubic hair begins to grow;

their parents say it is from a hernia operation they underwent at the age of three. This same scar is reopened at the age of sixteen, when they have their gonads removed from their abdomen. They are told that this is necessary. They are told these little globes of tissue produce too much testosterone for a body raised girl. They are told they could become cancerous. The scar that is reopened grows longer, the incision deeper this time, and wide, because of the keloid from that much-earlier operation. A companion scar is made this time, too, a fraternal twin resting delicately on the other side of their abdomen—smaller, less conspicuous. The child is, at this late point, shocked into an intense awareness of their *indeterminate sex*. Told so by a team of medical practitioners in their now-metropolitan, subtropical dwelling place. At night, before bed, they stroke their scars and meditate on both whether and how, given this new information, living is at all feasible. A stranger to the emotive style of the typical American teenage girl, they begin to slip sometimes into a baroque kind of despair, brooding in a small bedroom with the blinds drawn, crying themselves to sleep. Most of the time, their mood is more contemplative: A quiet meditation, internal, deeply considered, shrouded in a certain silence. A socially sanctioned silence. Each of their doctors—and there were quite a few—had told them this silence was important. They had been told to not mention their *condition* unless absolutely necessary. Avoid disclosure. Evade intimacy. Be a good girl; be delicate; be cautious with this aberrant body. They had been told, implicitly, that no one wanted to talk about it; they had learned, explicitly, that this was true, at least within the confines of their birth family. When their mother spoke of it, her speech was comprised of intricate gaps, slights, and euphemisms; they, however, preferred to dwell in the brutality of the *fact* that they were *neither a boy nor a girl*.

"THE DOCTORS SAID SO!" they would scream in one of their periodic tantrums. But that is not, in point of fact, what the doctors had actually said. They would have their medical records shipped to them years later, and they saw there the terms that had been carefully recited to them. The diagnosis: "testicular feminization," an outdated way of saying androgen insensitivity syndrome that makes it sound as if the testicles got all dolled up in girl-drag. The doctors had certainly not sat them down and said, "You are not a boy or a girl." They had said this: "We have to take a few steps to help you along the right developmental path, to make sure you develop *like other girls*." The doctors had asked them if they were sexually active (they were) and what kind of partners they had (then, mostly boys; soon after, mostly girls). They had told them to take pills, pills made from the urine of pregnant mares. The pills were supposed to make their breasts swell, their hips expand. They couldn't decide if they wanted their body to start behaving like that. They did, for a while, but then they didn't. They took the pills for a while, but then they didn't. They told their family it was because they were vegan. It was really because the pills elicited those late-night crying jags that gradually transitioned to a stolid and numb confrontation with the unlivability of their life. They didn't want to kill themselves but could see very few other possibilities.

Depression is sometimes a side effect of orally ingested conjugated estrogens. Were they depressed on account of the pills or because of the brutality of that one unalterable fact, that knowledge that sat heavy on their sternum like a concrete block, like the onset of a panic attack—their inhabitation of a *body of indeterminate sex*?

In any case, they stopped going to the offices of the battery of medical specialists they'd been seeing.

They stopped taking Premarin.

They started wanting to live again.

They are, of course, me.

3 Gone, Missing

Queering and Racializing Absence in Trans and Intersex Archives

Who appears in the medical archives that document the treatment of intersex and trans subjects? Who is missing? What can we learn from these absences?

This chapter takes on these questions, examining the phenomena of patient disappearance and the broader archival absence of queer folks and folks of color in the archives of U.S.-based sexologists—particularly John Money—who served as the primary architects of trans and intersex medical pathologization. I read these absences and disappearances as, at least in part, a method of resistance to the imposition of what María Lugones has termed the colonial/modern gender system and explore the implications of the fact that folks whose desires for transformation run counter to hegemonic, white, bourgeois understandings of masculinity and femininity were systematically prevented from accessing technologies of transition, deemed unacceptable candidates or noncompliant patients.[1] By "technologies of transition," I refer to the ensemble of medical practices utilized in the process of transition, both hormonal and surgical. This exclusionary, highly regulated system of medical gatekeeping has prompted two linked phenomena: a legacy of trans folks tailoring experiential narratives—lying—to fit the heterosexist, highly binarized logic utilized by what are now understood as classic models of transsexuality, as well as a history of intersex folks critiquing the pathologization of intersex traits and refusing to be interpellated by the medical establishment as disordered or deformed, in need of surgical and hormonal gender normalization.

Building on these insights, I position racialized, classed, and queer absences as central to understanding how access to technologies of transition have become intensively compromised for poor folks, trans folks of color and gender-nonconforming, nonheterosexual folks while they have simultaneously been coercively imposed on intersex folks in the interest of normalizing our ostensibly unruly forms of sexed embodiment. This selective utilization of technologies of transition helps explain why we lack holistic approaches to trans and intersex health that move beyond surgical and hormonal techniques of gender normalization and focus more heavily on the quotidian and structural violence that so often compromises the life chances of trans and intersex subjects.

Repairing Gender: Tactics of Medical Normalization

John Money opened the first clinic in the United States that specialized in intersex and trans conditions—the Johns Hopkins Gender Identity Clinic. This clinic began performing gender reassignment surgery on trans and intersex folks in 1966 and enabled him to become one of the first sexologists to engage in the substantive study of trans and intersex conditions, treatments, and long-term outcomes. In 1968 he published *Sex Errors of the Body: Dilemmas, Education, and Counseling*; in 1969 he co-authored with Richard Green *Transsexualism and Sex Reassignment*. These books laid the theoretical and practical groundwork for contemporary forms of intersex and trans diagnosis. They were rapidly translated; Money quickly became an international authority on intersex and trans counseling, surgery, and continued care. He also coined the term *gender role*, which we've come to throw around very casually today; our contemporary conceptual habit of separating sex from gender is rooted, in part, in his work.

I approached his archives—housed in the Kinsey Institute for Research in Sex, Gender, and Reproduction at Indiana University—skeptically. As an intersex person I am deeply critical of his treatment protocol, which advocated binary gender assignment (usually as female because surgically speaking, "it's easier to dig a hole than build a pole") and genital reconstructive surgery. These surgeries were (and are) performed on infants and toddlers nonconsensually because Money believed gender identity was solidified before the age of three and that it would be too psychologically destabilizing for intersex folks to grow up after that age with atypical genitalia. He argued in a 1955 article that "gender role is so well established in most children by the age of two and one-half years that it is then too late to make a change of sex with impunity."[2]

For Money, as articulated in the previous chapter, a "normal" vagina was one capable of intromitting an average-sized penis. This is his gold standard for a well-realized genital reconstruction, and in the case of intersex patients, it always came coupled with the surgical removal of the clitoris (which was considered "abnormally large," too phallic for someone being reared as female). He argued that this was totally cool, an a-okay practice that didn't compromise sexual sensitivity in the least: "There has been no evidence of a deleterious effect of cliteridectomy. None of the women experienced in genital practices reported a loss of orgasm after cliteridectomy. All of the patients were unanimous in expressing intense satisfaction at having a feminine genital morphology after the operation. . . . There is considerable evidence that an amputated clitoris is erotically sensitive."[3] It is apparent that for Money, gender-typical aesthetics trumps erotic functionality; his musings here also raise an important question: how can something missing— the amputated clitoris—be "erotically sensitive"? This question presages a broader question entertained in this chapter: what are the effects of absence? While I certainly don't buy Money's assertion that a missing clit is erotically sensitive, I do want to think about the effects—in the form of afterlives, hauntings—of other forms of missing in relation to coercive forms of medicalized transition: patients that go missing, that refuse to show up for medical appointments, as well as those beings who can't get their foot in the door of the clinic because they're too poor, too queer, too gender nonnormative.

In the same article, Money argues for the importance of referring to vaginas, reductively, as "baby tunnels" when discussing anatomy with intersex children.[4] His logic was that if you avoid mentioning the clitoris, intersex children won't realize it exists and thus won't be upset that theirs had been removed! He also advocated years of invasive continued care, including regular manual dilation of the reconstructed vagina by the child's caretakers (until they were old enough to do so themselves) and a lifelong hormonal regimen meant to "normalize" secondary sex characteristics. He encouraged doctors and family members to lie to the child about their intersex condition. In other words, parents were encouraged to go to great lengths to obscure the realities of Money's invasive forms of gendered normalization and to do so in the name of protecting intersex folks from the supposedly devastating truth of their own nonconventionally sexed embodiment. As if we wouldn't figure it out!

The literature within the growing field of intersex studies, not surprisingly, has unequivocally critiqued the medical protocol developed by John Money. Anne Fausto-Sterling in her landmark volume *Sexing the Body* reviews the modern medical management of intersexuality and concludes with no uncertainty, "stop infant genital surgery." Suzanne Kessler in *Lessons from the Intersexed* asserts that this method of treatment implements a medical fix—surgical and hormonal gender normalization—for what is actually a social dilemma: a body that doesn't fit neatly within the parameters of sexual dimorphism, our prevailing narrative of biological sex differentiation. In her important history of the medicalization of intersex conditions, Alice Dreger examines the contemporary autobiographical writing of adult intersexuals and concludes that "despite the effort to make intersexed children look and feel 'normal,' the way intersexuality is treated by doctors in the United States today inadvertently contributes to many intersexuals' feeling of difference and defectiveness." More recently, Elizabeth Reis has argued that "ever since the early nineteenth century, when doctors began to professionalize and publish their cases in medical journals, we can trace not only their cruelly judgmental descriptors of these conditions and people but also the damaging therapeutic treatment they have dispensed. The ways intersex bodies have been scruti-nized and pathologized have been negative, harmful, and based not on med-ical necessity but on social anxieties about marriage and heterosexuality and on the insistence on normative bodies." Rounding out this chorus of academ-ics against the medical pathologization of intersex conditions is Georgiann Davis, a sociologist as well as someone with an intersex trait, who asserts that the gendered expectations that "force intersex people, who do not fit neatly into the gender structure, to undergo medically unnecessary and irreversible surgeries that . . . may be intended to help but are often quite harmful."[5]

Relatedly, within trans studies, there is a growing number of scholars insisting on grappling with the harm caused by forms of medical gatekeeping that green-lit transition only for folks who provided a straightforward life narrative that relied heavily on gender stereotypes to claim they were trapped in the wrong body, had a high likelihood of effectively passing as cisgender posttransition, and could attest to their lack of queerness—that is, promise exclusive heterosexual behavior posttransition and demonstrate both chastity and sexual disgust with their bodies pretransition. Historian Joanne Meyerowitz summarizes, in brief, the foundational premises of a more recent generation of trans scholars:

> As a group they tended to start with premises that early twentieth-century theorists had only begun to outline: that sex, gender, and sexuality represent analytically distinct categories, that the sex of the body does not determine either gender or sexual identity, that doctors can alter characteristics of bodily sex. Some disputed binary definitions of biological sex. . . . Some saw in transsexuals an evolving core sense of self and others a postmodern fluidity. . . . Many combined the feminists' critique of the constraints of rigid gender dichotomies and the gay liberationists' goal of freedom of expression, and rendered healthy the variations that doctors had routinely cast as illness and disorder.[6]

Meyerowitz's intellectual touchstones here are such scholars, activists, and performers as Susan Stryker, Sandy Stone, Kate Bornstein, Henry Rubin, Jason Cromwell, and Riki Anne Wilchins—names now associated with the emergence of both trans studies and contemporary transgender activism. Critiques of binary gender, rejection of the pathologization of trans embodiment as a form of deviance or disorder, and deconstructions of the disciplinary regulation of access to technologies of transition are integral to the field, taken up across the landscape of contemporary trans scholarship.

Legal theorist Dean Spade, for instance, offers an intimate account of his failure to provide the correct gender narrative to psychiatric professionals as he was seeking access to technologies of transition:

> From what I've gathered in my various counseling sessions, in order to be deemed real I need to want to pass as male all the time, and not feel ambivalent about this. I need to be willing to make the commitment

to "full-time" maleness, or they can't be sure that I won't regret my
surgery. The fact that I don't want to change my first name, that I haven't
sought out the use of the pronoun "he," that I don't think that "lesbian"
is the wrong word for me, or, worse yet, that I recognize that the use
of any word for myself—lesbian, transperson, transgender butch, boy,
mister, FTM fag, butch—has always been/will always be strategic, is
my undoing in their eyes. They are waiting for a better justification of
my desire for surgery—something less intellectual, more real.[7]

Spade highlights the enormous difficulty medical professionals have in
cognizing forms of gender variance that don't subscribe to classic narratives of transsexuality and articulates the realization of his own naiveté
in believing that he could actually communicate the complexities of his
own desires and experiences to medical professionals invested in these
narratives. He becomes involved with a trans support group and realizes
that this space—not the doctor's office—is one open to honest, complex,
and mutable truths about queer forms of trans embodiment: "I have these
great, sad conversations with these people who know all about what it
means to lie and cheat their way through the medical roadblocks to get the
opportunity to occupy their bodies in the way they want."[8]

While Spade excoriates the medical establishment as a regulatory system deeply invested in stereotypical binary gender, he also complicates
transnormative narratives of transition that are invested in the reification of
hegemonic medical constructions of transition as a linear, teleological path
(from male to female or female to male). By *transnormative*, I mean subjects
who, save for their status as trans, are otherwise highly assimilable—gender
normative, heterosexual, middle class, well educated, racialized as white.
It is transnormative subjects who populate the medical archives of transsexuality most heavily, and it is transnormative subjects that have the least
mitigated access to medical technologies of gender transition—hormones,
surgery, and continued care. Conversely, it is nontransnormative subjects
who are systematically exposed to institutional and interpersonal violence,
up to and including death—by homicide and suicide, yes, but also by lack
of access to quality, affordable, trans-competent health care.

I understand—perhaps controversially—the use of technologies of transition by both intersex and trans folks as forms of gender transition. While the medical rhetoric surrounding the surgical and hormonal normalization of intersex folks frames these procedures as correcting or repairing an "unfinished" (that is, not unequivocally male- or female-typical) form of sexed embodiment, these experiences are lived as major reconfigurations of one's gendered reality and thus signify as a form of transition. With this in mind, I apply the concept of transnormativity to both intersex and trans experiences, using it as a shorthand means of indexing narratives that embrace gender stereotypes, understand technologies of transition simply as a means of deliverance into the promised land of gender normativity, and utilize heterosexuality as a means of shoring up and verifying this gender normativity. We find transnormative narratives of gendered becoming in both contemporary accounts of transition as well as in the archives of medical sexology, issued by intersex and trans subjects alike—though, as Spade points out so eloquently above, often under conditions of coercion, as a means of playing into and verifying the medical establishment's investment in gender and sexual normativity.

Transnormative Structures of Feeling

Popular accounts of gendered becoming—particularly those that are focused on the use of estrogen, progesterone, and testosterone—rely heavily on what I understand as *transnormative structures of feeling*. The stories folks tell about the affects and effects of hormone use operate as dense transfer points between the epistemological and the ontological—that is, they illustrate how what we think about hormones informs our embodied experience of them, and vice versa. I think that there is something we can learn about the transformations experienced through the use of hormones from the tales folks weave about them; I also think that these stories inflect and help shape the affective experience of microprosthetic hormonal use.

I want to focus on two narratives that operate paradigmatically in the context of contemporary trans accounts of gendered becoming. The first is from Julia Serano and appears in *Whipping Girl*, in the chapter "Boygasms and Girlgasms: A Frank Discussion about Hormones and Gender

Differences," which is very much concerned with moving discussions of hormonal affect beyond oversimplified, reductive determinisms while still granting them significant experiential influence. She writes:

> When testosterone was the predominant sex hormone in my body, it was as though a thick curtain were draped over my emotions. It deadened their intensity, made all of my feelings pale and vague as if they were ghosts that would haunt me. But on estrogen, I find that I have all of the same emotions that I did back then, only now they come in crystal-clear. In other words, it is not the actual emotions, but their intensity that has changed—the highs are way higher and the lows are way lower. Another way of saying it is that I feel my emotions more now; they are in the foreground rather than the background of my mind.[9]

She goes on to discuss her experience of a heightened haptic inclination—a more intense desire to touch—as well as an immensely increased sensitivity to the nuances of scent. Her account of affective shifts concludes with a significant discussion of a transformed sexual sensitivity—longer plateau periods prior to orgasm, more diffuse full-body orgasms, and a newfound propensity for multiple orgasm—descriptors anyone, post–Masters and Johnson, would say mark a more feminized experience of orgasm. This shift in the affect of orgasm comes coupled with a marked decrease in sexual drive (three to four times a week, she says, rather than one to three times a day). She concludes:

> Some people—particularly those who favor social, rather than biological, explanations of gender difference—will be somewhat disappointed at the predictable nature of my transformation. . . . [However,] not only are similar experiences regularly described by trans women, but trans men typically give reciprocal accounts: they almost universally describe an increase in their sex drives (which become more responsive to visual inputs), male-type orgasms (more centralized, quicker to achieve), a decrease in their sense of smell, and more difficulty crying and discerning their emotions.[10]

Paul Preciado's 2013 *Testo-Junkie*, particularly the chapter entitled "Becoming T," corroborates Serano's assertion that "trans men typically give reciprocal accounts." This chapter is an affective account of taking consistent—though relatively low—doses of testosterone in gel form, and its narrative arc is compelling. Preciado begins with an account of life pre-T. He writes, ruminating on the gender and sexual transgression that shapes this moment of his personal history, that "none of the sexes that I embody possess any ontological density, and yet there is no other way of being a body. Dispossessed from the start." He also describes this moment as a sort of tense holding pattern wherein he anxiously awaits the advent of masculine realness testosterone will provide: "Waiting for my beard to grow, waiting to be able to shave, waiting for a cock to grow from my loins, waiting for girls to look at me as if I were a man, waiting for men to speak to me as if I were one of them, waiting to be able to give it to all the little sweeties, waiting for power, waiting for recognition, waiting for pleasure, waiting . . ."[11] Contrast this, then, with his affective account of actually taking testosterone:

> An extraordinary lucidity settles in, gradually, accompanied by an explosion of the desire to fuck, walk, go out everywhere in the city. This is the climax in which the spiritual force of the testosterone mixing with my blood takes to the fore. Absolutely all the unpleasant sensations disappear. Unlike speed, the movement going on inside has nothing to do with agitation, noise. It's simply the feeling of being in perfect harmony with the rhythm of the city. Unlike with coke there is no distortion in the perception of self, no logorrhea or any feeling of superiority. Nothing but the feeling of strength reflecting the increased capacity of my muscles, my brain. My body is present to itself.[12]

Each of these narratives are shaped by transnormative structures of feeling: they both describe the experience of hormone use as one that confirms, in some significant sense, hegemonic conceptions of masculine and feminine modes of feeling. Serano feels more intensely, with a degree of emotional acuity not present before taking estrogen and progesterone. Preciado is released from the passivity, stasis, and lack of ontological heft that characterized his pre-testosterone gender expression and becomes possessed of a new capacity for action. His passage reads as a kind of neo-futurist melding of the human and the machinic, a narrative of the intensification of mental and physical strength that elicits a feeling of oneness with the city—not a false megalomania but a sustainable, even-keeled sense of belonging to the urban rhythms that so many find depleting, exhausting, necessary to guard against or retreat from. It's worth noting that this narrative is also underwritten by whiteness—his oneness with the city is possible only in the absence of intense surveillance and policing. In both descriptions, there is an emphasis on increased clarity; they echo the visual rhetoric of SSRI ads that are shot in greyscale and then, suddenly, with the prescription of the antidepressant, go full color.

What I want to highlight is that these narratives are popular and palatable because they confirm certain truisms regarding the biology and psychology of sex difference. The narratives offered up most consistently within John Money's case studies do the same sort of confirmation work, shoring up his idea that gender is a matter of indelible psychological imprinting at a young age. His preferred examples are those that testify to indelibly male-typical or female-typical gender roles, and he relies on narrations of childhood memory that conform to transnormative structures of feeling. For instance, one of the few patients cited at length in his case studies—a male-identified intersex person with hypospadias who had been reared as male—recounts, "'I remember myself squirting the hose. I think I squirted my father in the process. And it was lots of fun.' This memory, dating from the age of two, had been reinforced from a photograph taken on the occasion; 'and yet, when I look at it, it kind of brings me back, you know, that wonderful feeling of power you have when you're watering something! Well, it kind of brings back something of being a master in your own domain as you squirt this blasted hose around.'" Not only does Money's paradigmatic patient enjoy the rush of power that comes with squirting the hose, he also explains that he is heavily preoccupied with sex, but only the strictly heterosexual variety, and he also manifests some concern about being too sex-positive: "I would think about all kinds of sex, what kinds there were, and then I would wonder if I was safe or not. Whether I would find myself liking it too much or something. Yet, if I ever started making any image of homosexuality, I could never get myself into it." This narrative shores up the dominant expectations regarding male sexuality of that era—a man was a person who had to, for the social good, reign in sexual drive and make sure his preferred objects were exclusively of the opposing gender. It is no surprise, then, that Money—in his (troublingly) assumed role as the arbiter of the truth of gender identity—declares "all in all, beyond every possible doubt, this person was psychologically a man. He was fortified with a diplomatic arrogance which adjusted to the human demands of the occasion, yet enabled him to choose and select his standards rather than run with the herd."[13] Diplomatic arrogance! Pronounced individualism! A natural-born leader, this patient, possessed of all the hallmarks of rugged American machismo. We need no further proof of the immutability of psychological gender, even in cases of ambiguously sexed individuals. In other words, all intersex people have an "indelibly imprinted" psychological gender; it is the job of the medical sexologist to discern what that is and green-light technologies of transition accordingly. His function is, then, only one of enhancing the potential of intersex and trans persons to live unremarkable, gender-typical and sexually normative lives.

One of the great risks of late gender assignation, for Money, is the possibility of queer sexuality. In a 1965 article, he writes, "after a child has entered school, a sex reassignment is extremely perilous psychosexually and is liable to produce a person who lives socially in the reassigned sex but falls in love as a member of the other originally assigned sex—and thus has all the outward appearances of being homosexual. These late sex reassignments also may issue in nonspecific, moderate to severe psychopathology of the personality."[14] To put it bluntly: not only does Money think late gender reassignment might make you queer, it might also produce mental disorders.

This rigorous effort to guard against any association with queer sexuality is not only present in intersex cases, but—as mentioned above—in trans cases as well. The aim of intersex and trans medical treatment was—and in many cases, remains—the production of gender-normative heterosexuals. Given that treatment centers have historically been located exclusively in metropolitan areas, this also meant that most rural folks had no access. If we couple this heterosexist, gender-stereotyped gatekeeping with the prohibitively high costs of surgical transition, we have a situation wherein those folks who are most vulnerable to transphobic and queerphobic violence—poor folks, queer folks, rural folks, folks of color—are also those with the least access to the technologies of gender transition that would render them more passable, thus less subject to these forms of gendered violence. This is not an argument for the importance of passing but a pragmatic admittance that to be read as heterosexual and cisgender is to evade both micro- and macro-aggressions. It also means that the legacy of policing access to technologies of transition is implicitly both classist and racist.

Trans Necropolitics and Archival Absence

What if technologies of transition sometimes make us feel like shit, but we utilize them because of the more intense social cost of not being passable as cis? What if we reject hormonal therapy? What if we have reservations about submitting to technologies of gender normalization? What if we can't afford or can't geographically access technologies of transition? What if transition, for intersex and trans folks alike is not always a triumphal narrative but instead a sort of necropolitical calculus wherein negative effects are weighed one against the other? Trans necropolitics, as theorized by Jin Haritaworn and C. Riley Snorton, refers to the exposure to violence, debility, and death that shapes nontransnormative lives.[15] Trans necropolitics is a useful concept in thinking through how intensely stratified access to medical care is for trans and intersex subjects, how the rise in trans visibility comes coupled with an intensification of violence toward nontransnormative subjects, and how the livability of transnormative lives is interwoven with institutional mechanisms that expose less privileged trans and intersex subjects to systemic violence and disenfranchisement.

Could we understand decision making that takes place within this milieu as an instance not of willed, autonomous self-making but instead as consent compromised by conditions of coercion? These are the questions that motivate my effort to compile an archive of trans, intersex, and gender-nonconforming feelings regarding medical transition that foregrounds the experiences of affect aliens—those folks who, as Sara Ahmed writes, "do not experience pleasure from proximity to objects that are attributed as being good."[16] Why have we not paid more attention, as scholars, to the historical incidences of folks who experience trauma in their interface with medical professionals rather than validation? Those who reject the notion that medical specialists are also, somehow, saviors?

I began thinking about this while working on a project documenting my own experience growing up intersex. As I recounted in earlier, I was diagnosed late—around the age of sixteen–and promptly put on Premarin, a conjugated estrogen that was at the time commonly used to treat intersex conditions, as well as for hormone therapy in both cis and trans women.[17] This was meant to normalize my intersex body along female-typical lines, resulting primarily in breast growth and fat redistribution. After months of severe depression, including suicidal ideation, I stopped taking it, and I haven't been on hormones since. It's difficult, existentially speaking, to tease apart the side effects of that particular drug from the general trauma of grappling with an intersex diagnosis, but I do know that my decision to cease hormonal treatment was directly linked to a substantial decrease in the intensity of depressive symptoms I experienced. I also understood my refusal of hormone therapy as a refusal, more broadly, of medical tactics of gender normalization aimed at intersex youth and adults, a refusal of the notion that, as I understand it, my corporeal queerness needed to be fixed or remediated.

When some years later I visited the archives of the medical sexologists who produced the treatment protocols I'd been subjected to—and run away from—I found my experience mirrored, though obfuscated by the curatorial impulses of these medical professionals, veiled by their desire to protect and render watertight their theories. I discovered a lot of anger on the part of intersex patients and quite a lot of trauma at the hands of the medical establishment. Patients repeatedly refuse to return for further examination, finding their own gendered and sexual inclinations at odds with Money's recommendations for treatment. Several patients, when slated to have their genitalia photographed by Money's assistants for medical publications, simply don't show up. One patient—an androgen insensitive person reared as male whom Money, in concert with this boy's parents, insisted on reassigning as female—went so far as to call Money on the coercion evident in his treatment methods:

> I think you're a rotten guy. I told my father that you were trying to make me do what he wants. And I think the same thing of you. . . . You're trying to make me say what you want me to say. And I don't want to say that. . . . I told you what I want. You said we won't mention nothing about the other sex that I don't want to be. . . . What you're saying is to imagine that I'm the other sex, that's what you're saying, and I don't like imagining that way.[18]

What is shocking is that Money doesn't interpret this anger as directed at him, as stemming from the patient's profound disagreement with his dogged insistence on gender reassignment. Rather, he believes it is the product of a wrongly assigned gender, believes this child is mad because he was reared as male despite being intersex and thus not possessing what, for Money, was the ultimate arbiter of manhood—a "normal-looking" penis. Money concludes the case history by noting the patient's eventual suicide, which he argues would not have happened had this patient heeded his advice and accepted gender reassignment as female. This misreading of patient affect is consistent across Money's case studies. I became concerned that in trans and intersex narratives alike the palliative effects of hormone replacement therapy were overdetermined, the elements of coercion involved in medical procedures of gender normalization were elided, and the deleterious effects of these procedures were downplayed.

Historically speaking, folks whose desires for transformation run counter to hegemonic, white, bourgeois understandings of masculinity and femininity were systematically prevented from accessing technologies of transition. The forms of gender normativity utilized by the medical establishment were—and remain—undergirded by race, insofar as what was understood as a normative gender ideal was implicitly white, shaped by the typologies of masculinity and femininity that apply to what decolonial feminist philosopher María Lugones has called the "light side" of the colonial/modern gender system.

Lugones reasons that white bourgeois ideals of gender embodiment have been shaped by a deeply dimorphic understanding of gender complementarity that emphasizes white female sexual submissiveness, domesticity, minimized agency and access to the public sphere, and white male providence, epistemic and political authority, virility, and naturalized dominance. This light side of the colonial/modern gender system stands in contrast to a dark side constituted by the ways in which the sexualities, embodiments, and kinship forms of colonized peoples were constructed within the colonial imaginary. As Lugones writes in "Toward a Decolonial Feminism," "the hierarchical [gendered] dichotomy [that characterizes the 'light' side] also became a normative tool to damn the colonized. The behaviors of the colonized and their personalities/souls were judged as bestial and thus non-gendered, promiscuous, grotesquely sexual, and sinful."[19] In short, the gendered norms and mores that have determined the telos of biomedical logics of gender transition are also those that have framed the kinship forms, sexualities, and embodied intimacies of peoples with legacies of colonization as aberrant and in need of rehabilitation and assimilation.

Emily Skidmore in her media analysis of mid-twentieth-century representations of transwomen argues that those women with the most "proximity to bourgeois white womanhood" were represented most frequently, so their stories "came to define the boundaries of transsexual identity."[20] Moreover, access to technologies of transition was, and remains, doubly compromised for trans folks of color; as Delisa Newton attests in a 1966 issue of *Sepia* cited by Skidmore:

> Because I am a Negro it took me twice as long to get my sex change operation as it would have a white person. Because I am a Negro many doctors showed me little sympathy and understanding. "You people are too emotional for such an ordeal," one doctor told me. But finding medical attention wasn't the only problem complicated by the color of my skin. Even with my college and nursing education, I couldn't get a good, steady job to raise money for the operation.[21]

My own work in the Kinsey archives verifies this phenomenon of compromised access, which manifests most often as archival absence. Trans and intersex folks of color are conspicuously missing from the medical archives of sexology; moreover, many folks—white folks and folks of color—appear only briefly in medical records, never to return, going AWOL from the medical protocols of transition and gender normalization. Despite this, never in the work or correspondence of either of these massively influential sexologists I've researched was there any reflection on the partiality of knowledge manifest in such a racially homogenous, Eurocentric archive. In the rare moments that folks of color appear in these archives, they are framed, in accordance with the logic of the dark side of the colonial/modern gender system, as deviant, sexually perverse, and culturally aberrant and anachronistic. Take figure 1, an image of an indigenous American—a member of the Diné people—that appears with little context other than what's typed beneath the image.

I found this in a box of photographs marked "intersex" in the archives, though this person may not have an intersex condition, but may possibly be nadleeh—a Diné conception of embodiment that is not accurately translatable into Western gendered logics, though it is often referred to as a type of third gender. This was the only photograph of a nonwhite subject in that box, as well as the only photograph that was not formally composed and set indoors in a photo studio or medical clinic. The text reads as follows:

A Navajo Indian. Age 27, ht. 5'7, wt. 150, length 2.0", diameter 0.3. No hair on body and no sign of testes. Scrotum contained only a soft mass of indistinguishable tissue. Erection and orgasm possible but orgasm slight with emission of a few drops of what appeared to be semen. Intelligent and normal in other ways. He had attended Indian Boarding School. Was rejected by army draft board because of his sex organs. He tries coitus and enjoys it. Gets most satisfaction with little girls, but prefers adult women. They ridicule him because of the size of his organs. He feels his condition deeply, and begged to be told how he could "make it grow, so he could get married and have babies." His concern was over the size of his penis, not seeming to attach much importance to the lack of testes. He is probably one of those individuals who some tribes develop for pederasty through non-instrumental castration while small boys, although he denied it. If he is, he apparently has rebelled and desires to be normal. They

FIG. 1. Photographer unknown. "A Navajo Indian." Date unknown. Black and white photographic print. Courtesy of the Kinsey Institute for Research in Sex, Gender, and Reproduction archives, Indiana University, Bloomington.

are usually very effeminate in appearance and actions, but he was not. He is experienced in fellatio and pederasty, the anal muscles being quite relaxed. Adult male organs attract him very much and he delights in handling and gazing at them. He is particularly fascinated by semen, which, however, is not unusual in Indians. He was reluctant to pose which, combined with lack of seclusion, prevented more and better pictures.

This man is framed as living proof of the sexual and gendered deviance of the Diné people; he is presented as both irrefutably perverse in relation to Western gendered and sexual norms, engaging in nonheterosexual, age-inappropriate sexual activities, but also as victimized by the ostensibly strange sexual customs of the Diné and desperate for the forms of gendered normalization Western medicine can provide. His desire for gendered and sexual "normalcy" is implicitly linked to his time spent in the viciously assimilatory Indian boarding school system. White, Western-centric gendered and sexual normalcy is aspirational for this person; the medical specialist is simultaneously the gatekeeper and the benevolent colonial patriarch, able to make these dreams come true.

Racialized, classed, and queer absences and misrepresentations of this sort are central to understanding how access to technologies of transition have become compromised for poor folks, folks of color, and gender-nonconforming and queer folks. Popular understandings of trans and intersex identity are linked indissolubly to medicalized transition. Access to medicalized technologies of transition is too often understood as the sine qua non of trans and intersex livability and health. We are in dire need of holistic approaches to health that move beyond surgical and hormonal techniques of gender normalization and focus instead on remediating the quotidian and structural violence that so often compromises the life chances of trans, intersex, and gender-nonconforming subjects. It is imperative to interrogate this exclusionary legacy of medical treatment as the trans-national market for medicalized transition grows while the communal nonprofit networks of support, advocacy, and assistance that are able to address the exigent needs of trans and gender-nonconforming subjects remain relatively stagnant.

While I examined questions of archival absence, erasure, misrecognition, and partiality here, in the following chapter I analyze photographic tropes that actively dehumanize those subjects who are present in the archives of medical sexology. I examine the function of medical imaging technologies in producing intersex embodiment as a condition in need of remediation. Drawing on the work of Donna Haraway, Foucault, and Deleuze and Guattari, I focus on how medical photography desubjectivizes the intersex patients that it documents, though its ostensible purpose is to document the corporeal truth of sex abnormality and the supposed success of sex normalization procedures. Faces are obscured; genitals are exposed. I argue that the use of the visual trope of the "black bar" or circle that covers the eyes or face of the subjects of medical photographs is a means of absenting them from forms of legible personhood. While the pragmatic function of this trope is to ensure the anonymity of the patient, it works to further stig-matize intersex bodies through entrenching the idea that the visibly intersex body must remain secret, covered, socially and politically invisible—it cannot be attached to a person. Theorizing this way of viewing intersex bodies as a form of dispassionate detachment (what Haraway has called "modest witnessing") that shores up cisheteronormative understandings of embodiment, I then turn to instances of trans, queer, and intersex visual art practice that offer up alternative possibilities for depicting our various passionate attachments to forms of queer corporeality, analyzing the visual work of the queer feminist collective LTTR, Carrie Moyer, Ginger Brooks Takahashi, Amos Mac, and Del LaGrace Volcano as they passionately, empathically, and lovingly render forms of non-cishetero embodiment and desire.

on sight

I entered a private room at the urologist's office, leaving my mother paging through *Golf Digest* in the lacquered-wood waiting room. The assistant instructed me to lie down on the examination table; I did, noting the familiar crinkle of those awful paper sheets. I wasn't quite sure what the examination was for—I had already had ultrasounds performed, we already knew that I didn't have a functioning reproductive system, and I assumed that this doctor—who had been charged with the task of removing my gonads—ostensibly because "they could become cancerous" but really because they produced more testosterone than was acceptable for a person being reared female—knew where they were and how to get them out. But he had ordered this examination, which I knew would feature hysteroscopy—the insertion of a small camera into my body through my genitals. This was a completely mortifying phenomenon for my sixteen-year-old self to consider.

He entered the room. He wasn't alone. He had brought a friend, a visiting physician from a place my anesthetic-fogged memory cannot recall, to observe the procedure, a man who had a "very intense interest" in cases like mine. He explained to me that given the relative rarity of my condition, it was important that I allowed other physicians access to both my case history and, well, my body. He explained that today the goal was to get "the lay of the land"—a metaphor that I found really poorly chosen. I wasn't a territory to be discovered and colonized. I wasn't the mute terrain on which some doctor-explorer got to adventure alongside his brothers-in-arms.

Or was I? Years later, I read Anne McClintock's *Imperial Leather: Race, Gender, and Sexuality in the Colonial Contest,* the first chapter of which is entitled "The Lay of the Land." In it, she writes, "all too often, Enlightenment metaphysics presented knowledge as a relation of power between two gendered spaces, articulated by a journey and a technology of conversion: the male penetration and exposure of a veiled, female interior; and the aggressive conversion of its "secrets" into a visible, male science of the surface."[1] McClintock brought me immediately back to that examination table, back to that feeling of radical disempowerment in the face of medical objectification, that feeling of being shelved in a cabinet of curiosities only to be brought out, dusted off, and shared with dinner guests over a glass of sherry. What an unusual specimen! Such grotesquery to behold! We must find out what makes them so *unusual*!

While hysteroscopy isn't always performed under general anesthetic, mine was. I was skittish, young, ashamed of my body, and unused to sharing it with strangers. I consented to the visitation of this younger doctor as the anesthetic set in. Here I was, offering up my body to science, allowing these strange physicians access in the name of research, in the name of enhancing their specialized knowledge of my ostensible malformation so future physicians could know—without having to be in this room—what the "lay of the land" was.

I'm twenty, and a friend of mine, a photographer, wants to put together a short film about, well, me—about my being intersex, about my experience with doctors, about resisting discourses of disorder and deformation. The idea was to take a poem of mine (from my short-lived time as a teenage slam poet) and make a sort of slideshow of photo stills. He wanted me to pose nude; I wouldn't, feeling still shy, still sheepish, still ashamed of my body. We compromised—I would buy a body stocking that matched my flesh and pose in that. I did, and afterwards I cried and refused to meet up with him to finish the project.

I wasn't familiar with the idea of being triggered then, but I was definitely being triggered. The whole mise-en-scène was reminiscent of that urologist's office. I had lost control, again, of how I was represented, how I was interpreted. Here I was with another man who wanted to capture images of my unusual body, to disseminate them in order to build up his portfolio, to enhance his career.

It's 2010. I've received a travel grant that allows me to drive from upstate New York, where I'm finishing my PhD, to the Kinsey Institute at Indiana University. Housed in one of IU's characteristic ornate limestone buildings, the institute holds many, many artifacts from the heyday of U.S. sexological research, including medical and artistic photographic portraits of intersex subjects. I had brought a good friend—an art historian, a Latinx queer who loves minimalism and rasquachismo—along with me, thinking he'd be as interested in these images as I was. We started sorting through the first box of photos (loosely collated, with minimal, if any, information regarding their genesis), passing images back and forth, sometimes murmuring commentary but mostly not saying anything. Some of these images are ornately posed, with intersex folks draped in fabrics reminiscent ancient Greek statuary— clichéd framings of us as the mythical Hermaphroditus. Most of them, though, are medical photographs where our eyes are blacked out and we're positioned, nude, in front of a wall marking our height: medical mugshots.

After a few hours, we were both overwhelmed and left the mauve reading room of the Kinsey to grab something to eat. I asked him how he felt. He said, "I don't know. I don't know if I'm turned on or angry." I understood. Intersex bodies are beautiful; the ways they are depicted when intersex folks are not in control of their representation, though, have been incredibly ugly.

4 Black Bar, Queer Gaze
Medical Photography and the
Re-visioning of Queer Corporealities

Once upon a time, queer bodies weren't pathologized. Once upon a time, queer genitals weren't surgically corrected. Once upon a time, in lands both near and far off, queers weren't sent to physicians and therapists *for being queer*—that is, neither for erotic reform, gender assignment, nor to gain access to hormonal supplements and surgical technologies. Importantly, when measures to pathologize queerness arose in the nineteenth century, they did not respect the now-sedimented lines that distinguish queernesses pertaining to sexual practice from those of gender identification, corporeal modification, or bodily abnormality. These distinguishing lines—which today constitute the intelligibility of mainstream LGBT political projects— simply did not pertain. The current typological separation of lesbian and gay concerns from those of trans, intersex, and genderqueer folks aids in maintaining the hegemony of homonormative political endeavors. For those of us interested in forging coalitions that are attentive to the concerns of minoritized queer subjects, rethinking the prehistory of these typologies is a necessity. This chapter is an effort at this rethinking, focused particularly on the conceptual centrality of intersexuality to the development of contemporary intelligibilities of queerness.

It is necessary to give some shape to this foregone moment. It exists prior to the sedimentation of modern Western medical discourse and practice. It is therefore also historically anterior to the rise of a scientific doctrine of sexual dimorphism. To paraphrase Foucault's famous assertion in his prologue to the diaries of nineteenth-century French hermaphrodite Herculine Barbin: folks have not always been forced into one of two ostensible "true" sexes but were at one point perceived as simply *having two*.[1] With this assertion,

Foucault counterposes a notion of queer corporeality—that is, a body comprised of both male *and* female elements—as predating a dimorphic system of bodily intelligibility. The rise of sexual dimorphism establishes a rubric for understanding bodies that offers only two strictly opposed understandings of what a body can be: male *or* female. The epistemological ascendancy of sexual dimorphism means that the queer understanding of intersexuality that Foucault indexes is gradually placed under erasure—an erasure I've been mapping over the course of this book. The sexually mixed body becomes an epistemic impossibility. It is necessary, then, to ask after the agglomeration of forces, techniques, and objects that have worked to fabricate this impossibility.

To orient and guide this inquiry, I analyze two phenomena that attest to this profound shift in the logic of understanding sex, sexuality, and the abnormal body: the medical pathologization of the intersex body and the professional popularization of reproducible imaging techniques. Intersex infants—that is, infants born with nonstandard genitalia or reproductive organs—are frequently interpellated within a medicalized, pathological understanding of their bodies as well as captured by imaging technologies from the camera to the X-ray to the ultrasound. These seizures of the intersex body are composite parts of the same apparatus of capture. Following Giorgio Agamben's gloss on Deleuze and Guattari's theorization of the apparatus of capture, we can think of it in broad terms as "literally anything that has in some way the capacity to capture, orient, determine, intercept, model, control, or secure the gestures, behaviors, opinions, or discourses of living beings."[2] Imaging technologies work in conjunction with biomedical etiologies of sex as an apparatus of capture that reworks the legibility of queer corporealities to render them compatible with a strictly dimorphic understanding of sex and gender. The interpellation of the intersex body by biomedicine is enabled and supported by the visual documentation of sexed aberrance, insofar as this documentation is made to function as evidentiary proof of sex and sex disorder. Photographic technologies are put to work in the service of biomedical understandings of the constitution of sex, and every attempt is made to fix the meaning of the image so as to confirm—and *only* to confirm—diagnosis of pathology and the supposed rectitude of assignation of sex.

A brief account of how queer corporealities were understood before this dovetailing of Western medical authority and photographic technologies will help us grasp the import of this shift in intelligibility. In this "once upon a time," this long moment before the rise of medical authority in the metropoles of the West, bodies were understood according to a schematic of sex "inversion" formulated by the second-century Roman physician Galen of Pergamum. This understanding of how bodies are sexed demonstrated considerable staying power throughout subsequent epochs. Within the Galenic schema, intersex bodies were perceived as composed of both male and female elements—located between genders, as it were. This understanding of sex is what we could term bimodal rather than dimorphic. Imagine a vertical line as the hierarchy of sex, with the male as the apotheosis and the female as the base and varying degrees of hermaphroditism located between the two. One's position within this schema is concordant with one's degree of bodily heat, that amorphous something said to force what were conceived of as analogous genital and reproductive structures out rather than allow them to remain internal. The more heat one possessed, the nearer one was to this male apotheosis; the less, the closer to the female base. Heat was equated with bodily perfection, reinscribing a familiar schematic of sex hierarchy. It is important to note, however, that within this system of somatic intelligibility, intersex bodies were considered legitimately mixed, rather than dissimulating or obfuscating an underlying true—that is, male or female—sex. Thomas Laqueur has deemed this mode of intelligibility a "one-sex" model, and this model served as foundation for both premodern and early modern research on the biology of sex. Laqueur persuasively articulates how it was that early modern anatomical discoveries were incorporated within, rather than disruptive of, this preceding conceptual understanding. When ovarian structures were discovered, for instance, they were construed as internal analogs of the testicles, not as markers of an incommensurable difference between the sexes. This began to shift gradually in the late 1830s, with the introduction of the notion of a "spurious" hermaphrodite by British physician James Young Simpson. Spurious hermaphrodites "possessed genitals that were 'approximate in appearance' to those of the opposite sex, whereas true hermaphrodites had a mixture of male and female organs."[3] The concept of genital dissimulation—that is, of genital structures that would seem to signal one's status as belonging to an intermediate sex—is introduced as the lynchpin of a process of interrogation in a move that renders queer corporealities as nothing more than the proposition of a riddle of sex to be solved by medical practitioners, framed here as privileged interventionists capable of discerning the "true"—that is, male or female—sex that lay hidden beneath these dissembling genitals.

Simpson's invention of the spurious hermaphrodite was elaborated upon by T. A. E. Klebs, who reconfigured the taxonomy for intersex bodies, articulating three divisions: the male pseudohermaphrodite, the female pseudohermaphrodite, and the true hermaphrodite. Sex, in this classificatory schema, was determined by the gonadal tissue present in one's body, regardless of genital configuration or the varying presence or absence of secondary sex characteristics. Given that only one form of intersex condition (what is called "mixed gonadal dysgenesis") results in the copresence of ovarian and testicular tissue in the gonads, nearly all intersex bodies came to be seen as "pseudohermaphroditic," as bodies masking an underlying true sex.[4] This ushered in what I think of as the Reign of the Gonads, when the tissue present therein was the mighty arbiter of one's sexed ontological status, the revelator of biological and social being.

This diagnostic shift and concomitant purging signals more than a move away from the one-sex model and its discursive admittance of a certain degree of sexed mixity. It also marks the consolidation of medical authority in matters of gynecology and obstetrics, as well as a movement away from the primarily female institution of midwifery. With midwifery, which exists (both historically and currently) in a significant sense beyond the stranglehold of biomedical intelligibility, the solution in instances of intersex births hinges on what we now understand as performative aspects of gender. When faced with sexed mixity, a preferred gender of rearing is selected by the parents and then ostensibly consistently enacted and encouraged. In the absence of surgical and hormonal maneuvers to intervene in sex constitution, the success of this assignation was judged along the lines of dress, comportment, gestural habit—all techniques of recurrent and quotidian subjective constitution currently examined beneath the rubric of performativity. As such, this method of gender assignment prefigures what I consider a noninstitutionalized mode of dealing with intersex bodies. This method, given its lack of surgical intervention and reconstruction, is one potentially much less psychosomatically damaging than the prevailing mode of treatment that recommends infant genital surgeries that are often botched and repeated numerous times, which results in both pain and desensitization, and that are coupled with the recommendation of lifelong hormonal regimens. It is a particularly invasive treatment protocol, given that the ostensible necessity of these treatments is not a matter of bodily wellness but is shaped fundamentally by *social and aesthetic* concerns that fear the disruptive potential of these queer bodies.

Summarily speaking, in the epochs preceding the consolidation of modern medical authority in matters of sexed and sexual irregularity and abnormality (that long moment of Galenic bodily intelligibility spanning from the second to the nineteenth century), the treatment of intersex bodies was one of both juridical and informal (but *not* explicitly medicalized) gender assignment and subsequent performative conscription to a social (male or female) gender. It is not yet one of dimorphic corporeal truth. Before the 1800s sex was a social rather than ontological category. In large part, this is because the body was not yet construed as an epistemological object with its own truth to tell, a truth only able to be discerned by medicoscientific specialists in anatomy. This particular mode of corporeal objectification was not salient until the advent of Enlightenment-era scientific positivism, which sought—through close anatomical analysis of both living beings and increasingly available corpses—to establish biological facts *from the body up* rather than viewing the body as merely *reflective* of larger cosmological truths. While intersex bodies certainly presented enfleshed signs that bespoke an unusual corporeality, comprised of elements that are conventionally perceived as neither wholly male nor female—for instance, large clitorises, blind vaginal canals, hirsutism, small breasts, and the presence of descended testicles in the labial folds—these elements were not yet orchestrated into a full diagnostic symptomatology of a medically classifiable entity.

In the nineteenth century these queer corporeal signs come to constitute a symptomatology, thanks to the calibrated perception of the medical clinician. This finely tuned mode of perception is not simply comparative but wholly engendered by a drive to articulate an original and natural order, to achieve an exhaustive, clear, and complete reading of the body with no ambiguity or ineluctability. This intense clinical gaze is considered to be isomorphic with the transparent and fully denotative language of diagnosis and disease. Together, they guarantee the truth complex of medical science. It is in this way that nineteenth-century medicine shrugs off its speculative yoke and becomes an explicitly positivist endeavor. Further, this isomorphism calls into being a certain stranglehold on what had heretofore been posited as the caprice of nature. The notion of the natural irregularity or error of nature is done for. Nature can no longer produce *Homo sapiens* that are anything other than male or female. In keeping with this, there are no more mysterious, unusual, monstrous, or wondrous bodies. Rather, these bodies are now seen as merely deformed, and the richness of their possible meanings are sacrificed to a eugenic conception of etiology that takes as its standard-bearer that phantasm known as the *normal body*. The normal body becomes the gauge for the exacting articulation of somatic pathology, which all bodies are measured against. Within this schema, intersex conditions come to be seen as desperately in need of intervention, as disordered, and thus as privy to the infinitesimal explorations and discourses on both the etiology of hermaphroditism and the recommended courses of action relevant to diagnosis.

In keeping with this transition, the intersex body must be recuperated to a position *within* the diagnostically mappable realm of the natural, not perceived as special or preternatural. As discussed earlier, this recuperation happens by way of the near-erasure of the possibility of a diagnosis of "true" hermaphroditism, the elaboration of a discourse on pseudohermaphroditism, and the divvying up of what appears to be aberrance within a pre-given conceptual schematic predicated on sex dimorphism in order to secure the correlation between the medical gaze and the language of diagnosis. Later in this chapter, I examine an example from the late 1800s that vividly dramatizes this process, wherein the body of an intersex patient is photographed and presented as diagnostic evidence of a discernible "true sex" to a council of gynecologists.

We can think of this process as a sort of *significatory kidnapping* wherein the intersex body loses its sexually mixed and, to a large extent, ineluctably wondrous and monstrous status and is instead submitted to a clinical gaze that intently maps this queer corporeality with the intent of discerning, once and for all, its "true" sex, as well as the etiological path of its abnormal development. For with the death of the notion of the true hermaphrodite, we also witness the beginning of an increasingly fine-tuned diagnostic machinery that will refine the taxon of sex abnormality into multiple categories. The queer body is ensnared within the scientific logic of sexual dimorphism and as a result has a new subjective truth mapped onto its flesh. The guarantor of this truth is the denotative language given to the medical gaze that "circulates within an enclosed space in which it is controlled only by itself," a gaze that fantasizes and fetishizes its autonomy, rationality, and powers of adjudication and is aided in this endeavor by an imaging technology once imagined to be fully denotative, entirely commensurate with the real: the camera. The "enclosed space" Foucault writes of indexes the construction of a distinct medical realm that is centralized in its structure and sovereign in terms of its knowledge production. Within this contained realm, medical knowledge is produced not through a doctor's encounter with a patient nor through a confrontation between "a body of knowledge and a perception" but through the establishment of a realm in which an endless feedback loop is created between medical observation and medical judgment and adjudication.[5] Medical professionals build a world wherein only they may knowingly investigate and observe the body and declare their theorization of what is observed as diagnostic truth. The first level of observation is constantly and continuously mapped homologously to the second level of judgment and knowledge production. It becomes difficult to intervene in the truths created by this closed epistemic loop, and the utilization of photographic technologies within medicine only enhances the supposed veracity of the knowledge produced.

This relatively long backstory is necessary to grasp the import of a photo documenting the abnormal or aberrant genitals of Eugénie Rémy, a photo which is paradigmatic of the ways intersex genitals are documented within medical archives. This image, which circulated among medical professionals in France in the late 1800s, was initially published as part of a paper on hermaphroditism given by gynecologist Fancourt Barnes of the British Gynaecological Society in 1888. The photograph features the body of an intersex person, who had been raised and was living as female, with their skirts pulled up to the waist, exposing the genitals, where a physician's hand gingerly holds up what appears to be a microphallus. The upper body and face of this "living specimen" are out of focus, while the doctor's hand and the genitals of the Rémy are positioned both clearly and centrally.

This image entered into an intensely contestatory field of medical discourse and was accordingly read in widely varying manners. These genitals were a hot topic, eliciting arguments that recursively referenced both Simpson's conception of spurious hermaphroditism, dependent on the contradiction of genitalia with other physiognomic features that spoke one's real sex, and arguments that presaged the entrenchment of Klebs's gonadal taxonomy. Barnes himself recommended male sex assignment, arguing that this "living specimen" was clearly male on account of "the undoubted existence of a well-formed prepuce and glans penis [and] the imperfectly formed urethra running down from the tip of the glans and passing into the bladder." While Barnes was arguing for sex assignation based upon the apparently male formation of the genitals, within Simpson's framework privileging the genital configuration as evidentiary of true sex, other conference attendants protested his method of rectal examination, the relative femininity or masculinity of the "specimen's" facial structure, and the amount of body hair present. These counterarguments were taken into consideration by the attending members, resulting in a highly divisive resolution wherein the physicians in attendance essentially agreed to disagree. Dreger writes that they were "dramatically unable to decide what they had seen and felt, incapable of agreeing on the nature of sex and its proper diagnosis."[6] Counterintuitively, perhaps, the inconclusiveness of this meeting precipitated *not* a reconsideration of the now-entrenched doctrine of univocal sex in cases of hermaphroditism but an increasingly fervent search for a "true" material determinant, resulting in the full-on entrenchment of gonadal determination.

Given this intensely contestatory field, what is there to make of the actual photograph? What *do* these genitals signify? It is obvious that they are meant to testify in some way. The image reads as a scene of capture, the physician's tastefully cuffed hand raising the enlarged phallo-clit to facilitate a clearer view of the genital surface, the hiking up of Rémy's skirts, the obfuscation of their face. Through what eyes, however, can this photograph work as evidence of something other than undecidability? How would it be that that image spoke in order to unify agreement as to Rémy's true sex? Undoubtedly, it would first need to be coupled with that endless and transparent clinical discourse of which Foucault wrote—a precise and rigorously descriptive discourse that maps and fixes the seen.[7] This is provided by Barnes's written account of this photograph, particularly through his use of descriptors coded as masculine. This attempt at incorporeal transformation—that is, a naming that effects a shift in perception without material reorchestration—ultimately results in dissent.

So what exactly does this image depict? The genitals of the intersex body are rendered spectacular while the person replete with these genitals is desubjectivized—in the blurring of their face, they become subjectively unidentifiable. The image, in its intent focus on Rémy's genitals, definitively testifies to a burgeoning drive to document congenital sex deformity, but it also does much more. If we turn away from the apparatus composed of the camera, the doctor, and the "deformed" genitals of the intersex subject—all signifiers working in conjunction to produce the medical intelligibility of the intersex body—and instead focus on the frame of the image and what it absents, we can begin to parse some of the other work being done here. The demonstrative hand of the physician signals two pointed disappearances— that of his body and face. What do these absences mean?

They visually index the physician's intellectual integrity, the noninterferential character of his observation and analysis. Put more simply, these absences establish his being a modest witness. Donna Haraway provides a thorough account of this disappeared modest witness, arguing that modesty, as a trait of comportment, is a crucial underpinning of scientific claims to objectivism. I read this modesty as a means of signaling a distinct lack of pomposity in cultures of science and medicine. Scientific method itself attempts to cap grandiosity and the triumph of the individuated genius, the great brain, by procedurally in-building both a culture of empiricism and a logic of progressive supersession. The culture that produces the modest witness is one "within which contingent facts—the real case about the world—can be established with all the authority, but none of the considerable problems, of transcendental truth." The modest witness, produced by the Enlightenment-era scientific "culture of no culture," is constituted by the fundamental sameness of his subjectivity and objectivity. As Haraway writes, his modesty is "the virtue that guarantees that the modest witness is the legitimate and authorized ventriloquist for the object world, adding nothing from his mere opinions, from his biasing embodiment. And so he is endowed with a remarkable power to establish the facts. He bears witness, he is objective, he guarantees the clarity and purity of objects. His subjectivity is his objectivity." The modest witness, in the isomorphism of his subjectivity and objectivity, seems to be pure conduit, embodied only insofar as he is a ventriloquial medium, in possession of a body so unlike queer bodies, women's bodies, nonwhite bodies, and disabled bodies that it does not risk compromising his production of facts. In this capacity to possess a body that *doesn't matter*, the modest witness is what Haraway calls "self-invisible." He must inhabit the space of the unmarked, must be the witness who is never himself witnessed, never the object of a critical or incisive gaze. Thus, the modest witness is a ghostly figure, the producer of facts that do not, in fact, produce him. He is possessed of an ostensibly non-situated—that is, universal—knowledge, secured through the erasure of the "non-matter" of his (white, male, upper-class) body, through the construction of a scientific myth that assumes he adds nothing to the analysis that is derived from "his mere opinions, his biasing embodiment."[8]

To return to the hand that directs the scenography here while remaining otherwise disembodied—we follow it to the wrist, which the border of the image severs, invisibilizing the physician, diffusing medical authority, rendering it part of the miasmic milieu while sterilizing its violence. The corporeal absence of the modest witness is thus documented, along with his mastery, his literal factic grasp of the matter at hand, and the ostensible non-matter of his somatic matter.

There is another near-disappearance here—the face of Eugénie Rémy. Moving beyond a hoary assumption of the supposed negation of essence implied by a lack of eye contact, a better mode of understanding what this facial blurring signifies is offered by Deleuze and Guattari's theorization of faciality. "The face is a politics," they plainly state in A Thousand Plateaus.[9] So let us ask first what this politics is and second what the pixelated blurring of *this* face might mean.

For Deleuze and Guattari, faciality—the politics of the face—refers to how faces operate to signify identity. When they write of "the face," they are not referring to just any face but rather to a face that operates as a master code of sorts, one thoroughly Eurocentric and modern, geopolitically and historically contingent. They write that the "face is not a universal. It is not even that of the white man; it is White Man himself, with his broad white cheeks and the black hole of his eyes. The face is Christ."[10] The politics of the face, then, consists of the way that it marks a standard wherein all faces are intelligibly fixed through reference to their degrees of difference or deviation from this despotic signifier, this white man face. Importantly, it is through this reference to the white man face that faciality does the work of biunivocalization. *Biunivocalization* is a term specific to Deleuze and Guattari, used to make plain the power dynamics at work in dichotomous thinking, wherein two terms are linked to one another through the act of defining one term according to the other. Biunivocalization signals the process by which one term in a dyad overcodes or fixes the meaning of the other so that the two terms become yoked together by what is ultimately a unitary rather than a differential logic—hence, *bi-uni-*vocal.

Deleuze and Guattari claim that we read utterances through reference to a signifying face that is always "in biunivocal relation with another: it is a man or a woman, a rich person or a poor one, an adult or a child, a leader or a subject, 'an x or a y.'" It is through this biunivocal relation that the specificity of the face is transformed—biunivocal subjective positions become units of intelligibility that combine and recombine but always through an overcoded schema based on degrees of derivation from the white man face. Subjectivation works, then, through this process of (re)combination and is comprised of a second aspect: whether or not a given face passes, that is, can be slotted into a given regime of biunivocal sense. Deleuze and Guattari write of the faciality machine's "rejection of faces that do not conform, or seem suspicious."[11] This rejection of the inassimilable is often followed by the creation of new divergence-types, new etiologies of deviance that more effectively subjectify that which seems at first glance inassimilable, improper—intersex folks, for instance.

While the absence of the physician's face signals the invisibility of the modest witness, it also signals the diffuse omnipresence of the despotic signifier, the face that need not appear on account of its entrenchment as standard-bearer. It can sustain invisibilization without risking disappearance—its lack of visibility is not commensurate with its illegitimacy or nonexistence but rather shores up its position as arbiter of the real, as master code. It is, even in its absence, always already present, its gaze and discourse provident of the exegesis for this image of capture, the mask that the viewer is expected to adopt as its own, constituted by its possession of the gaze that legitimately territorializes, not the body territorialized by the gaze. The modest witness is part of a larger machine invested in processes of identification, recognition, and identification, and the facial absence of the modest witness only further positions him as part of the "abstract machine that has you inscribed in its overall grid."[12] The face may not be present, but this does not in the least signal an attempt at what Deleuze and Guattari call becoming-clandestine, a fugitive refusal of the politics of faciality, a refusal of identitarian belonging secured by and through the signification of the face. In the instance at hand, the absence of the face is conjoined with a bodily absence, the authoritative and privileged gaze of the medical professional becoming that of the intended viewer at the same moment it signals the disembodiment and isomorphic subjectivity-objectivity of the modest witness.

This is decidedly not the case with the intersex body in question. The blurred face, in concordance with this theorization of faciality, signals visually what we have already either intuitively deduced or assumed given the contestatory field into which this image initially entered—a suspension of subjectivity, a liminal body, a body in limbo. While this photograph is historically poised on the cusp of conventions for concealing the identity of patients—a set of practices that began only in the late nineteenth century, gradually supplanting earlier portrait-style images—it is nevertheless important not to reduce the meaningfulness of subjective concealment to the level of ensuring patient privacy.[13] If the face is a politics that overcodes the body, that forces the body to cohere beneath and with reference to the face, to form a coherent and unified appearance within a pre-given schematic of somatic intelligibility, then the blurring of the face is a visual strategy that decisively suspends subjective coherence. We know these genitals correspond to a person, present in the upper third of the image, but only tenuously does this person—as subject—exist. This tenuous existence is necessary if the purposive function of the image is to perceptively dissect the genitals to adjudicate sex. The suspension of subjectivity enacted by the blurred face highlights the ambiguity of the corporeality pictured and in so doing posits the body as inhabiting the space of a caesura, a pause while proper subjecthood is recalibrated in concordance with the developing parameters of biomedical thought. There is a certain tension here between the ostensible function of the image (to prove Rémy's "true" sex) and the undecidability and ontological unsurety called up by this blurred face.

These tropes of the absent modest witness and the subjectively suspended intersex body abide throughout the twentieth century. In certain instances, the physician's hands have been replaced by the hands of the patients themselves, while in others they are not only present in the image but inserted in the patient, ostensibly documenting "insufficient" vaginal depth. There are three other new introductions that operate as heightened instantiations of the aforementioned tropes. The face may be left entirely out of the frame, cropped at the eyes, or blocked at the eyes by the ubiquitous black bar. In certain images metric sets are inscribed, documenting the age, height, and weight of the intersex body. Finally, the images have proliferated in number and variety of perspective. In many ways, these shifts are merely logical extensions of preexisting tropes, the black bar doing the work of the blurred face, the metric sets further attesting to the flourishing microphysics of power operative in diagnoses of sex. What of the proliferation of shots though? Later, in the mid- to late twentieth century, photographs of congenitally queer bodies are presented in one of two ways—as shots documenting the patient over a succession of months and years as they underwent hormonal regimens and surgical treatment to "correct" sex, thus operating as documents of an enforced teleological journey toward the heteronormative promised land of proper dyadic, dimorphic sex; or as comparative images that document similar cases with dissimilar outcomes, or dissimilar cases with similar outcomes.

In this image set from the Kinsey archives, however, in the absence of comparative or developmental documentation, the multiplication of photographic perspective alludes to another increasingly emphatic trope—what Linda Williams, in her book on hardcore pornography, calls "the principle of maximum visibility." This principle manifests in hardcore's privileging of close-ups over other shots, the overlighting of too often easily obscured genitalia, and the selection of positions that aim to display the intricacies of bodies and organs. She goes on to compare this principle with Eadweard Muybridge's motion studies, with their prominent grid of measurement attesting to his attempt to "gauge the action of the body with increasing exactitude."[14] While this principle is certainly never estranged from medical photodocumentation generally, with its aim to establish purely denotative and factic materials for study and professional use, it dovetails particularly well with the aims of documenting intersex bodies. This drive for the clearest possible rendering of a chimeric body merges with what Williams frames as the motivation behind the same principle in hardcore. Both are efforts to stabilize and render apparent (or, perhaps more accurately, to stabilize *through* rendering apparent) ever-elusive somatic aspects—for intersex bodies, the slippery and elusive evidentiary truth of (dimorphic) sex; for hardcore, the documentation of what Williams calls *the thing itself*—visible proof of cis female orgasm.

This motivational conjuncture of hardcore and biomedicine is the place at which the assumption of observational detachment veers, belying another possible motivation as well as a different way of viewing these congenitally queer bodies. It introduces questions of affect, suggesting the possibility of a passionate attachment to these images, to these bodies, an engaged and visceral response that is about something other than sex determination. These multiple images, meant to map the vicissitudes of what biomedicine terms sex deformity, speak also to the difficulty of drawing a line between

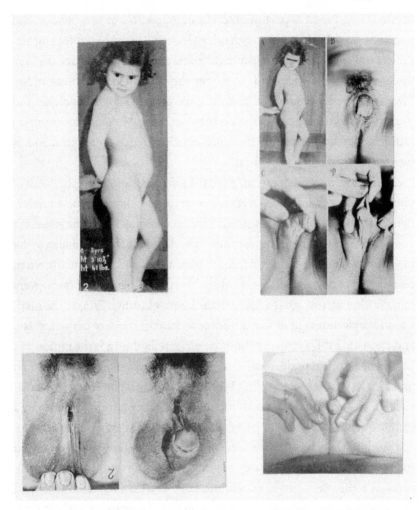

FIG. 2. Photographer unknown. Untitled. Date unknown. Black and white photographic print set. Courtesy of the Kinsey Institute for Research in Sex, Gender, and Reproduction archives, Indiana University, Bloomington.

the clinical and the pornographic. As someone who is not an anti-porn feminist, not sex-negative, and decidedly queer, I find this difficulty profoundly interesting.

Williams positions hardcore as a genealogical derivative of Foucault's *scientia sexualis* insofar as it relies on a fascination with unearthing somatic mysteries and secrets pertinent to the composition of sex, gender, and sexuality—a drive to concretely render and stabilize the heretofore ineluctable, from the discovery of ovaries to etiologies of genital structures. She understands the stag film and the money shot as close cousins to sexology. Given the overlapping of the photographic practices of biomedicine and porn, how can we think the relation between the medical photodocumentation of intersex bodies and the representation of gender atypical bodies beyond the realm of the medical?

This is an important question, given the long institutional deployment of photographic technology as an apparatus of capture that attempts to clearly delineate and fix the meanings and practices of queer bodies—whether congenitally queer, in the case of intersex bodies, or otherwise queer, in the case of trans, queer, and gender-nonconforming folks, particularly when one discovers that each of these ostensibly separate species of queer were initially filtered through the figure of the hermaphrodite. Prior to the medical and social intelligibility of the homosexual, the modern gay or lesbian, and consisting still as parcel of homosexual intelligibility, is the notion of a "hermaphroditism of the soul," that which Foucault, referencing German psychiatrist and neurologist Carl Westphal's 1870 work on "contrary sexual feeling," understands as defined "less by a type of sexual relations than by a certain quality of sexual sensibility, a certain way of inverting the masculine and feminine in oneself, in the form of an 'interior androgyny' onto which the practice of sodomy is transposed."[15] Coinciding with the flourishing of medical discourse on the constitution of transsexuality in the 1950s and 1960s, we find that John Money writes on the diagnostic use of the term *psychic hermaphroditism*. In a paper entitled simply "Hermaphroditism" in the 1961 *Encyclopedia of Sexual Behavior*, Money submits both a synopsis of the differential deployment of this term and an intervention of sorts:

Although its use is questionable, it is used from time to time as a synonym for homosexuality, transvestism, or contrasexism, the compulsion to have the body surgically and hormonally transformed to that of the other sex. The idea is that in these three allied conditions the patient is psychologically of one sex and morphologically of the other, and so is a hermaphrodite. . . . The term psychic hermaphroditism implies a physical or constitutional basis for the discrepancy between sexual psychology and morphology. Theoretically and morally, the three disorders become more respectable, to some people, as a result of this implied physical etiology.[16]

Money calls our attention to a few important aspects of the deployment of "psychic hermaphroditism." The equation of homosex, transvestism, and "contrasexism" (a diagnostic entity we now call transsexuality) with a disorder of sex that has a physical or constitutional—that is, visible, apparent, and thus irrevocably "real"—basis grants a certain legitimacy, at once biomedical and social. These attempts to legitimize queernesses that aren't immediately mappable as sex abnormalities through recourse to medical facticity is heard repeatedly today in ongoing battles fought to secure queer legitimacy within conservative institutional and social realms, for instance, "born that way" explanations of queerness and the flourishing of genetic and neurological research on queerness and the constitution of "brain sex" as a means of explaining trans identities. Interestingly, Money refers to these conditions not as practically and theoretically separate but as "allied conditions," conditions that rely, for their own biomedical intelligibility as disorders constitutive of discrete modes of being, on linked discourses that work unilaterally to mark queer patients as *both subjectively distant from* and *failures with reference to* heteronormativity (understood as a total match of morphology, psychology, and desire along dimorphic, heterosexual lines).

This is how hermaphroditism becomes the conceptual center of queerness, the figure that nonnormative genders and desires are, and have been historically, so often understood through and in relation to. It is as if the spectrum of queer being is strung up between, at one pole, the dyad of the dimorphic heterosexual couple and, at the other, the hermaphroditic body. The conceptual centrality of hermaphroditism to both biomedical and popular queer intelligibilities is often overlooked within the arena of LGBT politics, shaped as it is by efforts to firmly distinguish shifting lines—of both amity and enmity—between these queer beings while attempting to maintain what is increasingly a solidarity of the homonormative. Gender studies pedagogy, too, devises heuristics to explain the dangers of conflating queer identities, of reading lesbianism into transgender practices, of confusing the concerns of intersex folks with those of genderqueers. There is a portion, a subset, perhaps even a subculture, however, that has formed against this endless entrenchment of queer separability, of identitarian sects and boundary policing and has instead aimed to blur these lines, to mediate against the enforcement of stagnant and categorial conceptions of queer being. This blurring is activated by a reclamation of queer corporeality that refuses the notion of a transparent and mappable body as source and revelator of gendered truth. This refusal is the first step toward activating a process-oriented practice of relational queer becoming, without firm itinerary, without a final (male, female, or "other") telos, that utilizes technologies of representation and reproducibility, not to proffer homonormative or transnormative "positive" representations, nor to transparently document the texture of queer lives, but as part-objects in assemblages that concatenate in processes of queer autopoiesis—that is, processes of becoming something other than taxonomic beings rooted in a long history of biomedical narratives of pathology, illness, and bodily impropriety.

Queer Gazes and TransGenital Landscapes

To parse assemblages of queer becoming and coalitional autopoesis, I turn first to a text that appears in the fourth issue of LTTR, the journal produced by the self-described "genderqueer feminist artist collective" of the same name. Released in 2005, the issue—entitled "Do You Wish to Direct Me?"—is marked, like other LTTR projects, by repeated reference to what Abigail Solomon-Godeau has termed the first wave of an avowedly feminist art practice historically concurrent with the late 1960s to early 1970s women's liberation movement (typically indexed as second-wave feminism) and tied (albeit in complex ways) to this pre-psychoanalytic and pre-poststructuralist moment in feminist theory and political praxis, wherein dominant currents vacillated between hardline and tendentiously Marxian, socialist, liberal, and radical feminisms. Vacillation is the key term here, as a detailed reading of the history of U.S. feminist political movement in this historical moment is one of constant rift, fracture, contestation, and reconfiguration. To yoke seventies-era feminist art practices to a neatly delineated set of political theorems would be a drastic mistake. LTTR's citational practice is marked by a far more complex set of references that speak to a desire to construct a counter-genealogy for contemporary queer art and activism, one that merges radical feminism, queer liberation, and sex positivity. In their words: "LTTR is dedicated to highlighting the work of radical communities whose goals are sustainable change, queer pleasure, and critical feminist productivity."[17] It is through this eclectic and critical citational practice that they avoid the reinscription of sectarian understandings of queer identity while simultaneously refusing to elide the specificity of the bodies, subjects, and practices of political resistance and critique curated in the space of their journals.

The specific text I'm interested in is Anna Blume's "Mesh: The Tale of the Hermaphrodite," which provides a brief literary and art historical account of hermaphroditic representation. Blume moves from Ovid's *Metamorphosis* through the second-century AD sculpture *Sleeping Hermaphrodite* and on to Nadar's medical photographs of intersex genitals from the folio *Examination of a Hermaphrodite*, images whose scenography is recognizably akin to the photograph of Eugénie Rémy and Fancourt Barnes discussed prior. Blume names a tension running throughout these documents: a fascination with the queer reconciliation of masculinity and femininity concretized in the body of the hermaphrodite, paired with an impulse either to relegate hermaphroditism to the realm of the purely mythic or to posit it as a somatic state of loss and punishment rather than one of imagined fulfillment. Blume ends with a queer call to arms that resonates deeply with LTTR's critical revision of queer inheritance, begging the reader "not to carry this doom any further" nor to "allow our deep and dual sexualities [to] be relegated to a sleeping or faceless state." This echoes, in the register of queer resistance, the earlier privileging of the hermaphroditic body as conceptual centerpiece, with an important twist. With Blume, the hermaphroditic body is one that signals a set of possible yet feared and foreclosed desires that, in her words, Western civilization has spent the better part of three thousand years "running away from."[18]

What Blume calls our attention to is that, concurrent with the centuries-long thread of mythification, clinical detachment, and social and scientific abhorrence that has shaped typical perceptions of intersex bodies is the possibility of an illicit attraction, a passionate attachment, a reading of them as positively queer rather than interstitial and lacking. This possibility of a queer embrace of the interstitial, the refusal of sexed and gendered discourses of lack, passivity, and genital and psychosexual immaturity in favor of an embrace of bodies in their complex, textured, malleable, and mutating surfaces marks a double distancing—not only from normative popular and biomedical readings of hermaphroditic bodies but from certain historic strands of feminist and lesbian theory and praxis as well. This distance becomes both important and fraught within the field of contemporary queer and trans visual culture.

The traces of this radical feminist matrilineage are tendentious and definitively not done justice by a simple split between two moments in feminist art practice conceived as yoked to second- and third-wave feminisms that remain divided by an embrace of essentialism and discourses of global sisterhood on the one hand and a refusal of second-wave feminism as essentialist and politically naïve on the other. It is true that certain of the more banal tropes of seventies feminist art are burdened with an essentialism that is also coded as straight: iterations of Judy Chicago's central core imagery, glossed as "cunt art" by Faith Wilding and Miriam Schapiro (participant and faculty, respectively, of the short-lived Feminist Arts program at CalArts in the early seventies) is perhaps the most obvious instantiation. Richard Meyer offers a useful reading of this phenomenon in the companion book to 2007's WACK!: Art and the Feminist Revolution exhibition at MOCA, writing that "however transgressive, the Feminist Art Program's formulation of 'cunt art' seems rarely to have acknowledged lesbian sexuality. Vaginal imagery was called upon to signal the common experience (or 'sensation') of female embodiment rather than the explicitly sexual desire of one woman for another."[19] The essentialism lies in the assumption of a commonality of affect that would adhere around the ostensibly shared vicissitudes of possessing a vagina. Central core imagery is motivated by the assumption of a common somatic experience that, while sensual, is decidedly arelational, involving no other bodies and rather laterally and crudely equating the experiential with the genital.

Not all vaginal representations are produced with the same intent, however. As an instructive point of contrast, we can turn to Tee Corinne's drawings collected in the *Cunt Coloring Book*, initially published under the title *labiaflowers*. Corinne went on to become one of the better-known photographers of lesbian erotica, working for *On Our Backs* throughout and beyond the infamous feminist Sex Wars of the 1980s. In her early work, Corinne demonstrates a commitment to specificity and difference within the context of debates around women's sexuality, evident in the detail and attentiveness involved in her renderings. This is counterposed to the elision of queer desire enacted by an essentialist presumption of bodily sameness we see in central core imagery. While these images are detached from a person, a discrete subjectivity, the intense specificity of their rendering refuses essentialist abstractions about something we could call the "nature" of women's experience and desire. These are not the abstract and heavily symbolic genitals of Judy Chicago's *Dinner Party*, nor are they the captured evidence of deformity, depravity, or potential perversion so common in medical documentation. They are counterposed to blatant and reductive sexual symbologies. One reviewer wrote, "instead of obdurateness she gives us labial interface, clitoral hood, flesh, texture, wrinkles, different thicknesses of skin, and so on. Corinne's [work] is about specificity, sensation, vulnerability, and voluptuousness."[20] In its graphic articulation, Corinne's genital renderings rhyme with the historically concurrent reclamation of the material specificities and trajectories of women's bodies enacted by the women's health movement. A project begun while Corinne was working at San Francisco's Sex Information Hotline in the early 1970s, the *Cunt Coloring Book* was drawn with the practical intent of being utilized as a tool in feminist health and sex education courses, as well as an intervention staged against the typically misogynist and heterosexist bent of medicoscientific attitudes and treatment evinced in the realm of women's reproductive and sexual health. Insofar as Corinne links these pragmatic health concerns with a decidedly lesbian gaze, her work is a foremother to the work of contemporary queer artists who critically interface with the pathologization of trans and intersex bodies and pair this resistance with attempts to document the realities, ephemeralities, and vicissitudes of trans, intersex, and gender-nonconforming bodies, spaces, and desires.

Looking back to work like Corinne's and that stemming from the Feminist Art Program helps establish intergenerational bonds and set new critical stakes. To this end, the recent work of Carrie Moyer and Ginger Brooks Takahashi is deeply compelling. Both aim to complicate the 1970s feminist re-envisioning of the body, in particular the representation of genitals. Both take the phenomenon of the genital portrait as a starting point for their interventions. Carrie Moyer's work, which resonates as an ironized wink to central core imagery, renders this core in acrylic and glitter, flattening the dimensions and shifting the register of iconicity. The flows and puddles cohere in shapes reminiscent of what Moyer has termed the "invented avatars" of feminist new age kitsch, captured in a format she calls "worthy of a 1960s Supergraphic."[21] She is lovingly critical of invented avatars of fertility meant to signal the life-affirming productivity of Woman with a capital W, highlighting their cis-sexism and problematic emphasis on reproduction while honoring the critical spirit they were produced in, which is the feminist legacy contemporary queer artists like Moyer claim. This legacy is subject in part to the vicissitudes and vagaries of funding trends and shifting tides of critical reception and re-evaluation, tides and trends that threaten 1970s feminist art practice with disappearance and dissolution. These works are thusly part genealogical, part archival—hence the playful periodization of Moyer's titles for them: *The Crux, The Stone Age*.

Ginger Brooks Takahashi, too, is cognizant of this need for archiving and remembering. For instance, some of her recent paintings of Catherine Opie photographs attest to a means of documenting an artistic and political heritage that refuses stagnation and sedimentation, that is in movement and subject to critical redeployments. These queer feminist artists are not beholden to past strategic essentialisms. They see as their primary artistic and political task the rendering of spaces for dialogue and action that aren't contingent on the exclusion of trans and intersex folks but instead work to expand the parameters of queer communal articulations set by prior movements and moments. In keeping with this reformulation, "cunt art" becomes,

FIG. 3. Ginger Brooks Takahashi. *Genital Portraits, $25 per sitting.* 2008. Mirror, leather-covered toilet seat on pedestal, additional pedestal as step; found color pencil drawings on paper, with directed light. Dimensions variable. Courtesy of Ginger Brooks Takahashi.

in this work of Brooks Takahashi's, unfixed, named more inclusively as "genital portraits." This piece, instead of simply faithfully rendering diverse genitals, also constructs an apparatus for artistic genital documentation and positions this apparatus as a node around which diverse bodies and artists can gather, publicly, to more inclusively recapitulate that liberatory, communal, and eroticized practice of genital self-examination practiced by feminist women's health collectives. Given Brooks Takahashi's embeddedness in queer countercultural life—as co-editor of LTTR and as member of the band MEN, among other projects—we can understand this practice as pushing the parameters of inclusion beyond what Rosi Braidotti has called the "female feminist subject" while still paying a counterhistorical homage to the radical feminist birth of this practice of collective genital-gazing.[22]

These contemporary works may also be considered part of what has been posited by Jack Halberstam in *In a Queer Time and Place* as a turn taken as early as the late 1960s by many queer and female artists "to use representations of the body to resist the move to total abstraction and, by implication, to return a representational mode of political urgency to the practice of making art."[23] More than responses to art historical tendencies toward abstraction and the dissolution or dispersal of a coherent, readily identifiable subject of representation, these works also answer to trajectories of medical and popular spectacularization of bodies thought to display marks of sexed and sexual aberrance. As such, they can be read as a set of concerted attempts to wrest control over bodily intelligibility and technologies of representation away from mechanisms of institutional pathologization. Evident in this work is a queer effort to both critique the laws that compose bodies as well as to document an ecstatic movement *beyond* the stranglehold of these forceful norms of intelligibility.

On this tip, the photographic work of Amos Mac is particularly interesting. A transman and cofounder of the zine *Original Plumbing*, which is dedicated to documenting the "sexuality and culture of FTM trans guys," he was also one of the participants in the 2009 "Queer Gaze" photographic exhibition at Fontanelle Gallery in Portland, Oregon. This exhibition responds both to feminist film theorist Laura Mulvey's classic work on gaze theory as well as to the 2009 "Female Gaze" show at Cheim and Read in New

FIG. 4. Amos Mac. *Seth, from Austin*. 2009. Color photographic print. Courtesy of Amos Mac.

York through moving beyond the male/female dyad of gaze theory and into a space less codified by conventional understandings of gender and orchestrated alternatively around the act of queers looking at queers. In curating the show, Leslie Miller (co-owner of Fontanelle) selected artists already deeply involved in the representation and documentation of queer subcultures, already embedded in these alternative world-senses, documenting what composes the quotidian erotics of our lives. While a number of photographs included in the exhibition are quite obviously staged, they are contextualized as belonging to the realm of the intimate, the personal, the known and non-estranged. They are not spectacles of androgyny, nor are they merely exemplars of gender parody that aim only at destabilization and transgression—though many of the images do indeed do that. There is an earnest intensity to these images, a sense of erotic playfulness that is not deliberately or primarily contestatory. One photograph of Mac's in particular seems to forget the dominance of both male and conventionally heterosexual gazes; rather, it exists comfortably in a space of visual recognition shaped by a refusal to play what Foucault has called the "truth game" of sex. In it, a trans man, bare chested though covered by a frilly apron, hold out a plate of cookies, beckoning the viewer. In an interview Leslie Miller gave to Eva Lake, host of Oregon's ArtFocus on KBOO community radio, she provides the backstory to the image: the apron is borrowed from the girlfriend of this gentleman (called simply in the interview "Seth, from Austin"), and the cookies being made are *for* her. The domesticity here moves not only beyond the heteronormative but also beyond the staged. The setup of this image is in no way separate from the everyday domestic flirtations of the subjects so lovingly documented. A long way from Marcel Duchamp's Rrose Sélavy, Mac's images are about performances of queer and trans *authenticity*, rather than mere destabilizations of the real. They do not seem to attest to what Halberstam has argued is a dominant trope of queer representation that frames the "*transgender* body as a paradigm for the impossibility of bodily comfort."[24] Rather, they assume that trans and queer bodies are at home otherwise, secure in their inhabitation of normatively impossible corporealities. They highlight the way we build this comfort and belonging as outsiders with and through each other. This gaze doesn't work in an insular or rarefied circuit that actively excludes but does perceive according to erotic protocols that, in their lack of anxiety about and address of masculinist and heterosexist modes of perception, would tend to estrange or unsettle the uninitiated viewer, those unfamiliar with the relational modes and micrological etiquettes of queer and trans spaces, bodies, and desires. In this context, sexual objectification is something other than, as Mulvey would have it, a burden to be borne. The *to-be-looked-at-ness* of the transmasculine body in this image is no cross to bear but perhaps is the *point*—the point around which intimate and communal relations come into existence, however permanent or ephemeral these relations may be. A measure of erotic objectification can be life affirming, validating the ostensibly improper belonging of nondimorphic subjects, and actively (re) cognizing the bonds of passionate attachment that render lives outside the bounds of sexed and sexual propriety possible.

This politics of graphic affirmation is evident in the photographic work of Del LaGrace Volcano as well, in a much more explicit interchange with the practice of medical photodocumentation. For instance, in a series entitled "TransGenital Landscapes," Volcano proffers photographs of their own hormonally enhanced queer genitals, centering on what they call a "dick-lit," well-lit, closely cropped so that the entirety of the photograph is taken up by a lush vista of trans sex organs. There is no gingerly demonstrative physician's hand, no textual exposition as to what one is seeing, only an unflinching document that details what in medical and otherwise heter-onormative realms is urged to remain hidden, secret, shameful, that which at all costs should avoid public exposure. In another piece, entitled *Herm Torso* (figure 5), the grid of measurement that so often forms the backdrop of medical photographs of trans and intersex bodies is transposed onto the chest of an intersex body and transformed into a tic-tac-toe board of sorts. In this image, the grid of sexual intelligibility becomes material for play, determined interactively, by oneself and with various and multiple partners of one's choosing. Visual theorist and trans studies scholar Eliza Steinbock writes that Volcano's *Herm Body* series (of which *Herm Torso* is a part) offers "visual and affective traces of the medico-cultural processes of depersonalization" yet "diverges sharply from early medical photographs

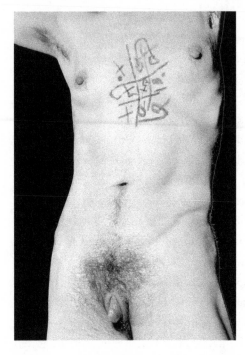

FIG. 5. Del LaGrace Volcano. *Herm Torso*. 2009. Black and white photographic print. Courtesy of Del LaGrace Volcano.

of intersex people in one crucial aspect: herm does not document herm's genitalia." These shots "recall and displace medical photography" by drawing on the visual tropes of medical photography while wresting control of the image away from the heterosexist fraternity of medicine.[25]

Despite the embrace of intersex and trans bodies in contemporary queer visual culture, the affirmation of queer somas isn't quite happening in the spaces of intersex activism. Given the traumatic rounds of medical photodocumentation many intersex bodies have forcefully undergone, contemporary activist depictions of intersex folks counter this ongoing legacy of forced medical photodocumentation by creating an alternative paradigm of intersex figuration governed by an almost exclusively domestic studium. The aim is to normalize intersex folks, documenting them as just like other folks, with families, partners, and overwhelmingly normal lives—with "normal" visually connoted by the pairing of intersex and nonintersex folks linked either by blood or adoption, fully clothed and smiling, in an unremarkable family snapshot. A representative instance is the cover of the *Handbook for Parents*, published in 2006 by the Intersex Society of North America as a practical guide for the families of intersex children or in more recent and problematic parlance, children with disorders or differences of sex development. This trend toward a tamed representative practice is understandable as a subjectively caring response to those people traumatized by years of more or less forced medical exposure. However, it entails a politics of subjective assimilation radically counterposed to the artistic practices discussed above, practices that take on—rather than attempt to disengage from—histories of problematic and often violent representation by *actively intervening* in visual culture, by creating alternative depictions of intersex bodies that don't shy away from a politics of corporeal reclamation, that are unafraid of visibility. The work of LTTR, Carrie Moyer, Ginger Brooks Takahashi, Amos Mac, and Del LaGrace Volcano embraces a queer politics of corporeal reclamation that refuses to pass as normative, that refuse the idea that the nondimorphic body is something better kept under wraps.

Moving from questions of representation to questions of epistemology and practice, the following two chapters analyze first how the concept of gender was developed, utilized, and justified by practitioners of hegemonic medicoscience in fundamentally biopolitical ways, deployed to discipline corporeally queer bodies in order to tame the threat they pose to dominant logics of social reproduction. I then build on the distinction between biopower and biopolitics (or "biopower from above" and "biopower from below") developed by post-Marxist philosophers Michael Hardt, Antonio Negri, and Maurizio Lazzarato and connect these terms to Deleuze and Guattari's distinction between a fundamentally regulatory form of scientific knowledge-praxis they term "state science" and a potentially resistant knowledge-praxis they coin "minor science." This theoretical scaffolding helps me to theorize gender transition as a complex phenomenon both deeply wedded to biopolitical forms of corporeal governance and radically enabling of forms of embodied becoming that have the power to contest and undo such forms of conservative corporeal control.

on record

It's summer 2006. I'm spread out on the floor of my tiny, sweltering apartment in upstate New York, just north of downtown in the Rust Belt city that's become my new home. I've spent most of the summer reading zines (about bicycle maintenance, polyamory, the imminent collapse of neoliberalism), drinking Genesee Cream Ale (on my brother's recommendation—"the best sixer you can find under four dollars!"), and listening to the new Gossip album, which I think is maybe the best thing I've ever heard. I'm nervous about graduate school, which is about to commence, and also shocked that I—a first-generation student from poor white folks born and raised in the Adirondack foothills—actually made it this far.

My new place is quiet. I've got time to myself before the semester begins. I'm learning how to actually cook, learning to live off of something more nourishing than boxes of semolina pasta and Diet Coke. It seems like a good time to unpack something other than endless boxes of books. I write an email to the office of my former pediatric endocrinologist and primary care physician and request my medical records.

I'm not sure how traumatic receiving them is going to be, and I'm not sure I want to find out. When the large manila envelope arrives in my mailbox, I bring it inside, toss it on the kitchen counter, and wait a few days to open it. When I finally do, I realize the records are arranged chronologically, the most recent records at the top of the stack. Paging back to the earlier stuff, I find a heartbreaking portrait of a kid who had no idea what was happening to their body, who was confused and seeking some logic or rationale for why it hadn't begun menstruating, for why it was growing hair in places that weren't normal for girls.

My endocrinologist noted, "Hilary believes that the reason she did not begin to menstruate is that her step dad died at about age 12. At that time she stopped eating and had some other problems which she thinks prevented her period from coming." When my stepfather died, my family and I were homeless—the house we lived in was still in his ex-wife's name, and she wanted us out. We lived in a motel for a little while, until a friend of my stepfather took us in. I did indeed stop eating and shrunk rapidly, from a size 10 to a size 2 in a matter of months. I was stressed out, couldn't control any of the external factors that pushed my mother, brothers, and I from one tenuous domestic situation to the next. I could control what I put in my body though, and I did. The fact that, four years later, this was still my rationale for amenorrhea meant that that form of self-abnegation wasn't just an unfortunate chapter I'd wrapped up; it had become the explanatory principle for the gender anxiety I was experiencing. I thought that *I* was the cause of my supposed abnormality, that my formerly beleaguered body begat my currently beleaguered body. In other words, I blamed myself for being intersex before I knew what that word meant. I believed it was a kind of curse I'd brought upon myself.

The later reports document the prescription of Premarin after my gonadectomy. While my doctors had told me that the gonadectomy was necessary because said gonads had a high risk of becoming cancerous, it becomes obvious, paging through my records, that they were removed because of the testosterone they produced. I'm not sure how I feel about this. Medical professionals had misled me again.

But I, too, was misleading the doctors. In the report issued before I ceased visiting my medical team altogether, my pediatric endocrinologist wrote:

Hilary is a 17 and 9/12 year old female with probable partial testicular feminization, who was seen in my office for continued follow up. Hilary is status post a gonadectomy in January. She was started on Premarin 0.3mg daily about 2.5 months ago. Hilary does state that since starting the Premarin, her mood seems to have improved significantly. . . . She is doing quite well on her estrogen replacement. I have recommended that we continue her on the Premarin 0.3mg for 2 more months and then increase the dose to 0.625 mg. Subsequently down the road, we will be adding Provera.

I had told her I was doing just fine, feeling better now that I was jacked up on estrogen after the sharp drop in testosterone that followed my gonadectomy. I felt cajoled into presenting myself as an increasingly well-adjusted girl, happy to have been given these opportunities to normalize my body. The reality, however, was that I was completely miserable, sick of seeing doctors, sick of being pathologized, sick of being prescribed hormones that made me feel erratic and sad, that transformed my body in ways that felt misfit, dissonant, undesirable.

Reading the medical report, you wouldn't know such negativity was roiling beneath my forced chipper demeanor. The endocrinologist notes that "the clitoral examination was deferred at this point in time until her next visit." There was no next visit. She had asked if she could examine my genitals the way she and several others had done before. I said no for the first time. It was liberating, the realization that you could actually say no to a medical practitioner. At seventeen, I hadn't fully realized that. My burgeoning feminism aside, I hadn't internalized the idea that I was the expert on my own body, that I decided what I did and did not want to do with it. That I had that autonomy, if I only chose to assume it.

5 State Science

Biopolitics and the Medicalization
of Gender Nonconformance

In my earlier examination of the research of John Money, I suggested that the concept of gender—particularly as developed and deployed within mid-twentieth-century Anglo-American sexology—doesn't always herald increased freedom and autonomy in its movement away from biological essentialism. In this chapter I delve further into this assertion, exploring the disciplinary, regulatory functions of gender that emerge from John Money's work and proliferate throughout the entirety of the medical apparatus designed to treat intersex and trans folks. I draw on Foucault's elaboration of biopolitics, which I understand as tactics of individual disciplinarization in the service of mass forms of social control, tactics that "work at the juncture of the body and the population" to regulate sexuality, reproduction, illness, health, familial organization—indeed, all the major domains of life experience.[1] The early elaboration of gender undertaken by Money is significant with respect to biopolitics, as it opens up new terrains of intervention, regulation, normalization, and disciplinarization that are targeted quite specifically at intersex, trans, and gender-nonconforming persons. The forms of political contestation and resistance undertaken by populations affected by the biopolitics of gender are animated by a deep critique of the forms of coercive treatment uniquely enabled by such intense and intimate corporeal regulation. Therefore, understanding the biopolitics of gender is an important and necessary step in grappling with intersex and trans contestations of the problematic medicalization of gender nonconformance.

In 1955 John Money, along with companion researchers Joan and John Hampson, published several articles in the Bulletin of the Johns Hopkins Hospital detailing his research findings on what he calls "the evidence of human hermaphroditism." The first of these articles, entitled "Hermaphroditism: recommendations concerning assignment of sex, change of sex, and psychological management," concerns itself primarily with rectifying what Money refers to as "the homespun wisdom of medically unsophisticated people" who, when confronted with an intersex infant, proceed to "assign the baby to the sex which it most resembles in external genital appearance." Positioning this practice as a technophobic, anachronistic extension of "the age old practice of inferring, on the basis of a single glance, that the reproductive system in its entirety is either masculine or feminine," Money proposes what he frames as a thoroughly enlightened approach to the treatment of "human hermaphroditism," drawing on "modern surgical and microscopic techniques," Freudian psychoanalysis, a Darwinian-derived theory of human bisexuality, and behaviorism.[2] It was out of this complicated cocktail that gender—that term we use frequently to separate heuristically the biological from the cultural, the "raw" from the "cooked"—emerged, with radical implications for the existential possibilities of those beings located on the crux of this fault line between the newly minted "gender" and old-fashioned biological "sex": intersex and trans folks.

Money was at this point in time working as a professor of pediatrics and medical psychology at Johns Hopkins, on the heels of a recently granted PhD from Harvard where he wrote his dissertation on much the same topic covered in these early articles: the revision of protocol for understanding and treating "human hermaphroditism." While it would still be a decade before Money was instrumental in founding the Johns Hopkins Gender Identity Disorder Clinic, these early articles presage—indeed, form the epistemological underpinnings of—the work that would take place in the space of that clinic. His research is based on the interrogation and medical investigation of "seventy-five hermaphroditic patients manifesting somatic ambisexual [read: androgynous, mixed-sex, hermaphroditic] anomalies." These patients were evaluated according to six "variables of sex," using a possible seventh variable provided the preceding six are inconclusive in determining the univocally sexed constitution of the patient. The six core variables of sex were as follows: assigned sex and sex of rearing, external genital morphology, internal accessory reproductive structures, hormonal sex and secondary sexual characteristics, gonadal sex, and chromosomal sex.[3] Looking at these core variables allows us to map Money's engagements with the history of intersex diagnostic protocol, as he takes a multi-causal approach that incorporates nearly all prior frameworks for the determination of sex. These frameworks have been most commonly considered in terms of supersession, with each new discovery of sex determination threatening to unseat earlier framework: the privileging of external genital morphology being taken over by the discovery of the function of the gonads in sex determination; the priority of the gonads being unseated by the discovery of the work of hormones in sex constitution; and the privileging of the hormonal determination of sex being overtaken by a prioritization of so-called sex chromosomes.

The novelty of Money's approach lay in his uniquely syncretic understanding of sex determination, wherein he refused to engage hoary old debates about singular determinants of "true sex," whether they be genitals, hormones, gonads, or chromosomes. Rather, he included all of these as significant factors of sex constitution but granted trump power to a seventh and final variable that would be introduced only in situations wherein there was some degree of ambivalence after examining the six "core variables." The seventh variable, then? "Gender role and orientation, established while growing up."[4] Money and his co-researchers clarify what they mean by this new term, offering one of the first systematic accounts of those factors that determine gender in a manner capable of contraindicating the prior six core variables. It's worth revisiting their initial articulation of the concept of "gender role," which I quoted in chapter 2, given that the criteria listed will become the crux of what is surveilled and adjudicated upon in sexological practice concerned with intersex and trans individuals:

> By the term, gender role, we mean all those things that a person says or does to disclose himself or herself as having the status of boy or man, girl or woman, respectively. It includes, but is not restricted to sexuality in the sense of the eroticism. Gender role is appraised in relation to the following: general mannerisms, deportment and demeanor, play preferences and recreational interests; spontaneous topics of talk in

unprompted conversation and casual comment; content of dreams, daydreams and fantasies; replies to oblique inquiries and projective tests; evidence of erotic practices and, finally, the person's own replies to direct inquiry.[5]

All of these diverse phenomena—indeed, every thought and utterance of those subjects under medical investigation on account of their sexed nonnormativity—come to be read as evidence of gender identity. What this means is that the manifold meanings possible when it comes to comportment, gesture, desire, fantasy, and casual conversation become intensely overdetermined by their relation to stereotypical forms of maleness and femaleness. Every aspect of one's being becomes medical evidence in the determination of gender. This evidence is then put to work in the service of gender normalization, as a means of taming threats to the sexed and sexual order of the broader population. As Jemima Repo argues, Money's elaboration of gender works by "strategically interfering in the contingent cognitive processes of the behavioral control system of the mind, and by cutting up and reordering ambiguous genitals into normative and normalizing stimuli. By providing new explanations for the misalignment of psychological sex and physiological sex, gender provided physicians with a framework with which to diagnose potential cognitive and structural sexual threats to the management of the life of the species."[6] In this initial articulation of gender role, the conflation of sexuality and gender is also pronounced—sexual identity, verbalized accounts of sexual practices, and erotic fantasies are all taken into account in the process of parsing gender, attesting to a profound entwinement of heteronormativity and early theorizations of gender identity. While the use of sexual desire to parse gender identity has come under significant criticism in the past two decades— queer and trans activists and academics have vehemently insisted on the separation of sexuality and gender identity, directly refuting the assumption that sexual desire for the opposite gender is integral to the assumption of gender role—it was (and remains, to some degree) integral to medical perceptions of gender. Appearing alongside considerations of mode of dress, gesture, and play preference, the complex of factors that constitute sexual inclination is woven tightly into the fabric of this foundational iteration of the concept of gender and is in fact integral to it.

On account of this centrality of sexuality to gender role, we witness across Money's body of work (published case studies, patient interviews, the books in which he systematizes his system of gender diagnosis) an intense focus on discerning the truth of a patient's sexuality, and a positing of that sexuality as absolutely integral to discovering the gendered inclinations of a given patient. Insofar as his research attests to the production of the truth of gendered subjectivity through the proliferation of scientific discourse on sexuality, Money's work is one of the most important and influential instantiations of what Foucault has called scientia sexualis. Foucault understood scientia sexualis as a "science made up of evasions" insofar as it refused to speak "of sex itself"—the manifold pain- and pleasure-inducing practices that constitute sexual action, something more akin to an *ars erotica*—and, by way of skirting "sex itself," focused primarily on "aberrations, perversions, exceptional oddities, pathological abatements, and morbid aggravations." This focus on the aberrant, the perverse, and the pathological is often operative in sexological practice, particularly in the mid-twentieth century. Practitioners placed at the center of analysis those beings and behaviors thought of as estranged from sexual and gendered normativity and, too frequently, prescribed reparative action (surgical, hormonal, therapeutic) to bring patients back within the heteronormative fold. For Foucault this process speaks to the ways in which scientia sexualis is governed by "the imperatives of a morality whose divisions it reiterated under the guise of the medical norm."[7]

In other words, the proliferation of taxonomies of gendered and sexual deviance—the parsing of deviance into myriad and distinct pathologies—that we witness in nineteenth- and twentieth-century sexological archives operates in the service of a specific morality lacquered with the veneer of objectivity (read: moral disinterestedness) afforded by an embrace of scientific protocol. It is my project in this chapter to discern the constitution and aims of this medicoscientific morality and to examine the ways in which it was and is linked, intimately, to state regulation of gender identity, sexual identity, and sexual practices.

The concept of gender is fundamentally, constitutively biopolitical—it is invented to monitor, regulate, and control deviant segments of the population. This is, perhaps, a bizarre way to consider the concept of gender, given its long history of embrace by much feminist and queer theory-praxis as a liberatory concept insofar as it moves us beyond the constant essentializing of bodies, the constant subordination of male-female distinctions to the biological. I don't wholly disagree with this understanding of gender as a concept, but I do think that in our collective embrace of it we've lost sight of the immense disciplinary power it has in the lives of gender-nonconforming folks. The invention of gender did not herald, for all of us, an era in which we would no longer be yoked to the political, economic, and emotional expectations placed upon us on account of our sexed corporealities, though it did help denaturalize the meanings ascribed to those corporealities. Rather, it worked unevenly, subjecting those beings who, to hearken back to Money, exhibited some discontinuity in the "core variables of sex" to intense medical and juridical regulation *at the same time* as it enabled a larger range of existential choices for other gender-nonconforming folks. For instance, while the invention of gender enabled certain folks newly understood as transsexuals access to technologies of transition, it severely curtailed *who* had access to these technologies and thus reinscribed the logic of heteronormativity and corporeal dimorphism as standard in the lives and collectivities of trans and gender-nonconforming folks.

To think the concept of gender as constitutively biopolitical is to think about its productivities, which are both disciplinary and liberatory, constraining and freeing. It is to think about the concept of gender according to a both/and logic that examines the selective enfolding of certain intersex and trans subjects within the terrain of the normative while also remaining mindful of the violence and trauma engendered by this consistently expanding medicoscientific regulation of gender nonconformance.

Biopower from Above, Biopower from Below:
Theorizing Intimate Regulation and Creative Resistance
In order to consider the multi-potential work of gender as a biopolitical phenomenon, we should perhaps take a detour through two influential

theorizations of biopolitics. The first, routed through the work of Michel Foucault, focuses on biopolitics as a phenomena of individual discipli-narization in the service of mass social control. The second theorization, routed through the work of thinkers who merge an Italian autonomist line of thought with this Foucauldian conceptual figuration, is concerned with the conditions for collective resistance in a milieu shaped by intense biopolitical regulation. While what these related theorizations of the biopolitical have to do with the practices of mid-twentieth-century sexology in the United States may be opaque at first, they are nevertheless integral to cognizing the imbrication of gender pathology with state control, as well as contem-porary instantiations of resistance to these regulatory processes. My hope is that this detour proves useful both theoretically, in terms of providing a framework for understanding the rather Janus-faced history of trans and intersex medical treatment, and praxically, in providing a methodology with which to think contemporary projects concerned with the reforma-tion and transformation of technologies of gender and the apparatuses in which they are embedded.

To begin, what is the Foucauldian figuration of biopolitics? One of the more systematic accounts of this concept is provided in the closing pages of *Society Must Be Defended*, the English translation of his lectures at the Collège de France in the academic year 1975–76. He makes an initial dis-tinction between biopolitics and disciplinary power, the form of power that targets individual bodies in order to regularize their operations, routinize their habits, and maximize their economically productive force. This disci-plinarization of bodies was enacted through a series of *dispositifs* (appara-tuses) that utilized "a whole system of surveillance, hierarchies, inspections, bookkeeping, and reports"; these *dispositifs* were utilized within, indeed formed the very fabric of, the sorts of disciplinary institutions Foucault spent much of his academic career investigating—prisons, schools, clin-ics.[8] Much of his conceptual corpus is based upon careful investigation of the material traces of these systems of surveillance, hierarchization, and inspection—legal documents, case reports, and the like.

Foucault locates the emergence of disciplinary power at the close of the seventeenth century, marking it as coterminous with the emergence of what we tend to gloss, however problematically, as "modernity." He submits that it develops its ganglia throughout the eighteenth century and dovetails in the midst of this century with another emergent technology of power that begins to embed "itself in existing disciplinary techniques." This new technology of power, unlike disciplinary power, is "applied not to man-as-body but to the living man, to man-as-living-being; ultimately . . . to man-as-species." In other words, while disciplinary power is individuating, focused on the regulation of specific bodies, this emergent technology of power is massifying, concerned with populations, the regulation of exponentially increasing human agglomerations, and ultimately with the monitoring, tailoring, and control of the human-as-species. Foucault, in a telling figuration, posits disciplinary power as an "anatamo-politics of the human body" that begins to be gradually combined with this new technology of power that Foucault tentatively submits he "would like to call a 'biopolitics' of the human race."[9]

Biopolitics begins, thus, with investigations into life and death considerations as they traverse and shape human masses, including birth and death rates, fertility issues, the transmission and spread of endemic diseases, public hygiene reforms, and the like. As part and parcel of these considerations, biopolitics concerns itself with "accidents, infirmities, and various anomalies"—those phenomena that take individuals "out of the field of capacity, activity" as in the case of old age or debilitating illness. It also concerns itself with elements in a given population that pose a threat to the continued enhancement of productive capacities within that population. This is where the initial articulations of discourses on genetic inheritance and degeneracy can be situated, as well as the earliest iterations of modern racism, which operated according to a fundamentally eugenic logic that had nothing at all to do with "victory [over] political adversaries" but instead was concerned with "the elimination of the biological threat to and the improvement of the species or race."[10] Colonial and neocolonial fears of métissage and miscegenation, the constitution of scientific discourses on polygenesis that racialize species, the mass extermination of racialized constituencies in colonial milieus, and the death-camp all figure as instantiations of biopolitical racism.

Scientia sexualis and, by extension, sexology as a definitive instantiation of scientia sexualis occupy a special place in Foucault's theorization of biopolitics. The science of sex works as a sort of hinge between individual disciplinarization and populous or species-oriented biopolitics, the center point of a Möbius strip that circulates between individuating and massifying effects. Foucault writes of sexuality that "it is . . . the privileged position it occupies between organism and population, between the body and general phenomena, that explains the extreme emphasis placed upon sexuality in the nineteenth century." It is this privileged position as the hinge between organism and population (and thus between disciplinary power and bio-power) that renders sexuality ripe for medicalization. Foucault writes that medicine constitutes a "power knowledge that can be applied to both the body and the population, both the organism and biopolitical processes, and it will therefore have both disciplinary and regulatory effects."[11] The medical *dispositif*, then, in its dual disciplinary and regulatory capacities, is perfectly suited to become the primary vehicle for discursive and mate-rial control of that unique set of phenomena that links up organism and population: sexuality.

Following Foucault, the task becomes how to articulate the biopolitics of sexuality, the becoming-biopolitical of sex. Moreover, this exploration must remain attentive to the individuating, disciplinary processes implicated in the becoming-biopolitical of sex. We must think about the population-level effects of particular knowledge-productions; we must place individual case studies in their contingent milieus and think about the shifting terrain of conceptual and material regulation at work in each instance. For instance, the nineteenth-century consolidation of medical knowledge production and authority indexed by the term *scientia sexualis* had two foundational concerns that shuttled vertiginously between individual and population, between what Foucault cites as "two levels," the level of the body and the level of population:

> At the level of the body, of the undisciplined body that is immediately sanctioned by all the individual diseases that the sexual debauchee brings down upon himself. A child who masturbates too much will

be a lifelong invalid: disciplinary sanction at the level of the body. But at the same time, debauched, perverted sexuality has effects at the level of the population, as anyone who has been sexually debauched is assumed to have a heredity. Their descendants also will be affected for generations.... This is the theory of degeneracy: given that it is the source of individual diseases and that it is the nucleus of degeneracy, sexuality represents the precise point where the disciplinary and the regulatory, the body and the population, are articulated.[12]

Here the theory of degeneracy operates as the sanction that legitimates the disciplinarization of the body of the sexual debauchee. Through linking individual pathology to species-life, the regulation of perversity and deviance is executed in the name of maintaining and improving the life chances of the social more broadly. In other words, disciplinarization always happens in the name of social maintenance and reform. While the particular explanations that sanction specific processes of disciplinarization may mutate and shift, this conservative and protectionist structural logic remains in force. Thus, when thinking about individual instances of disciplinary power, it is necessary to seek out the particularities of this structural logic. For instance, while theories of degeneracy certainly no longer sanction the *medical* rehabilitation of various forms of perversion, there remains in force a discourse on the rightness of the social censure of perversion on account of its capacity to torque, infect, and corrupt normative moral codes. Perverts are still disciplined, then, in the name of the family, in the name of the father, in the name of the child. Foucault was deeply attentive to these structural logics that sanction discipline for the sake of the population—they form what we've become accustomed to calling *power/knowledge regimes*. These regimes intersect and co-articulate and in doing so become a dense weave that constitutes the fabric of biopolitical regulation capable of constructing and controlling not just citizen-subjects but life itself.

What Foucault names with the term *biopolitics* is more than merely population regulation; it is the targeting of bodies—both individual and collective—to transform them according to the imperatives of the state and thus bring them into line with the imperatives of capital. It is easiest to see this absolute merger of statist imperatives with biopolitics if we look to Nazi Germany, which is precisely what Foucault does in parsing this concept. In Nazi Germany, he writes, we witness the ascendancy of a racism that is unexplainable in strictly economistic terms (and thus unthinkable with any of the analytical apparatuses provided by traditional Left political formulations-communism, socialism, etc.). This racism grants the power to take life not to a single, isolatable sovereign power but to a "whole series of individuals (such as the SA, the SS, and so on)"; racism, in other words, is another name for the process whereby "murderous power and sovereign power are unleashed throughout the entire social body."[13] With this unleashing, countless individuals are charged with the task of understanding themselves as state agents defined by and through their capacity to regulate, coerce, and control—up to the point of death—beings who were essentially neighbors, folks in quite close proximity, in the name of maintaining the moral and economic health of the nation. This transformation of normative citizens into a racist police force is a process of total subsumption—the very logic of social constitution and belonging is wedded to the immediate objectives of the Nazi regime, and the search for signs of nonbelonging, threat, or corruption extends to all arenas of social life, all interpersonal relations.

It is in this way that biopolitics, and its intimate linkage with racist and otherwise taxonomizing modes of perception, operates through the proliferation of what Foucault termed in his preface to Deleuze and Guattari's *Anti-Oedipus* "microfascisms," the fascisms "in us all, in our heads and our everyday behavior, the fascism that causes us to love power, to desire the very thing that dominates and exploits us."[14] Microfascisms are intimate implantations, mutations on the level of the lived body that corral desire in ways compatible with hegemonic interests. Another way of considering this phenomenon is to think of biopolitics as a way of marking the intimate regulation of bodies, desires, and affects in ways compatible with the shifting demands of neoliberalism. It allows us to think more concisely about deep complicities between capitalism and familial organization, the regulation of sexuality and gender norms, and the formation and reformation of institutions of all kinds—hospitals, mental institutions, schools, universities, prisons—in the context of mass-mediated culture.

Hardt and Negri, throughout the three-volume opus often referred to as the Empire trilogy (composed of *Empire, Multitude,* and *Commonwealth*), have remained committed to considering the implications of this notion of biopolitics in the theorization of political resistance to neo-imperial capital. While a substantive detour through this work is beyond the scope of this particular project, I do think that an address of the distinction worked out between what Hardt has termed a "biopower from above" and a "biopower from below" is worth grappling with.[15] This distinction has also been termed one between biopower (understood as synonymous with this biopower from above) and biopolitics (a sort of shorthand for political resistance that takes on, in a mode simultaneously intimate and immanent, resistance to a situation of total subsumption). Maurizio Lazzarato, a fellow traveler of Negri's in Italian Autonomist circles, has set about the task of theorizing this distinction through dialogue with the later work of Foucault in a brief article entitled "From Biopower to Biopolitics." He grounds this distinction in Foucault's theorization of power as productive, as involving sets of strategic relations rather than operating in a strictly top-down, dictatorial manner. Lazzarato cites and provides commentary on Foucault's 1982 interview that appeared in 1984 in the gay-oriented magazine *The Advocate* under the title "Sex, Power, and the Politics of Identity":

> "A power relationship, on the other hand, can only be articulated on the basis of two elements that are indispensable if it is really to be a power relation; that the 'other' (the one over whom power is exercised) must be recognized and maintained to the very end as a subject who acts; and that, faced with a relationship of power, a whole field of responses, reactions, effects and possible inventions may open up." The only way that subjects can be said to be free, in keeping with the stipulations of this model, is if they "always have the possibility to change the situation, if this possibility always exists." This modality of the exercise of power allows Foucault to respond to the critiques addressed to him ever since he initiated his work on

power: "So what I've said does not mean that we are always trapped, but that we are always free—well, anyway, that there is always the possibility of changing."[16]

While Hardt and Negri have asserted repeatedly that Foucault has been only concerned with biopower from above, Lazzarato here submits that Foucault was, particularly at the end of his career, concerned with thinking not only the institutional and structural operations that established systems of intimate regulation and control—that is, microfascisms—but also with the conditions of creative resistance in this context. If Foucault seemed heavily focused on the theorization of biopower from above, this work was engaged in order to more adequately consider the shifting terrain of political resistance in the context of strategic relations of power. If biopower from above is productive, so must be biopower from below; effective biopolitical resistance can never be merely negative, merely an act of naysaying, but must also be comprised of creative elements. It must make other modes of being possible. Lazzarato proposes that these methods and practices of creative resistance deployed to develop these "possibilities of changing" should be termed biopolitics—they compose a politics concerned with resisting the operations of biopower. The development of a creatively resistant biopolitics is the constant concern of Hardt and Negri as well; their entire theorization of the resistant potential of the multitude hinges on thinking the transnational development of conditions for massive acts of creative resistance that redeploy the forces of affective and immaterial labor in liberatory ways.

Hardt has written that "biopower is the power of the creation of life; it is the production of collective subjectivities, sociality, and society itself."[17] Biopower, conceptualized both from above as well as from below, operates on the level of the ontological, on the level of being itself. It is the ontological effects of biopower that I aim to keep at the forefront of my theorization of the biopolitics of gender, both while considering, in this chapter, the biopower from above at work in the medicalization of gender nonconformance and, in the next, a praxis of queer being in creative resistance developed in efforts to undo the stranglehold of institutional logics.

What is State Science?:
Biopower and the Biomediated Body

As an aid in thinking the biopolitics of gender, particularly as it plays out in and upon the bodies of trans and intersex folks, I'd like to introduce two helpful companionate concepts culled from the work of Deleuze and Guattari: state science and minor (or "nomad") science.

Minor science is a concept counterposed to state science that appears in the twelfth plateau ("1227: Treatise on Nomadology—The War Machine") of Gilles Deleuze and Félix Guattari's *A Thousand Plateaus*. These terms offer two distinct, incommensurable ways of thinking about bodily matter and embodied form. Minor science emphasizes the malleable, fluid, and metamorphic nature of being, while state science conceptualizes being as solid, essential, and unchanging. Given the anti-essentialist focus of minor science, it is a particularly helpful concept in thinking transgender, transsexual, and gender-nonconforming modes of embodiment, particularly those that exceed or actively contest medical understandings of trans identity. Conversely, state science is a useful heuristic for considering the medical and psychiatric pathologization of trans, intersex, and gender-nonconforming subjects.

Minor (or "nomad") science is in dense dialogue with Deleuze and Guattari's theorization of nomadology. Nomadology is the study of wandering subjectivities, of beings that drift from predetermined or normative paths, particular those paths determined and regulated by apparatuses of the state. For Deleuze and Guattari, nomadism is a form of life that is shaped by continual embarkation on lines of flight—that is, modes of escape, moments of transformation, ways of becoming nonnormative, and ways of acting in excess of, or insubordinately in relationship to, repressive forces. Lines of flight have the capacity to *deterritorialize*, to undo, to free up, to break out of a system or situation of control, fixity, or repression.

Minor science, by extension, concerns itself with experiments and inventions that are fundamentally *deterritorializing*, while state science is, by counterpoint, fundamentally *reterritorializing*. To territorialize an entity is to set and define its limits, to organize component parts into a coherent whole determined by a specific end. Deleuze and Guattari write that "state science continually imposes its form of sovereignty on the inventions of nomad science."[18] In other words, state science imposes a particular logic of organization on beings that wander, curtailing and taming the creative inventiveness of these beings.

Deleuze and Guattari outline the salient aspects of this imposition: state science privileges the fixed over the metamorphic; it seeks to establish transhistorical, universally true theories rather than exploring specific, singular instances. In doing so, it fetishizes the eternal, the stable, and the constant and thus develops fixed, immutable, and essential understandings of being. State science is incapable of conceptualizing beings as they are caught up in fluid processes of becoming.

Fluids are known for their malleability, their capacity for transformation, their capacity to adjust and recalibrate at the molecular level; when one investigates fluid phenomena, one asks after what a fluid is doing in a given situation, interaction, or milieu. That is, one focuses on *the hows and whys of transformation*. When investigating solids, on the other hand, very different properties are assumed, and these assumed properties generate very different sets of questions. Solids are firmly delimited entities. They have stable boundaries rather than blurred or porous ones; they exist as beings-unto-themselves. Thus, a science concerned with solids tends to also be concerned with establishing the characteristics that make delimited entities *what they are*. Unlike dealing with fluids, where the emphasis is on transformation, with solids the emphasis falls on questions of essence that seek to establish attributes that render a solid what it is through contradistinction with what is not.

The tactic of establishing essence through contradistinction is central to the medical pathologization of trans and gender-nonconforming subjects, which utilizes this tactic to produce the gender stereotypes that are utilized in the diagnoses of gender identity disorder (GID) and gender dysphoria. These stereotypes are necessary to the functioning of the state science of diagnosing gender difference; they are utilized to establish dyadic essences of gender that are then codified within diagnostic criteria. Just look at the criteria that constitute gender dysphoria, the diagnosis used to allow trans folks access to surgical and hormonal procedures.

In order to be considered a being with gender identity disorder, one must meet six of the following criteria, as laid out in the most recent version of the *Diagnostic and Statistical Manual of Mental Disorders* (DSM-5):

> 1. a strong desire to be of the other gender or an insistence that he or she is the other gender; 2. in boys, a strong preference for cross-dressing or simulating female attire; in girls, a strong preference for wearing only typical masculine clothing and a strong resistance to the wearing of typical feminine clothing; 3. a strong preference for cross-gender roles in make-believe or fantasy play; 4. a strong preference for the toys, games, or activities typical of the other gender; 5. a strong preference for playmates of the other gender; 6. in boys, a strong rejection of typically masculine toys, games, and activities and a strong avoidance of rough-and-tumble play; in girls, a strong rejection of typically feminine toys, games, and activities; 7. a strong dislike of one's sexual anatomy; 8. a strong desire for the primary and/or secondary sex characteristics that match one's experienced gender.[19]

I'd like to focus on the a priori assumptions at work in these criteria. They rely, first of all, on the phantasm of an "other gender" without ever delimiting what the constitution of these opposing genders consists of. Leaving open this aporia around the notion of "the other gender" allows all sorts of culturally normative, commonsense understandings of masculinity and femininity to shape the determination of gender identity disorder. In the absence of specification, this terminology tacitly abdicates to the most conventional understandings of gendered subjective constitution. In doing so, it renders all gender-nonnormative behavior potential evidence of GID and reifies the most hackneyed cultural stereotypes of masculinity and femininity, rendering these typologies the ground upon which the scaffolding of gender-nonconforming pathology is built. These gender-normative assumptions are buried deep, and destabilizing them rocks the entirety of the foundation upon which medical understandings of GID, trans identity, and the "reparative" treatment of intersex folks sits.

There are multiple consequences to this project of rendering all gender-nonnormative behavior as potential evidence for GID, adequately outlined by Dean Spade in his 2003 essay "Resisting Medicine, Re/Modeling Gender." After citing the numerous gender-normative statements utilized within the DSM-4's definition of GID (which is very, very similar to that outlined in the more recent DSM-5), ranging from positing girls with GID as those sorts of girls who prefer "contact sports [and] rough and tumble play" to framing male-born GID patients as prone to "drawing pictures of beautiful girls and princesses," he goes on to assert several consequences of this diagnostic criteria. First, the definition produces "normative childhood gender … by creating and pathologizing a category of deviants: normal kids are simply those who do the opposite of what kids with GID are doing." In doing so, it instates a regulatory mechanism that proliferates beyond the boundaries of the clinic. Spade writes that "because gender nonconformity is established as a basis for illness, parents now have a 'mill of speech,' speculation, and diagnosis to feed their children's gender through should it cross the line." It produces, in Foucauldian terms, a microfascist mode of gender policing. Finally, the medical model of transsexuality fixed in place through this definition—or, really, any definition—of gender identity disorder profoundly separates "gender from cultural forces."[20]

Spade precisely articulates here the logic through which gender nonconformance is established as a regulatory mechanism and frames the generation of this conception of gender insubordination as precisely the province of the medical establishment. The issue—for Spade, as well as for me—is not reforming the criterion that constitutes current institutional conceptions of gender identity disorder; the aim of criticism is not to construct a kinder, gentler GID. Rather, what Spade exposes is the idea that the very conception of gender identity itself—whether normative or otherwise—is called into being through the phenomenon of medicalization. Gender identity disorder needs a stable, essentialized understanding of what male and female genders are in order to remain intelligible, but it calls into being—indeed, substantiates—these genders in the act of conjuring up the specter of gender nonconformance.

What we end up with is an essentialized, transhistorical, acultural medical understanding of gender. While it of course grants the possibility of corporeal transformation on the level of matter, it remains committed on the level of form to binary understandings of gender. The matter of the body, in this hylomorphic formation, remains subordinate the master code of legible, essentialized binary forms. Gender identity disorder is the mechanism through which unruly matter—matter in excess of this master code—can be brought back into line with the binary hylomorphism of gendered being.

If the binary hylomorphism at work in the medical regulation of gender relies on a privileging of solid rather than fluid conceptions of gendered being, it also helps instate the second aspect of state science—a fetishization of the universal, the identical, and the constant. A commitment to search for the constitutive criteria of gendered form—what makes a woman a woman and a man a man—is, as Spade reminds us above, also an effort to universalize and ahistoricize these gendered forms. The establishment of medical criteria for gender nonconformance (and, by extension and unavoidably, of gender normativity as well) seeks to remove gender from the force of culture. To establish diagnostic criteria is to parse out certain aspects of disease or disorder from the contingencies of cultural perception, embroidery, and elaboration. To establish diagnostic criteria for a disorder or disease is to build a corpus of medical facts for use in the training of medical practitioners transculturally, transnationally, and—provided these criteria aren't supplanted by ostensible "advances" in technological, medical, or scientific knowledge—transhistorically. These facts are established through a process of what Brian Massumi has termed "diagnostic de-situation," which is the cornerstone of medicoscientific empiricism. He writes that

> diagnostic de-situation gives the empirical its formidable practical power. Diagnosing a condition is the first step to "correcting" or "improving" it. But empiricism's practical power is also its philosophical weakness. The clinical or experimental context produces a backdrop of generality. It does this simply by building an assumption of comparison into the situation. It produces standardization by assuming its possibility and institutionalizing the assumption. Anomalies that do not conform to the applied standard, or do not follow standardizable deviations from it (identifiable "deficiencies" or "diseases"), are thrown out, discounted as "exceptions." Statistics is the methodological instru-

ment for identifying and discounting exceptions. Statistical method squeezes out the singular in a pincer movement between the general and the discounted. It closes the circle between the assumption of the standard and its practical production. The singular is left out of the loop.[21]

Diagnostic de-situation refuses to dignify the quirks, anomalies, particularities, and contingencies of the singular life. It does so in the service of producing universalizable diagnostic knowledge. All instances that do not submit or cannot be grafted onto the processes of standardization involved in the phenomenon of generating a diagnosis are dismissed as irrelevant, unimportant, or unnecessary to understanding the particular disease or disorder under investigation.

This process of diagnostic de-situation—the amassing of statistical information, the movement of developing a general diagnosis from collated and analyzed statistics, and the institution of a regularized workhorse understanding of what constitutes gender nonconformance, medically speaking—is writ large across the history of scientific sexology concerned with intersex and trans persons. Historian Joanne Meyerowitz documents the vicissitudes of this process of developing diagnostic criteria, specifically for transsexuality in the United States, in her important work *How Sex Changed*. The developmental path charted by the Gender Identity Clinic at Johns Hopkins, parsed in some detail by Meyerowitz, provides an exemplary instance of this process of diagnostic consolidation.

Throughout the 1950s and early 1960s, accessing doctors who were sympathetic to or at minimum who didn't heap moral approbation upon transsexual subjects was a difficult task. There were only a small handful of medical practitioners in the United States interested in providing access to hormonal and surgical treatment during this period—notably, urologist Elmer Belt at UCLA, psychiatrist Karl Bowman at Langley Porter Clinic in San Francisco, and doctor Harry Benjamin, the figure chiefly responsible for the intellectual importation of European sexology to the United States. Following the publicity of the Christine Jorgensen case in the 1950s, folks desiring transition submitted countless appeals to those doctors rumored to be amenable to providing recommendations, performing surgeries, and prescribing hormones. Demand far outstripped supply. Doctors were far more likely, Meyerowitz reports, to perform vaginoplasty if significant self-harm had already occurred—that is, if MTF persons had already attempted a DIY castration. "According to one review of the medical literature, published in 1965" she writes, "18 of 100 MTFs had attempted to remove their own testicles or penises, and 9 had succeeded."[22]

Even if trans folks didn't resort to unsafe measures in order to cut through the extensive formal and informal red tape barricading access to technologies of transition, they still had to demonstrate their commitment to properly normative iterations of femininity or masculinity. They had to exhibit a staid, not-too-sexual brand of conservative gendering, and they must not, under any circumstances, demonstrate a commitment to fringe groups of sexual minorities. Folks had to "convince doctors that they were not just garden-variety homosexuals or transvestites" and "persuade the doctors that they would lead 'normal' and quiet lives after surgery." In order to pass muster, many trans* folks fabricated desires for entirely conventional modes of gendered life—marriage, children, picket fences, vanilla sex on Sunday afternoons. This practice of lying, generated by draconian gatekeeping, was so widespread that "by the end of the 1960s, the medical literature on transsexuals regularly noted that transsexuals shaped their life histories and even fabricated stories that might convince doctors to help them."[23] And even after submitting to this discursive demand for total gender normativity, one had to be able *pay* for the access. This was prohibitively expensive and not covered by medical insurance, mostly qualifying as a series of elective procedures.

The opening of the Johns Hopkins Gender Identity Clinic provided a brief glimmer of hope in this relatively desolate landscape. In 1965 John Money and colleagues, in close collaboration with Harry Benjamin, formed a special committee on gender identity that would eventually become the clinic. In the year before going public with news of the clinic, this committee had "received more than a hundred referrals"; the number of referrals and requests for access to the clinic expanded greatly after the publicization of the clinic's opening (via a favorable front-page *New York Times* article meant to stave off any bad press). Despite this deluge of requests, the clinic planned on evaluating "only two patients a month" and "perform[ing] surgery on even fewer." The clinic, in practice, essentially "turned away almost all the applicants for surgery."[24]

So what was the purpose of this Gender Identity Clinic? It seems to have been invented precisely in order to conveniently execute the process of diagnostic de-situation necessary to produce an etiology of gender nonconformance. Not only trans folks but also intersex people—Money's specialty—were systematically brought in and rigorously interviewed, their case studies and statistical analyses cribbed from these studies, published at a rather frenzied clip throughout the 1960s, 1970s, and 1980s. As Meyerowitz writes, "self-determination for transsexuals was not the first item on the doctor's agenda." Those medicoscientific practitioners researching gender nonconformance seemed to be concerned with expanding markets, establishing themselves as pioneers and exerting authority in the proliferating subspecializations concerned with pathologizing gender nonconformance. This research frenzy, spearheaded by Money and Benjamin, had generated by the early 1970s a diagnostic entity termed *gender dysphoria syndrome*. This would eventually become the GID we're familiar with today and was reportedly developed in order to assist, as one doctor reported, in the "liberalization of previously rigid and truly unrealistic diagnostic criteria."[25] But did it indeed do this?

Not particularly. While it certainly served to establish a legitimized, professionally recognized gatekeeping mechanism, it didn't necessarily liberalize constitutive criteria. The criteria for diagnosis still relies, as we've seen, on profoundly stereotypical understandings of gender difference; that is to say, it is still undergirded by a binary hylomorphism that refuses to admit of gender proliferation or diversity beyond a strictly dyadic model. Moreover, the establishment of professionally agreed-upon and codified diagnostic criteria has not resulted in a democratization of access to technologies of gender reconstruction. The liberalization of diagnostic criteria is not co-identical to the liberalization of access. Just because one can now be relatively easily recognized—provided one tailors their story smartly to match the logic of diagnosis—as a prime candidate for gender reassignment, that does not mean one can actually *afford* access to these technologies of reassignment.

What the establishment of firm diagnostic criteria for gender identity disorder does do, however, is codify how the medical industry deals with gender-nonconforming patients who seek access to hormonal and surgical modification technologies. This, to hearken back to Deleuze and Guattari's schematic, is an integral component of state science, which utilizes what they call theorematic approaches to diagnosis that rely on essences and finely grained taxonomies of species-type and forms of deviance. They juxtapose the theorematic approach to what they term "problematic" approaches. A problematic model of scientific process, they write, considers figures

> only from the viewpoint of the *affections* that befall them: sections, ablations, adjunctions, projections. One does not go by specific differences from a genus to its species, or by deduction from a stable essence to the properties deriving from it, but rather from a problem to the accidents that condition and resolve it. This involves all kinds of deformations, transmutations, passages to the limit, operations in which each figure designates an 'event' much more than an essence . . . whereas the theorem belongs to the rational order, the problem is affective and is inseparable from the metamorphoses, generations, and creations within science itself.[26]

A theorematic approach to understanding gender nonconformance proceeds from (groundless) essences—a conjuring of the notion of "opposite sexes" that, while given substance through diagnosis, is not based in anything more than conventional, normative typologies of masculinity and femininity that are substantialized through contraposition. The theorematic approach then establishes pathologized subspecies from those who trespass these invented essences. Trans and intersex folks are among these, but there are many, many others dotting the historical landscape of sexology: gynomimetics, andromimetics, transvestites, Uranians, the list goes on. The theorematic approach works through establishing criteria that serve to differentiate categorically these subspecies from one another by establishing a laundry list of properties common to each disorder, deviation, or perversion. Gender identity disorder is, on this reading, only the most recent instantiation of a long-lasting medical effort to rationalize queer and gender-nonconforming modes of being in the world, to bring them into line with conservative understandings of what it is to be a legibly sexed subject. With a theorematic approach, gender-nonconforming subjects are asked to restructure their subjective understandings in order to slot themselves into concordance with the prevailing theory of gender dysphoria and access technologies of corporeal modification. In other words, they are coerced into fabricating a gendered essence that accords with diagnostic criteria. A theorematic approach forces phenomena into alignment with its sovereign demands. It proceeds in a top-down, dictatorial manner, and it does so even while it pretends—through the amassing of statistical phenomena through patient interviews, for instance—to be proceeding from the experiential understandings of the patient, the specimen under analysis, as it were.

An understanding of state science shaped by the interarticulated aspects discussed—the privileging of the solid over the fluid, the fetishization of the eternal, the identical, and the constant, and the emphasis on theorematic, rather than problematic, approaches to diagnosis and treatment—is absolutely integral to thinking the contemporary biopolitics of gender nonconformance and, more generally, is necessary to the consideration of gender as a biopolitical conceptual apparatus. It allows us to parse more carefully the ways in which gender as a concept is far from being a merely liberatory category that distances subjects from the stranglehold of biological essentialist understandings of sexed being. Rather, deploying the analytic framework of state science, we can more ably examine the powerful scientific productions of solid, closed typologies, gendered essences, and universalizable and transhistorical conceptions of gender deviance. In so doing, we are on much better footing to understand the ways in which medical science has been granted authority over the bodies of trans, intersex, and gender-nonconforming subjects, the ways in which varying sorts of doctors (urologists, endocrinologists, sexologists) have been positioned—or rather, have positioned themselves—as possessing the hermeneutic key to queer modes of being in the world, as truly grasping the genesis of various subversions, resistances, and refusals to conform to heterosexist, homonormative, essentializing understandings of sexed subjectivity. Understanding these processes is integral to reworking, resisting, and refusing to be interpellated by them.

Although the medicalization of gender nonconformance has developed guidelines and protocol for transition and would thus seem to be linked to a more fluid conception of gender, these practical protocols are nevertheless built upon conservative typologies of maleness and femaleness. They are not concerned with transition as a (potentially always unfinished) process, but rather with the creation and suturing of firmly delimited, discrete, and binarily gendered entities. A minor science of transition, however, would focus on the specific, resistant, and creative ways in which trans* and gender-nonconforming subjects reinvent and reconstruct themselves in manners irreducible to the medical logic of transition. It is important to bear in mind that Deleuze and Guattari insist on framing this alternative understanding of materiality as a *science*. This is because they propose a formal conceptual system consisting of a set of theorems that help elicit a different understanding of embodiment. They propose a series of rules of thumb (rather than *laws*, eschewing the juridical language of conventional scientific practice) that enable one to *encounter* the physical world anew and to *counter* the hidebound cognition of materiality enforced by state science.

We can track a resonant preoccupation with thinking embodiment beyond static, dimorphic understandings of gender in a number of foundational texts in trans studies. Susan Stryker asserted early in her career that trans bodies should be understood as in excess of what is commonly understood as natural, and that they therefore destabilize "the foundational presupposition of fixed genders upon which a politics of personal identity depends." Sandy Stone, similarly, takes issue with the narrative of transsexuality offered by clinicians and calls for a counternarrative of embodiment, writing that "for a transsexual, as a transsexual, to generate a true, effective and representational counterdiscourse is to speak from outside the boundaries of gender, beyond the constructed oppositional nodes which have been predefined as the only positions from which discourse is possible." This shared conception of trans embodiment as in excess of conventional understandings of materiality has its afterlives in contemporary criticisms of the regulatory mechanisms of trans diagnosis and medical treatment. Dean Spade has written extensively on this topic, as has Lucas Cassidy Crawford, who utilizes the conceptual vocabulary of Deleuze and Guattari to think about trans embodiment as a kind of "affective deterritorialization" rather than a way of "coming home" to one of two ideal gender types.[27] These interpretations understand trans embodiment—and really all forms of gendered embodiment—through the concept of becoming. A minor science of transition would understand gendered embodiment as always about becoming—cycles of affective deterritorialization and reterritorialization—rather than realizing a predetermined essence. I elaborate the implications of rethinking gender as becoming in the following, concluding chapter, examining the Deleuzo-Guattarian account of becoming offered in *A Thousand Plateaus* in relation to feminist and transfeminist theorizations of the relational, nonsovereign, and built nature of gendered embodiment, focusing particularly on transfeminist deployments of monstrosity as a metaphor through which to understand trans and gender-nonconforming embodiments and our attendant experiences of alienation, ostracism, and isolation. If we can imagine and produce spaces that affirm our collective monstrosity—the fundamentally interwoven, co-constitutive *madeness* of our sexed and gendered selves—what forms of coalition, intimacy, friendship, and freedom might become possible?

mirrors

I can't remember where I was the first time I heard the Velvet Underground's "I'll Be Your Mirror," but I remember what I felt. The combination of the song's sugary arpeggios, like something straight out of the Monkees' discography, and Nico's husky account of bearing loving witness was intensely dissonant. She was singing about trauma, depression, and unutterable sadness, about desperately trying to bring someone she loves back from the brink of self-destruction, and she was doing it to a tune that made you feel like you were strolling arm-in-arm down a sunshiny country lane on an early spring morning with your best friend and a beloved puppy while chipmunks danced with bunnies in the bucolic fields around you. It became a song I listened to when I needed to be transported away from modes of self-perception that were insidious, harmful, and hard to shake, moments where I found myself deeply unbeautiful, deformed, grotesque. There were days I would drive to work or school, park, look at myself in the rearview mirror, and be so horrified by what I saw that I'd turn around and head home to stay in bed all day, avoiding everyone in order to avoid being seen.

Those days, mirrors were cruel. Nico reminded me that there were other mirrors, though—the folks you loved, the folks who saw you in all of your complexity, who spent time learning you and who you spent time learning: these were all more faithful mirrors. All of the queer and trans friends that populated my every day, who understood why I hated being gendered in binary ways, who understood why I had such difficulty going to see medical professionals, who knew why it was I preferred, most days, to stay at home and shoot the shit with a carefully curated group of friends rather than go out—even if the plan was to party at queer spaces (which were, at least in my neck of the woods, almost always cis-centric). Our trauma resonated, one to the other, but so did our resilience, our humor, and our grace. Nico reminded me to perceive myself through these mirrors, the mirrors built out of loving perception.

My mentor and friend María Lugones writes on loving perception in the context of world traveling. She thinks of world traveling not in the colonial sense of exploration and conquest, nor in the form of touristic, middle-class leisurely travel, but as movement between different worlds of meaning. To highlight this distinction, she always uses the word "world" in quotations: "Those of us who are 'world'-travelers have the distinct experience of being in different 'worlds' and of having the capacity to remember other 'worlds' and ourselves in them. We can say 'That is me there, and I am happy in that "world."' So, the experience is of being a person in a different 'worlds' and yet of having memory of oneself as different without quite having the sense of there being any underlying 'I.'" In some of these worlds, minoritized and marginalized folks may be constructed in ways we abhor, disidentify with, or simply do not understand. We may be overcoded by pernicious stereotypes; we may be misgendered; we may be subject to consistent hostilities and microaggressions. In others, we may be at ease, known in ways that allow us to be relaxed, inventive, playful. We are different selves in these different worlds, ontologically plural, but we carry memories of our way of being in certain worlds into those others we travel to or toward. Loving perception develops out of the practice of traveling to other people's worlds—doing so, you begin to understand them in their complexity, their multiplicity, and their fragmentation; as Lugones writes, only then "are we fully subjects to each other."[1]

Moving with each other through these differing worlds, we learn how our mirrors have cracked, how our ability to perceive ourselves has been compromised by the internalization of nonloving perceptions. We learn how to re-cognize and re-envision one another with a deep awareness of our selves in both hostile and loving milieus; in doing so, we repair each other. This is deep coalition, as political as it is intimate. Moving through the world with each other, learning how each other is constructed in different, sometimes disparate worlds, learning about the ambiguities, complexities, and difficulties those multiple constructions generate—this is how we build the bonds that make other worlds possible.

6 Toward Coalition: Becoming, Monstrosity, and Sexed Embodiment

> We know that many beings pass between a man
> and a woman; they come from different worlds,
> are borne on the wind, form rhizomes around roots;
> they cannot be understood in terms of production,
> only in terms of becoming.
>
> —Gilles Deleuze and Félix Guattari, *A Thousand Plateaus*

> Perhaps gender happens between bodies,
> not within them.
>
> —Indra Windh in conversation with Del LaGrace Volcano,
>   "Hermlove"

> In some ways, it is Kate Bornstein who is now carrying
> the legacy of Simone de Beauvoir: If one is not born a
> woman, but rather becomes one, then becoming is the
> vehicle for gender itself.
>
> —Judith Butler, *Undoing Gender*

Gender as Becoming

What does it mean to think of gender as becoming? What are the episte-mological obstacles we encounter as we try to reconceptualize gender in this way? What are the political and interpersonal stakes of this cognitive transformation? Who might it help, and how?

While considering gender as becoming is not a new phenomenon (it dates at least back to Simone de Beauvoir's well-known assertion that "one is not born, but rather becomes, a woman" and has quite a robust afterlife in Butler's corpus), it has an underexplored salience when thought in relation to intersex and trans subjects, for whom processes of becoming intelligibly gendered are often at the forefront of consciousness and daily experience.[1] The quotidian violence encountered by trans, intersex, and gender-nonconforming subjects often hinges on dueling conceptions of gendered realness. I consider these moments as epistemological clashes between an insistence on gender as being and alternative understanding of gender as becoming.

While it might be tempting index this distinction as a conflict between essentialist and social constructivist conceptions of gender, the being and becoming dyad operates a bit differently. What is targeted in many instances of trans and queer phobia is perceived gender nonconformance. This sometimes manifests as perceived contradiction between the biological "truth" of sex and performed gender, but it also often manifests as a perceiver's inability to place a subject stably with respect to both performed gender and biological sex. Accusations of being *"really* a man" or *"really* a woman" are as frequently uttered as hostile interrogations as to what kind of being one is: "are you a *boy* or a *girl*?" The former assertion relies, quite obviously, on a straightforward brand of biological essentialism, while the latter inquiry is underwritten by a conviction that one must mold oneself in the image of one of two morphological idealities and registers anger and aggression at the speaker's inability to read a subject along those lines. The former phobic response asserts an essentialist truth in the name of the subject under attack; the latter, faced with undecidability, positions the speaker as a grand inquisitor. Where both manifestations of hostility dovetail, however, is in their inability to think beyond dimorphism, either as biological truth or teleological manifestation. One must be either born a woman (or a man) and continue to manifest as such; if not, they damn well better become a passable, socially legible version of one or the other. Gender here must number no more than two, and it must be temporally stable, faithfully reiterated. Thus, underpinning each of those phobic locutions is a conception of gender as a stable, relatively static, durable, dimorphic phenomenon that provides the fundamental scaffolding of selfhood: gender as being.

To think gender as becoming is to think embodiment beyond sexual dimorphism, which is a lynchpin of gendered intelligibility regardless of whether one is utilizing an essentialist or a constructivist framework.

Re-cognizing gender as becoming means that the sex/gender distinction need be thought anew. It is quite possible to develop a social constructivist account of gender while leaving a dimorphic conception of biological sex in place, as we've seen in my earlier exploration of the implications of John Money's use of the concept of gender. Because the sex/gender distinction has been foundational for social constructivism, insofar as constructivist accounts focus on gender as a social and relational phenomena conceived as *distinct from* biology, a substantive engagement with the complexities of morphological variation falls by the wayside. As long as we remain wedded to the idea that there are two sexes, even if we grant that those sexes might manifest in multiply gendered forms, we remain committed to an understanding of corporeality that directly denies the existence of intersex subjects, as well as one that can only cognize trans persons as performing a gender *at odds with* birth sex. This renders the disjunction between biological sex and performed gender an origin story that undergirds hegemonic narratives of trans experience and that reads trans autobiographies in terms of traumatic disjunction, as lives shaped by wanting to be one morphological sex while being biologically affixed to the other. The tendency to consider trans experience as shaped primarily by this conflict means that trans lives are considered bifurcated by medicalized transition. Preoperative/postoperative or, more broadly, pretransition/posttransition becomes the narrative framework through which trans experience is understood, and stories of rebirth and radical subjective change trump more complex narratives of gendered embodiment.

Becoming encourages us to understand the body as inseparable from the milieu in which it comes to matter. If matter and milieu are inseparable, then the body can be thought in a framework focused on something other than its discursive legibility or the referents applied to and implied by its significations. If the truth of sex is not provided *by* the body, located *within* the body, but rather something that happens between bodies, in interactions and engagements that rework the materiality of the body itself, then we need to pay serious attention to this interplay, this *between*, particularly with reference to how it mutates our conception of the body as *the* source for the determination of sexed subjectivity.

This framework of bodily understanding is decidedly at odds with hegemonic understandings of sexed embodiment, and as such, must be thought in a register other than that that of institutional subjective legibility, which is characterized by discrete identity forms into which subjects are inserted, placed, and crosscut by. For Deleuze and Guattari, the very notion of two sexes belongs to what they call an arborescent understanding of sociopolitical organization. Arborescence refers to the rigid division of the social into discrete segments (or "rigid segmentarities") modeled on the figure of the tree. The tree: theorized by Deleuze and Guattari as "the knot of arborescence or the principle of dichotomy[,] ... the structure or network gridding the possible," this concept-figure hearkens back to Linnaeus's *Systema Naturae* and to taxonomic modes of thought more generally.[2] With these modes of thought, the tree is not *an* organizational model for representing the field of life, of the natural; it is *the* organizational model, separating and segmenting all manner of matter into discrete, hierarchical classes. It is this arborescent mode of thought, so salient across the natural sciences, that structures modern Western understandings of the intelligibilities of race, gender, the human, and the subhuman, understandings that have subsequently shuttled from their initial realm of articulation into all manner of modern Western institutions, thus engendering the difficulties we now face in terms of the contestations posed by trans, intersex, and queer bodies to dominant narratives of the human that are founded on this arborescent principle, producer of all manner of discrete dichotomies, not the least of which is the commonsense conception of sex as that which numbers two: no more, no less. Arborescence is what engenders both an institutionalized abhorrence of mixity—sexed, racialized, and otherwise— and an absolute incapacity to dignify folks so constituted, folks who've deliberately chosen, embraced, and inhabited bodies that both exceed and evade arborescent understandings of matter and who construct socialities and logics incommensurable with them.

The question is not, as Deleuze and Guattari write, whether the status "of those on the bottom [of intersecting, dichotomous social hierarchies] is better or worse, but the type of organization from which that status results." They ask a question that comes prior to those asked by strains of queer and feminist politics concerned with fair representation, formal equality, and institutional inclusion which refuse to interrogate the organizational roots of racialized, sexed, and sexualized social stratification. Rather, Deleuze and Guattari examine the ways in which the identity categories produced by arborescent logic "induce a molecularization of its own elements, relations, and elementary apparatuses"—that is, how these systems of classification produce master codes for embodiment, which then work to overdetermine the meaning of the elements that comprise embodiment.[3] It is in this way that hegemonic understandings of sex function—one is either a man or a woman, and one is that down to the last fiber of one's being. Contradictory signs, be they corporeal (e.g., the protrusion of an Adam's apple on a female-identified person, an enlarged clitoris on an intersex infant, a mixture of ovarian and testicular tissue in one's gonads) or otherwise significatory (e.g., the former New York City law allowing for the arrest of folks wearing more than two articles of clothing of the "opposite" sex), must be eliminated, and all microscopic corporeal elements come to be read in terms of this arborescent, dichotomous understanding of sex (e.g., the location of the truth of sex in the gonads and later discourses on sex as genetically or hormonally determined). Each cell, each chromosome, comes to be understood as dichotomously sexed. Every last molecule of one's being must, in this understanding, be made to speak univocally of either maleness or femaleness.

We can think of the transformation of matter into one of two sexes as an instance of what Deleuze and Guattari call "incorporeal transformation." Incorporeal transformations are instances of language effecting substantial transformations of social reality—for instance, when a guilty verdict is rendered or when a declaration of marriage is issued, quite similar to J. L. Austin's performatives.[4] While these utterances don't necessarily alter the body at the level of the material, they radically reform the social reality of the individual or individuals impacted.

Thinking of sex assignment as an instance of incorporeal transformation means that, while at the level of the corporeal bodies bleed, secrete hormones, produce gametes, house fetuses, grow hair in certain locations and not in others, it is through an incorporeal transformation that all of these actions come to constitute, and are united by, a dichotomous concept of sex. The dubbing of some bodily attribute or a body considered holistically in unitary terms, as "male" or "female" is an incorporeal transformation. Sex is in this way analogous to what Deleuze and Guattari write of aging: "Bodies have an age, they mature and grow old; but majority, retirement, any given age category, are incorporeal transformations that are immediately attributed to bodies in particular societies."[5]

Minoritarian Becomings

Rather than approaching sex as if it were a question of biological facticity, I'm proposing a theory of sex wherein it is conceptualized as *incorporeal*, as the product of a thoroughly historical and contingent transformation, related to the issuance of order-words, the attribution of the order-words to the body. If an incorporeal transformation is "recognizable by its instantaneousness, its immediacy, by the simultaneity of the statement expressing the transformation and the effect the transformation produces," then one can make much of the oft-vaunted biunivocal declaration of sex at birth—the "it's a boy," "it's a girl" emblazoned across all manner of party paraphernalia, the notarization of the birth certificate with a corresponding M or F, the pink and blue fleece. All of this is a matter of declarative ritual, an institutionally forced articulation that transforms and fixes, at least partially, our perception of the infant's body but does not determine its course of development, mutation, or desire. The medical establishment has not been interested in asking what systems of perceptual and conceptual organization produce sexual dimorphism; rather than asking this question, sexual dimorphism is assumed as matter of fact, as a natural biological reality, and the contrary—anomalous bodies, nonconforming bodies—are desperately reworked in keeping with the issuance of the incorporeal transformation that is the declaration of sex. The body is attributed as male or female, and then a series of interventions are proposed in order to render complex corporeal realities commensurable with the order-words of sexual dimorphism, to fabricate a static ontology of sex, one focused on being rather than becoming.

Regarding becoming, Deleuze and Guattari provide the following account:

A becoming is not a correspondence between relations. But neither is it a resemblance, an imitation, or, at the limit, an identification. . . . To become is not to progress or regress along a series. Above all, becoming does not occur in the imagination. . . . [It is] perfectly real. But which reality is at issue here? For if becoming animal does not consist in playing animal or imitating an animal, it is clear that the human being does not "really" become an animal any more than the animal "really" becomes something else. Becoming produces something other than itself. We fall into a false alternative if we say that you either imitate or you are. What is real is the becoming itself, the block of becoming, not the supposedly fixed terms through which that which becomes passes.⁶

In the conceptual figuration provided here, becoming is thought as that which refuses the referents provided by psychoanalysis: the distinction between the real, the symbolic, and the imaginary, the rift between one's ostensibly inaccessible and enigmatic psychic interiority and an outer external field—the world, one's material situation. For Deleuze and Guattari, dreams are perfectly real, the experience of oneself as other than human or in excess of the human is also perfectly real, and there is no recourse to discourses on mimesis, imitation, the dyad of the copy and the real; nor is there any telos, definitive goal, end, or aim that would secure or anchor, finally, the becomings (or, in existential terms, the projects) one engages, embarks upon. What is real, instead, is "the block of becoming," the process, the passing, the perpetual *between* counterposed to the rigid segmentarities of taxonomic, identitarian thought. Moreover, the terms through which one passes—woman, child, animal, molecule—are only *supposedly* fixed. Becoming undoes these suppositions. The notion of acting *like* a woman, *like* a child, *like* a lion has no purchase with reference to becoming—one does, one acts, affects, is affected by, and in these processes one continually produces "something other than [one]self," something that destabilizes the holisms that fix and determine that self in hegemonic logics that can only deal with minority identities, not processes of becoming minoritarian. In other words, hegemonic logic only recognizes the minority being through reference to the majority, or the normative, which then stabilizes and fixes said being as a minority. Or, alternately, it is only through the lens of the majority that the minority appears. This is why, as Deleuze and Guattari elucidate, it is necessary to "distinguish between the majoritarian as a constant and homogenous system; minorities as subsystems; and the minoritarian as a potential, creative and created, becoming." In other words, it is necessary to mark a break between the majoritarian construction of the minority and the minoritarian, which operates on very different terms and is not exhausted by its mode of construction as marginal and nonnormative but may be instead "thought of as seeds, crystals of becoming whose value is to trigger uncontrollable movements and deterritorializations of the mean or majority."[7]

To extend from this figuration of becoming to my more sustained, particular argument, the becomings engaged in by trans and intersex folks undo, irreparably, the suppositions of man and woman, male and female, but they also do much more than that. The motivations and processes through which these suppositions are undone are differential, complex, and stem from certain trans and queer infrapolitics, styles of resistance that are not readily visible to dominant culture, that appear as strange, illogical, but for all that are nevertheless resistant and productive when understood as projects of becoming minoritarian, as prefiguring a "deterritorialization of the majority," and as creating alternate sensibilities and logics that enable queer subjects to sustain nondominant modes of being, nondominant and resistant erotic and subjective logics. In part, what unites various queer and trans becomings is that each of them, in their own way, manage to affect a disarticulation of the organism, a wrenching of the body away from the stranglehold of dimorphism, away from the two-sex schematic. Through this disarticulation, new modes of joyful, irrevocable estrangement from stable, sexed ontologies of being are produced—though not without encountering difficulty, punishment, and censure.

I want to turn to a bit of Butler's writing on the violent psychiatric translation of trans becoming, with its demand for a sexual truth rooted in a static identity, as evinced in the diagnosis of gender identity disorder:

> The diagnosis . . . wants to establish that gender is a relatively permanent phenomenon. It won't do, for instance, to walk into a clinic and

say that it was only after you read a book by Kate Bornstein that you realized what you wanted to do, but that it wasn't really conscious for you until that time. It can't be that cultural life changed, that words were written and exchanged, that you went to events and to clubs, and saw that certain ways of living were really possible and desirable, and that something about your own possibilities became clear to you in ways that they had not been before.[8]

What won't do here is, exactly, the dignification of those various sources—queer dance parties, pop icons, an infatuation with pirates and damsels, a complex connection with Brando's character in *The Wild One*, a first reading of *My Gender Workbook*—out of which we can and do fashion, mutate, and reconstruct our selves, our desires, our flesh. What is demanded is the relegation of all of this found material to insignificant status, replaced with a narrative that speaks of lifelong yearning for a neat and normative masculinity or femininity, a yearning that is intimately tied to a desire to depathologize oneself.

Seeing Herm: Diffractive Perception and Gender Multiplicity

Deleuze and Guattari wrote, critiquing the arborescent logic of sexual dimorphism, that "the two sexes imply a multiplicity of molecular combinations bringing into play not only the man in the woman and the woman in the man, but the relation of each to the animal, the plant, etc: a thousand tiny sexes," or what they term *n-sexes*. My attempt to think queer becoming can be articulated, in shorthand, as an effort to think the ways in which these "thousand tiny sexes" engendered by trans and queer intimacies and interactions produce multiplicities of gender *between* bodies and can unsettle the "great binary aggregate" of sex while remaining, on the micropolitical level, unfixed, never fully determined by a stable identitarian logic.[9]

To develop this idea further, I'd like to look again at certain texts and images of Del LaGrace Volcano, who self-describes as "a gender variant visual artist who accesses 'technologies of gender' in order to amplify rather than erase the hermaphroditic traces of my body" as well as "a gender abolitionist, a part-time gender terrorist, an intentional mutation and intersex-by-design." Volcano is, in other words, negotiating the "great binary aggregate" of sex constantly, while refusing to be done over, made up in its image. Rather, herm accesses surgical, hormonal, and performative technologies in order to blur these binary scripts, reinventing and mutating constantly, or, in herm's words, "crossing the line as many times as it takes to build a bridge we can all walk across," engaging in queer transmogrifications, transmigrations with no permanent destination and no sense of or desire for a stable, concretized, sedimented sexed self. When herm's enactment of sex verges on conventionally intelligible, Volcano utilizes discourse on passing but with an important shift in emphasis. For Volcano, passing is not dissimulating, pretending to be something one is not—it is a survival strategy without recourse to an essence or truth beneath that which one presents. The passing herm engages in is not the more conventional practice of passing as the privileged term of a binary—it is passing as either male or female, when one knows intimately one is neither/nor, either/both. Herm writes, "In my daily life I pass. Usually as a male. Occasionally as female. Both passings are a compromise. . . . I'm not being seen but sometimes that's okay. I need to protect myself."[10]

Volcano's "not being seen," this attempted public invisibility or blending, is contingent, situational, and enacted, for herm, on account of the sensed necessity for safety in hostile transphobic and queerphobic spaces. Opposed to the account of a halfway normative sexual intelligibility aimed for in these spaces, Volcano writes of a differential enactment of gendered becoming: "in my own queer community I don't want to pass as male or female. I want to be seen for what I am: a chimera, a hybrid, a herm."[11] However, much of herm's work witnesses the irruption of this chimeric, hybrid, hermaphroditic becoming in ostensibly hostile—that is, highly regulated public (rather than counterpublic) spaces, disrupting the already unstable spatial division at work in Volcano's discursive separation of (normative) public and (queer) counterpublic. For instance, Volcano's photographic series *airportformance*, wherein herm and friends arrive at various western European airports such as Sturup and Heathrow in full-on queer peacock regalia, sometimes donning masks (those of monsters, tigers), sometimes dressed in hyperbolic transmasculine drag (as rockabilly boys, priests). The irruption of these chimeric performances in the transient, ephemeral space of the airport (a temporary site, a migratory node) works to underscore the nonproprietary, ephemeral, slippery notion of gender at work in herm's self-fashioning. For Volcano, gender is not only radically inessential, distinctly not a fixed set of attributions that socially stabilize a subject, but precisely these playful, differential articulations. Moreover, it is praxical, processual—a journey with no fixed destination, subject to delays, multiple departures, hiatuses and layovers, never fixed for long in just one site. The queer becomings witnessed in *airportformance* are, and are *only*, instantiations of the hybrid, the impure, and the confounding, risky and refusing to be underwritten by a stable ontology of sexed and sexual truth. A depathologized, nontaxonomic gaze, one that perceives beyond the rigidities of the great binary aggregate of sex and toward queer becomings of the self, reveals this.

This depathologized gaze is necessarily diffractive, in the sense in which Donna Haraway develops the term in "The promises of monsters: A regenerative politics for inappropriate/d others." Diffraction offers a way to see the chimeric, the hybrid, without reduction, without attempting to discern the truth behind appearances, a way that is simultaneously able to cognize the violence of pathologization and transphobia while still identifying the desirous, productive, resistant being forged in and through processes of queer becoming. This is because diffraction resists more traditional optics that see in biunivocal terms and concomitantly in terms of "hierarchical domination, incorporation of parts into wholes[,] . . . symbiotic fusion, antagonistic opposition," and so on. Refusing a dyad of sameness and difference, or normative and nonnormative, diffraction "does not produce "the same" displaced, as reflection and refraction do. Diffraction is a mapping of interference, not of replication, reflection, or reproduction. A diffraction pattern does not map where differences appear, but rather maps where the effects of difference appear." In this way, diffraction does not "invite the illusion of essential, fixed position" but is a more varied, fluid, and subtle optic mechanism that does not seek subjective truth and, moreover, can hold alternate realities and perceptions in a manner other than that of opposition.[12] With a diffracted gaze, Volcano's multifarious, playful becoming may be seen as a micropolitical practice at odds with the macro-intelligibilities of sex, a set of practices that provoke violent censure and threat of physical and psychic abuse, as a critical revision of modern tropes of monstrosity and aberrance, and as *sexy*: a mode of queer becoming at once dangerous, resistant, threatening, taunting, playful, and erotic.

The "we" posited in Volcano's work as the subject of herm's repeated bridge-building injunction has an unlikely yet deliberate and succinct texture that extends well beyond the confines of queer community writ large, or even a particular spatiotemporally fixed communal instantiation, coming to mean both "those of us who [choose] to live outside of [the sexual binary's] confines as well as those who were never given a chance to." Here, Volcano inverts the typical schematic that would establish tropes of normativity and deviance, displacing the centricity of binary sex as the master code for sexual intelligibility and framing "proper" enactments of sex as borne of a curtailed or distinctly lacking absence of *choice* or access to queer logics of the possible. Del writes of the taxon of sex as a prison, as a cage, a space of confinement—and herm's view from outside, from beyond this cage, displaces the entire schematic of sexed legibility, decentering it through a diffracted lens, through an understanding of oneself as diffracted—not represented within or by those confines, not locatable anywhere on the map of sexual intelligibility. It is in this way that Volcano occupies the position of what Haraway, building on Trinh T. Minh-ha's work, terms an "inappropriate/d other": "to be an 'inappropriate/d other' means to be in critical, deconstructive relationality, in a diffracting rather than reflecting (ratio)nality as the means of making potent connection that exceeds domination. To be inappropriate/d is not to fit in the taxon, to be dislocated from the available maps specifying kinds of actors and kinds of narratives, not to be originally fixed by difference. To be inappropriate/d is to be neither modern nor postmodern, but to insist on the amodern."[13] Volcano, as chimera, as hybrid, as "intersex-by-design," occupies this critical, deconstructive stance, engendering modes of relationality, erotic and otherwise, that do not seek as a politically desirable goal to become subjects of representation, as that engenders subjective fixity and curtails queer becoming. This is not to say Volcano is ignorant nor flippant about the available maps of sexed intelligibility. It is to say, however, that herm and cohorts are intent on flipping the script, on developing alternative maps of resistance, on *claiming* their dislocation from the taxon in order to forge further creative modes of dislocation, rather than dwelling or drowning in discourses of wounded subjectivity, of institutional exclusion, of depression, loathing, and self-destruction engendered by a hegemonic abhorrence of mixity, of anomaly. Volcano disrupts the taxon through the unabashed display of sexed mixity, the concomitant disruption of gender bipolarity, through experimentation and invention. The frame of reference for Volcano's diffracted position is not provided by any modern (nor postmodern) taxonomy of sex, of deviance, of perversion. Neither a man nor a woman; neither a bugger, a poof, a sodomite, nor a dyke; neither a faggot, a gender dysphoric, nor a woman-loving woman; neither physiologically abnormal nor psychically fucked up, Volcano is precisely what herm claims, what herm makes hermself: "a gender abolitionist, a part-time gender terrorist, an intentional mutation."

The question is: can you see herm? Diffractive perception allows us to do so, to witness chimeric and monstrous forms of becoming in all their complexity.

Monstrosity and Gender Nonconformance

In 1994, in the third issue of then-fledgling GLQ—the journal that would play a decisive role in the academic institutionalization and legitimization of queer theory—Susan Stryker published her essay "My Words to Victor Frankenstein above the Village of Chamounix: Performing Transgender Rage." This text, an expanded version of a performance Stryker gave at a 1993 conference at California State University, San Marcos, would go on to become an ur-text of sorts for what has come to be known as transgender studies. Stryker herself would go on to help found T*SQ, an academic journal that aims to be "the journal of record for the rapidly consolidating interdisciplinary field of transgender studies."[14]

This brief contextual description of the essay's publication is important because it signals that inclusion of transgender issues within queer theory and LGBT studies has come coupled with a critical mobilization of monstrosity. In other words, queer theory, trans studies, and "monster studies" are complexly intertwined. I'd like to think, through a close engagement with this foundational text of Stryker's, about why monstrosity has come to function as such a rich locus of intellectual and political investment for trans and gender-nonconforming folks. Why does monstrosity resonate so deeply for us? What can we learn from this resonance?

I wrote, at the outset of this book, that "what we need today, to resist the violences entailed by late modern disavowals of corporeal difference, is a coalition of monsters—those beings that embrace corporeal nonnormativity, hybridity, and mixity as a source of strength and resilience capable of challenging understandings of extraordinary bodies as pathological, aberrant, and undesirable." I now want to flesh out what I mean by a "coalition of monsters." Monstrosity is a powerful trope that indexes categorical excess, liminality, and a refusal of neat identitarian codification. Monsters are difficult to pin down, only ever partially classifiable, singular and unpredictable entities that work to trouble epistemological certainties and unsettle the ostensibly natural order of things.

The function of the monster as epistemological troublemaker is empowering and resonant for trans, intersex, and gender-nonconforming folks. In taking a critical stance in relation to the constitutive criteria for maleness and femaleness, one that troubles the distinctions between dyadic gender categories as well as the line between nature and artifice, we function as troublemakers, or what Sara Ahmed has termed "unhappiness causes."[15]

Ahmed analyzes the ways in which queer subjectivities are framed as both inevitably unhappy—on account of marginalization and ostracism by the dominant, heterofamilial social order—as well as "unhappiness causes," persons who generate unhappiness within the dominant order on account of their rejection of its rigidly gendered, heterosexist logics of inclusion, particularly those that manifest in the form of what Lee Edelman has called "reproductive futurism."[16] In other words, those beings that refuse to act in the name of the Child in order to reify and naturalize heterofamilial structure across generations, thus securing a future social order undergirded by the same heterosexist, reproductively oriented logic governing current hegemonic organizations of intimacy and belonging, are understood both as inevitably estranged from the promise of the "good life" and a source of affective dissonance and threat to those invested in the logic of reproductive futurism.

Long before Edelman authored his well-known polemic against the figure of the Child in *No Future*, long before Ahmed wrote about the unhappy queer, Stryker theorized a poignant exemplar of a being who troubled, railed against, caused unhappiness within, even decimated this dimorphic-ally gendered, heterofamilial, reproductively focused order: Frankenstein's monster. He is a product of positivist science whose existence far outstrips the intentions of the maker, a sentience called into being through the work of a man obsessed with replicating the wondrous, who turns against the maker and thus transgresses Frankenstein's fantasy of ontological mastery. A being thrown into a world with no habitable place for him. A destroyer of the heterofamilial order by way of revenge, murdering Victor Frankenstein's loved ones as retribution for being forced into this placeless, peripatetic, lonely existence. A being who wants company, wants intimacy, wants dis-course, care, empathy, and touch, but cannot easily access any of these on account of signifying as a repository of the dominant culture's greatest fears and phobias. A being who takes to the wilderness, finding some measure of solace in this outside dwelling absented from the judgment, fear, and derision of conventional humans.

It is the monster's rage, loneliness, and desire for an alternative social order that seems to motivate Stryker's identification:

The transsexual body is an unnatural body. It is the product of medical science. It is a technological construction. It is flesh torn apart and sewn together again in a shape other than that in which it was born. In these circumstances, I find a deep affinity between myself as a trans-sexual woman and the monster in Mary Shelley's *Frankenstein*. Like the monster, I am too often perceived as less than fully human due to the means of my embodiment; like the monster's as well, my exclusion from human community fuels a deep and abiding rage in me that I, like the monster, direct against the conditions in which I must struggle to exist.[17]

Identification with Frankenstein's monster precipitates something more than a desire for assimilation and inclusion within the normative "human community," however. While the comfort and security this mode of social organization affords are desired—for instance, the ability to not face consistent macro- and microaggressions in the realm of employment, housing, education, and everyday social interaction, or the ability to feel protected and supported both formally through legal and institutional reform measures and informally by accessible structures of interpersonal support—it is not yoked to an investment in inclusion that would leave the heterofamilial, dimorphic order of sociality unchanged.

Rather, the consistent and quotidian struggle to exist produces alternative pathways to community formation, support, intimacy, and belonging. This begins with a reclamation of monstrosity, a resistant rending of the term from its pejorative, Gothic, deeply othering associations:

> I want to lay claim to the dark power of my monstrous identity without using it as a weapon against others or being wounded by it myself. I will say this as bluntly as I know how: I am a transsexual, and therefore I am a monster. . . . Words like "creature," "monster," and "unnatural" need to be reclaimed by the transgendered. By embracing and accepting them, even piling one on top of another, we may dispel their ability to harm us. A creature, after all, in the dominant tradition of Western European culture, is nothing other than a created being, a made thing. The affront you humans take at being called a "creature" results from the threat the term poses to your status as "lords of creation," beings elevated above mere material existence.[18]

What does it mean to reclaim monstrosity? I think it is nothing short of the embrace of a specifically antihumanist ontology, one with possible decolonial potential. To embrace one's status as a "made thing" is to reject the fallacies of human autonomy, individualism, and self-sovereignty so central to modern Eurocentric conceptions of human being. This understanding of being as fundamentally "made" or "created" opens onto a conceptualization of the human as constructed, embedded in milieus not ever entirely of its choosing, fundamentally interrelational and nonsovereign. This reconceptualization of being stems from the deep ambiguity of monstrosity. On the one hand, the monster is a fabrication, a production of the dominant culture that serves to give flesh and form to otherness, to contain and manage the fear of difference, and to shore up through contrariety normative modes of being and identity. On the other, monstrosity is a semaphore of sorts, signaling the possibility of living otherwise or refusing dominant logics of gender, of the family, and of possessive individualism and inventing other styles of existence, other modes of embodiment and relation. Reclaiming monstrosity means, as Stryker writes above, coming to grips with one's status as a made thing, simultaneously understanding the dominant culture's fabrication of monstrosity while working this fabrication of alterity and otherness in resistant and liberatory ways, embracing as desirable the failure to assimilate to hegemonic modes of social belonging and social reproduction.

In other words, Stryker's essay enables us to reimagine monstrosity beyond the hackneyed conventions that typically shape it; chief among these is the relegation of the monster to a position of outsiderhood—whether, like Frankenstein's monster, the harsh terrain of the French Alps or, like medieval and early modern monsters, a dwelling at the margins of the colonial imaginary. What would it mean to think monstrosity beyond outsiderhood?

Beyond Outsiderhood:
Rethinking Tropes of Gender Nonconformance
We typically think of monsters as inhabiting borderlands, margins, peripheries, underworlds; if they dwell in the same spaces as normative beings, it tends to be in an illicit, mysterious, fugitive, or secretive way. This is also the way we tend to think of gender and sexual outlaws—even that term, *outlaw*, signifies a being outside of or in excess of social regulation and convention. However, when it comes to both monstrosity and gender (and the complex interweavings of these terms that I've been exploring), I don't think there is an outside. This is not a particularly popular claim in the field of women's, gender, and sexuality studies; those of us working in this area have learned and utilized, over and over again, heuristics that rely on a spatial

imaginary enabled through the dyad of centricity and marginality. Think of Rubin's formulation of the "charmed circle" of sexual normativity and the "outer limits" of perversion, deviance, and abnormality in "Thinking Sex" or Butler's theorization of the "constitutive outside" in *Bodies That Matter*. The outside, the margins, the limits: each of these overlapping tropes operates as a "domain of abjected bodies" or "field of deformation" that produces, through contradistinction, the highly regulatory gendered schema that Butler has termed "the heterosexual matrix."[19] It is important to remember that this matrix also accounts for the production of an expectation of continuity between birth sex and gender performance and could therefore just as easily be referred to as the cisgender matrix.

The spatial imaginary that informs this constitutive outside—that space of unlivability where gender and sexual transgressors, misfits, and weirdos supposedly dwell—seems somewhat like the margins of early modern European maps, where monsters (dragons and such) populate those unknown, partially known, much speculated-upon territories at the periphery of familiar lands. While I think that this framework for understanding the production of legible, properly gendered subjects has been enormously useful, I think it is also important to consider the limitations of the spatial imaginary that structures its logic.

Here's a question deceptive in its simplicity: where is this constitutive outside? Is it a mythic realm? Is it a set of locations interwoven with that familiar world that we, whether trans, queer, gender nonconforming or not, must navigate daily? Is it in those decentered, dispersed nodes—bars, bedrooms, queer communes, queer squats—where gender transitivity and transgression are (sometimes tenuously) valorized? Is it possible that it is, actually, nowhere, only a theoretical placeholder meant to explain the production of legibly gendered subjects but otherwise limited in its utility? I have a hunch that this may be so, mostly because I have no workable answer to this question of location. Who could possibly live in a non-place? Who could actually inhabit this "constitutive outside"?

What I'm suggesting, in other words, is that there is no *there* there; there is no non-place, no locatable constitutive outside, and that this spatial imaginary—even if we understand it only as a metaphor or heuristic tool—is actually quite unhelpful if we are concerned with ameliorating the conditions of unlivability and existential difficulty that contemporary gender-nonconforming and queer subjects experience. If there is no out-side, then there is no subject who dwells there; no subjectivity could form in an outside.

To reclaim monstrosity, to make it work as a resistant concept for trans, queer, intersex, and gender-nonconforming folks, we must imagine the monster differently, as something other than a being that exists beyond the realm of the natural order, that threatens to disrupt the logic of the natural from a position outside of it. Instead, perhaps we can imagine monsters in quotidian ways, consider their home places, the fraught complexities of their daily lives. We can try to think of monsters as communal, relational constructions enabled by, and in need of, networks of support, rather than considering them as extravagant, aberrant, abject, alone, misunderstood—the way they tend to be thought of by dominant culture.

Monsters conventionally operate as figures of outsiderhood. And I'm more and more convinced that thinking of trans, intersex, and gender-nonconforming folks as cultural outsiders is none-too-helpful in devel-oping intricate accounts of the existential difficulties we confront and how those existential difficulties are absolutely nonexceptional. Financial and emotional precarity, the debilitating effects of macro- and microag-gressions, difficulty accessing tools that enable holistic self-care—these linked phenomena shape many more lives than the trope of outsiderhood allows us to consider. If monstrosity is to be conceptually useful, it must be thought differently—as common, as quotidian, as a phenomenological orientation that enables more liberatory ways of building and inhabiting spaces of resistance and flourishing. Political philosopher Antonio Negri has argued, in a meditation on the reclamation of monstrosity (what he calls the "becoming-monstrous of life"), that "little by little in the history of the world, the monster, from his position 'outside,' comes to occupy the 'inside,'" drawing the conclusion that "the monster has been inside all the time, because his political exclusion is not the consequence, but the premise, of his productive inclusion."[20] The monster, even when posited as outside, is always actually serving a function internal to dominant culture; being labeled a monstrous being is a means through which a dominant culture exploits those beings within its domain of force through relegation to the status of sub- or nonhuman. Thus, reclaiming monstrosity is a mode of resisting the violence and denigration this entails without succumbing to assimilation, the demand to erase alterity.

I also worry that the marginality and centricity dyad is too closely yoked to reductive debates about radicalism and assimilation, in which outsiderhood is too neatly linked to queer radicality. My hunch is that this link produces a whole lot of posturing in relation to subcultural credibility and not as much pragmatic political action and empathic support as it could. Moreover, it presumes a neat division between normativity and resistance, a division ill-equipped to consider the complex complicities and concessions all subjects are forced to make in late-capitalist, neoliberal milieus. As José Esteban Muñoz reminded us well over a decade ago, a political terrain structured by assimilation and anti-assimilation is quite incapable of doing justice to disidentificatory practices, those modes of queer self-fashioning that are about tactical misrecognition, improper interpellations, and desire-with-a-difference that occur not outside but within, on, and, against fluctuating structures of power.[21]

Engaging these issues means developing a more relational ontology and in doing so building a different vocabulary to speak about trans and queer selfhood. Karen Barad's work on what she calls "agential realism," "quantum entanglement," and "intra-action" is useful in the line of inquiry I'm trying to sketch here. She moves beyond the treatment of materiality and discursivity as separate domains in order to think how matter is more than a "mere effect of discursive practices, but rather an agentive factor in its iterative materialization." Materiality and discursivity, here, are understood as ontologically inseparable, which means "body talk" is a transformative social and political force, not merely imprinted or molded and not ever able to be neatly relegated to a place beyond, outside, or squarely in the margins of the social. She considers what she calls the "world's performativity" as composed of phenomena and understands phenomena as an "entanglement of spacetimemagmatter," which means that, necessarily, it is quite difficult to decide the boundaries of phenomena; Barad goes so far as to claim that most objectifications are actually heuristic strategies that don't ever quite do justice to the reality of ontological entanglement.[22] Taking ontological entanglement seriously entails thinking about intra-activity rather than inter-activity. This means that parts—subjects, institutions, economic circuits—are never discrete but always enfolded, enmeshed, inextricably intertwined.

The spatial imaginary at work here is much more complex than the marginality and centricity dyad, and I think considering processes of queer and trans subjection and subjectivation through the analytic of entanglement or intra-action is capable of producing more robust accounts of experience, more useful political stratagems, and more intricate understandings of embodiment. By way of example, I'd like to consider a brief excerpt from Paul Preciado's *Testo-Junkie* on taking testosterone. It is very much written in the spirit of entanglement, becoming, and attentiveness to neoliberal complicities:

> Of all the mental and physical effects caused by self-intoxification based on testosterone in gel form, the feeling of transgressing limits of gender that have been socially imposed on me was without a doubt the most intense. The new metabolism of testosterone in my body wouldn't be effective in terms of masculinization without the previous existence of a political agenda that interprets these changes as an integral part of a desire—controlled by the pharmacopornographic order [Preciado's term of the technical/semiotic systems that mold and control the affective potential of bodies]—for sex change. Without this desire, without the project of being in transit from one fiction of sex to another, taking testosterone would never be anything but a molecular becoming.[23]

Here, transmasculine transformation is not about outsiderhood or marginality but rather a phenomenon that assumes meaning through a complex cocktail of biomolecular transformation, dimorphic fictions of gender, the circuits of hormone extraction and production (embedded as they are within neoliberal and neocolonial processes at work in production, drug trials, distribution, and access), the gray-market acquisition of hormones by uninsured subjects—the list could go on. The point is that, to do justice to the entangled, interwoven processes at work in the materialization of a gender-nonconforming body, we need an analytic that reconceptualizes Barad's "spacetimematter" in a mode not limited to the flat metaphor of center and margins.

The monster, at least within Stryker's reappraisal, is an excellent trope through which to think Barad's alternative ontology of phenomenological entanglement. Reclaiming monstrosity begins with the rejection of Western humanist conceptions of being, hyperindividualized and formative of subjectivities compatible with the violence and expropriation endemic to neocolonial capitalism, and pursues a reconceptualization of being that is creaturely, built, interrelational, and resistant to logics of dominance that devalorize and denigrate alterity.

Monstrosity as Coalitional Concept

The reclamation of monstrosity can work as a means of establishing connection and coalition between radical and progressive left movements that cohere around the realities of interlocking forms of oppression. While I don't want to suggest that monstrosity necessarily works as a common ground, I think it can denote a certain shared structure of feeling borne out of the experience of being marked, construed, or metaphorized as monstrous.

In suggesting that there may be a resonant structure of feeling common to experiences—historical and contemporary—of monstrous construal and that the predominant feelings that frame this structure are those of coping with derision and violence, rage, loneliness, lack of recognition, misunderstanding, and misinterpretation, I am not far away from suggesting that what is shared, or what connects trans, queer, and other forms of minoritarian struggle is traumatic experience. Positing trauma as an integral part of the weave that makes up radical coalition is necessarily a move to deindividuate and depathologize trauma. I follow Ann Cvetkovich in this; she has written extensively on trauma's role in the creation of queer public cultures and articulates trauma as "a social and cultural discourse that emerges in response to the demands of grappling with the psychic consequences of historical events."[24] Exploring trauma as a shared structure of feeling is one way of thinking about how we deal—and how we could deal differently—with the quotidian negativity that emerges from experiences of subalterity, being treated as less than or other than human. In understanding trauma as a complex response, simultaneously personal and public, to historicopolitical conditions of violence, abuse, censure, and delegitimization, we can think more adequately about how trauma can work as a prod to create empathic affective bonds that heal, that enable resilience, transformation, and flourishing.

Identifying resonant sources of pain, anger, and rage—monstrous construal among them—pushes political movements past a concern with formalized, institutional barriers to rights and attends to the affective dimensions of oppression. Cvetkovich's understanding of trauma blurs the distinction between the public and the personal, precipitating a focus on negative affect as public, shared, and deindividuated. Reclaiming monstrosity is a means of both distancing oneself from normalizing demands and embracing devalorized aspects of subjectivity and community as integral to inventing new styles of being and new ways of inhabiting the social. It is thus a means of coping with and perhaps healing from trauma communally in coalition and resistance.

To consider monstrosity in relation to coalition-building is to think of it in universalizing rather than minoritizing terms. It is to think of monstrosity as something that links folks across lines of difference. We should not think of monstrosity as a way of naming a ghettoized, delimited, and determinate subset of beings, but rather consider the ways we all negotiate monstrosity in the practice of building self and community, the ways in which we variously participate in the taxa that produce monsters. Monstrosity is a powerful trope because it is integral to the formation of proper citizen-subjects as well as those deemed sub-alter. It is also a mobile and mutable concept—as Asa Simon Mittman puts it, what makes a monster a monster is not its embodiment, location, or "the processes through which it enacts its being" but its *impact*. What is this impact? Mittman writes that "above all, the monstrous is that which creates this sense of vertigo, that which calls into question our (their, anyone's) epistemological worldview, highlights its fragmentary nature, and thereby asks us . . . to acknowledge the failure of our systems of categorization." What unites monsters, then, is this ability to force epistemological crises, to trouble "common" sense and "natural" orders, to prompt recognition of personal implication in oppressive systems of categorization. Monstrosity as coalition is not about identifying the discrete functions of specific manifestations of subalterity but about moving from those discrete manifestations toward a universalizing perspective that recognizes the ability of monstrous reclamation to disrupt and denaturalize heterosexist, cissexist, Eurocentric hierarchy and prompts those with naturalized privilege to confront that status as a made, constructed—and therefore fragile, contestable, and paranoiacally defended—phenomenon. As Stryker writes, "You are as constructed as me; the same anarchic womb has birthed us both. I call upon you to investigate your nature as I have been compelled to confront mine. I challenge you to risk abjection and flourish as well as have I. Heed my words, and you may well discover the seams and sutures in yourself."[25] Reclaiming monstrosity is a means of embracing agency in the process of fashioning new modes of being, affirming one's creaturely—made and nonsovereign—status, a way of refusing abjection in relation to hegemonic values, and a movement toward affirming and supporting alterity, linking struggles to construct an ethics of being-in-resistance. Siding with monsters, embracing the monsters we are, is a powerful means of inventing ways of inhabiting this world differently, within and against racist cishetero supremacy that understands different logics of being, relation, intimacy, and community as signs of tamable, correctable excess.

NOTES

Introduction

1. Foucault, *Herculine Barbin*, xiii.
2. Haraway, *Modest_Witness@Second_Millennium*, 23.
3. Schapiro and Wilding, "Cunts/Quilts/Consciousness."
4. Barad, *Meeting the Universe Halfway*. 33.

Prologue

1. McWhorter, *Bodies and Pleasures*, 4.
2. Fausto-Sterling, *Sexing the Body*, 7.
3. Fausto-Sterling, *Sexing the Body*, 252.
4. Butler, *Gender Trouble*, xix–xx.
5. Butler, *Gender Trouble*, 191.
6. Bartky, *Femininity and Domination*, 63–64.
7. Butler, *Gender Trouble*, 22.
8. Spade, *Normal Life*, 11.
9. Butler, *Gender Trouble*, 42.
10. Butler, "Imitation and Gender Insubordination," 310.
11. Butler, "Imitation and Gender Insubordination," 311.
12. Foucault, *History of Sexuality*, 1:10.
13. Grosz, "Bergson, Deleuze," 4.

1. Queer Monsters

1. I use *her* here as a provisional pronoun, not a declaration of the truth of Barbin's gender identity.
2. Butler, *Gender Trouble*, 127–50; McWhorter, *Bodies and Pleasures*, 199–208; Spivak, "Ethics and Politics," 17–31.
3. Muñoz, *Disidentifications*, 31.
4. While in contemporary parlance the preferred nomenclature for conditions of ambiguous or indeterminate sex is *intersex* or *disorders of sex development*, I have opted to use the problematic term *hermaphrodite* to refer to these conditions, as

it is historically accurate with reference to Barbin's case as well as being the term Foucault used in his mentions of folks with intersex conditions.

5. Sedgwick, *Touching Feeling*, 149.

6. Foucault, *Hermeneutics of the Subject*, 17.

7. Foucault, "On the Genealogy of Ethics," 254.

8. Foucault, "About the Beginnings," 203.

9. Foucault, "About the Beginnings," 203. Deleuze, *Foucault*, 104.

10. Allen, *Politics of Our Selves*, 47.

11. Foucault, *Abnormal*, 63.

12. Daston and Park, *Wonders and the Order*, 13, 14.

13. Daston and Park, *Wonders and the Order*, 63, 64.

14. For a thorough account of the development of the diagnosis of "pseudohermaphroditism" and the gradual eradication of "true hermaphroditism," see Dreger, *Hermaphrodites and the Medical*, 139–66.

15. Dreger, *Hermaphrodites and the Medical*, 16.

16. Foucault, *Herculine Barbin*, 127–28.

17. Foucault, *Herculine Barbin*, vii.

18. Dreger, *Hermaphrodites and the Medical*, 141, 142.

19. Fausto-Sterling, *Sexing the Body*, 36.

20. Dreger, *Hermaphrodites and the Medical*, 146.

21. Foucault, *Herculine Barbin*, xii.

22. Dreger, *Hermaphrodites and the Medical*, 23.

23. Foucault, *Herculine Barbin*, x.

24. Foucault, *Abnormal*, 64.

25. Foucault, *Herculine Barbin*, 119.

26. Proust, "The Line of Resistance," 27.

27. Roth, "Foucault's 'History,'" 44.

28. Foucault, *Herculine Barbin*, xiii.

29. Butler, *Gender Trouble*, 131, 135.

30. Butler, *Gender Trouble*, 134–35.

31. Foucault, *Herculine Barbin*, 119.

32. Mak, *Doubting Selves*, 84.

33. Mak, *Doubting Selves*, 68.

34. Jones and Stallybrass, "Fetishizing Gender," 90.

35. Foucault, *Herculine Barbin*, 99.

36. Foucault, *Herculine Barbin*, 99.

37. Foucault, *Herculine Barbin*, 103.

38. Garland-Thomson, *Extraordinary Bodies*, 55–63.

capacity

1. Young, "Throwing Like a Girl," 34.

2. Whitman, *Complete Poems*, 127.

2. Impossible Existences

1. Ariel Levy, "Either/Or," *New Yorker*, November 30, 2009.

2. Jeremy Hodges, "Dewey Takes up Semenya Case in IAAF Dispute," *Legal Week*, September 21, 2009.

3. Levy, "Either/Or."

4. Levy, "Either/Or."

5. Davis, *Contesting Intersex*, 14, 70.

6. Kessler, *Lessons from the Intersexed*, 132.

7. Holmes, *Intersex*, 138.

8. Holmes, *Intersex*, 155, 90.

9. Intersex Society of North America, "Dear ISNA Friends and Supporters," accessed January 2, 2018, http://www.isna.org/farewell_message.

10. Intersex Society of North America, "Dear ISNA Friends."

11. Fausto-Sterling, *Sexing the Body*, 59.

12. Intersex Society of North America, "Dear ISNA Friends."

13. Emi Koyama, "From Intersex to 'DSD': Toward a Queer Disability Politics of Gender," Intersex Initiative, http://intersexinitiative.org/articles/intersextodsd .html.

14. Geographic distance coupled with an institutionally engendered secrecy that often motivates a refusal to disclose of one's intersex condition in quotidian circumstances have rendered the constitution of an intersex community in "real" space-time difficult. Thus, any tenuous reference to intersex community must highlight its primarily virtual constitution or, as Morgan Holmes puts it, its "virtual situatedness" (Holmes, *Intersex*, 64).

15. Koyama, "From Intersex to 'DSD.'"

16. Feder, "Imperatives of Normality," 239.

17. Feder, "Imperatives of Normality," 239.

18. Feder, "Imperatives of Normality," 240.

19. Feder, "Imperatives of Normality," 240.

20. Alice Dreger, "Why 'Disorders of Sex Development'? (On Language and Life)," accessed January 2, 2018, http://alicedreger.com/dsd.html.

21. Money, Hampson, and Hampson, "An Examination," 302.

22. Money, Hampson, and Hampson, "An Examination," 310.

23. Money, Hampson, and Hampson, "An Examination," 310.

24. Money, Potter, and Stoller, "Sex Reannouncement," 215.
25. Howard Jones went on to cofound the Johns Hopkins Gender Identity Disorder Clinic with Money in 1965.
26. Karkazis, *Fixing Sex*, 50–51.
27. Rosario, "Quantum Sex," 280.
28. Dreger, "Why 'Disorders'"?

repair

1. Fausto-Sterling, Sexing the Body, 45.

3. Gone, Missing

1. Lugones, "Heterosexualism and the Colonial," 186.
2. Money, Hampson, and Hampson, "An Examination," 285.
3. Money, Hampson, and Hampson, "Hermaphroditism," 295.
4. Money, Hampson, and Hampson, "Hermaphroditism," 295.
5. Fausto-Sterling, *Sexing the Body*, 79; Kessler, *Lessons from the Intersexed*, 105–32; Dreger, *Hermaphrodites and the Medical*, 190; Reis, *Bodies in Doubt*, 157; Davis, *Contesting Intersex*, 157.
6. Meyerowitz, *How Sex Changed*, 284.
7. Spade, "Resisting Medicine," 21–22.
8. Spade, "Resisting Medicine," 23.
9. Serano, *Whipping Girl*, 67.
10. Serano, *Whipping Girl*, 72.
11. Preciado, *Testo-Junkie*, 134, 137.
12. Preciado, *Testo-Junkie*, 21.
13. Preciado, *Testo-Junkie*, 313, 315, 318.
14. Money, "Psychology of Intersexes," 187.
15. Snorton and Haritaworn, "Trans Necropolitics," 66–76.
16. Ahmed, *Promise of Happiness*, 41.
17. Premarin has come under heavy censure in the first decade of the twenty-first century following a longitudinal study documenting its link to endometrial cancer, strokes, blood clots, and breast cancer and is now prescribed less frequently.
18. Money, *Biographies of Gender*, 45.
19. Lugones, "Toward a Decolonial Feminism," 745.
20. Skidmore, "Constructing the 'Good Transsexual,'" 271.
21. Skidmore, "Constructing the 'Good Transsexual,'" 292.

on sight

1. McClintock, *Imperial Leather*, 23.

4. Black Bar, Queer Gaze

1. Foucault, *Herculine Barbin*, vii.

2. Agamben, *"What Is an Apparatus,"* 424–73, 14.

3. Laqueur, *Making Sex*, 135, 26–28, 10; Karkazis, *Fixing Sex*, 36.

4. Klebs, *Handbuch*, 718; Foucault, *Herculine Barbin*, ix.

5. Foucault, *Birth of the Clinic*, 30–31.

6. Dreger, *Hermaphrodites*, 20, 23.

7. Foucault, *Birth of the Clinic*, 29.

8. Haraway, *Modest_Witness*, 23–29.

9. Deleuze and Guattari, *A Thousand Plateaus*, 175.

10. Deleuze and Guattari, *A Thousand Plateaus*, 176.

11. Deleuze and Guattari, *A Thousand Plateaus*, 177.

12. Deleuze and Guattari, *A Thousand Plateaus*, 177.

13. Warner Marien, *Photography*, 42.

14. Williams, *Hard Core*, 49.

15. Foucault, *History of Sexuality*, 1:43.

16. Money, "Hermaphroditism," 483.

17. Solomon-Godeau, "The Woman," 337; LTTR Artist Statement, accessed April 16, 2018, http://www.lttr.org/about-lttr.

18. Blume, "Mesh," 24, 23.

19. Schapiro and Wilding, "Cunts/Quilts/Consciousness," 7; Meyer, "Hard Targets," 369.

20. Jerry Saltz, "The Venus of Long Island City," *New York Magazine*, March 27, 2008.

21. Moyer, "United Society of Believers," 392.

22. Braidotti, *Nomadic Subjects*, 191.

23. Halberstam, *In a Queer Time*, 105.

24. Halberstam, *In a Queer Time*, 111.

25. Steinbock, "Generative Negatives," 546.

5. State Science

1. Foucault, *History of Sexuality*, 1:147.

2. Money, Hampson, and Hampson, "Hermaphroditism," 284.

3. Money, Hampson, and Hampson, "An Examination," 319, 302.

4. Money, Hampson, and Hampson, "An Examination," 302.

5. Money, Hampson, and Hampson, "An Examination," 302.

6. Repo, "The Biopolitical Birth," 240.

7. Foucault, *History of Sexuality*, 1:53.

8. Foucault, *Society Must Be Defended*, 242.

9. Foucault, *Society Must Be Defended*, 242, 243.

10. Foucault, *Society Must Be Defended*, 244, 256, 242.

11. Foucault, *Society Must Be Defended*, 252.

12. Foucault, *Society Must Be Defended*, 252.

13. Foucault, *Society Must Be Defended*, 258.

14. Deleuze and Guattari, *Anti-Oedipus*, xiv.

15. Hardt, "Affective Labor," 99.

16. Lazzarato, "From Biopower to Biopolitics," 108–9.

17. Hardt, "Affective Labor," 98.

18. Deleuze and Guattari, *A Thousand Plateaus*, 385.

19. American Psychiatric Association, DSM-5.

20. Spade, "Resisting Medicine," 24, 25.

21. Massumi, *Parables for the Virtual*, 166.

22. Meyerowitz, *How Sex Changed*, 145.

23. Meyerowitz, *How Sex Changed*, 158, 161.

24. Meyerowitz, *How Sex Changed*, 220, 221.

25. Meyerowitz, *How Sex Changed*, 254.

26. Deleuze and Guattari, *A Thousand Plateaus*, 362.

27. Stryker, "My Words to Frankenstein," 238; Stone, "The Empire Strikes Back," 330; Spade, *Normal Life*; Spade, "Mutilating Gender"; Spade, "Resisting Medicine"; Crawford, "Transgender without Organs," 134.

mirrors

1. Lugones, *Pilgrimages/Peregrinajes*, 89, 97.

6. Toward Coalition

1. de Beauvoir, *The Second Sex*, 267.

2. Deleuze and Guattari, *A Thousand Plateaus*, 212.

3. Deleuze and Guattari, *A Thousand Plateaus*, 210, 215.

4. Austin, *How to Do Things*, 1–11.

5. Deleuze and Guattari, *A Thousand Plateaus*, 89.

6. Deleuze and Guattari, *A Thousand Plateaus*, 238.

7. Deleuze and Guattari, *A Thousand Plateaus*, 106.

8. Butler, *Undoing Gender*, 81.

9. Butler, *Undoing Gender*, 212.

10. Del LaGrace Volcano, "Artist's statement," accessed April 16, 2018, http://www.dellagracevolcano.com/statement.html; Del LaGrace Volcano and Indra Windh, "Hermlove," accessed April 16, 2018, http://www.dellagracevolcano.com/text2.html.

11. Volcano, "Artist's statement."

12. Haraway, "The Promises of Monsters," 300.

13. Volcano and Windh, "Hermlove"; Haraway, "The Promises of Monsters," 300.

14. Currah and Stryker, "Introduction," 1.

15. Ahmed, *Promise of Happiness*, 88.

16. Edelman, *No Future*, 4.

17. Stryker, "My Words to Frankenstein," 238.

18. Stryker, "My Words to Frankenstein," 240.

19. Rubin, "Thinking Sex," 267–93; Butler, *Bodies That Matter*, 3; Butler, *Gender Trouble*, 1–32.

20. Casarino and Negri, *In Praise*, 208.

21. Muñoz, *Disidentifications*.

22. Barad, *Meeting the Universe Halfway*, 71–96; Barad, "Nature's Queer Performativity," 13.

23. Preciado, *Testo-Junkie*, 143.

24. Cvetkovich, *An Archive of Feelings*, 18.

25. Mittman, "Impact of Monsters," 7, 8; Stryker, "My Words to Frankenstein," 242.

BIBLIOGRAPHY

Agamben, Giorgio. *"What Is an Apparatus" and Other Essays.* Stanford CA: Stanford University Press, 2009.

Ahmed, Sara. *The Promise of Happiness.* Durham NC: Duke University Press, 2010.

Allen, Amy. *The Politics of Our Selves: Power, Autonomy, and Gender in Contemporary Critical Theory.* New York: Columbia University Press, 2008.

American Psychiatric Association. *Diagnostic and Statistical Manual of Mental Disorders.* 5th ed. American Psychiatric Association, 2013.

Austin, J. L. *How to Do Things with Words.* Cambridge MA: Harvard University Press, 1975.

Barad, Karen. *Meeting the Universe Halfway: Quantum Physics and the Entanglement of Matter and Meaning.* Durham NC: Duke University Press, 2007.

———. "Nature's Queer Performativity." *Kvinder, Køn og forskning* (Women, Gender and Research), no. 1–2 (2012): 25–53.

Bartky, Sandra Lee. *Femininity and Domination: Studies in the Phenomenology of Oppression.* New York: Routledge, 1990.

Blacker, G. F., and T. W. P. Lawrence. "A Case of True Unilateral Hermaphroditism with Ovotestis Occurring in Man, with a Summary and Criticism of the Recorded cases of Tue Hermaphroditism." In *Transactions of the Obstetrical Society of London,* edited by W. B. Dakin and Percy Boulton, 38. London: Longmans, Green, 1897.

Blume, Anna. "Mesh: The Tale of the Hermaphrodite." LTTR 4 (2005): 20–24.

Braidotti, Rosi. *Nomadic Subjects: Embodiment and Sexual Difference in Contemporary Feminist Theory.* New York: Columbia University Press, 1994.

Butler, Judith. *Bodies That Matter: On the Discursive Limits of "Sex."* New York: Routledge, 1993.

———. *Gender Trouble.* New York: Routledge, 1990.

———. "Imitation and Gender Insubordination." In *The Lesbian and Gay Studies Reader,* edited by Henry Abelove, Michele Aina Barale, and David Halperin, 307–20. New York: Routledge, 1993.

———. *Undoing Gender.* New York: Routledge, 2004.

Bibliography

Casarino, Cesare, and Antonio Negri. *In Praise of the Common: A Conversation on Philosophy and Politics*. Minneapolis: University of Minnesota Press, 2008.

Consortium on the Management of Disorders of Sex Development. *Handbook for Parents*. Rohnert Park CA: Intersex Society of North America, 2006.

Crawford, Lucas Cassidy. "Transgender without Organs?: Mobilizing a Geo-Affective Theory of Gender Modification." WSQ: *Women's Studies Quarterly* 36, no. 3 (2008): 127–43.

Currah, Paisley, and Susan Stryker. "Introduction." TSQ: *Transgender Studies Quarterly* 1, no. 1 (2014): 1–18.

Cvetkovich, Ann. *An Archive of Feelings: Trauma, Sexuality, and Lesbian Public Cultures*. Durham NC: Duke University Press, 2003.

Daston, Lorraine, and Katharine Park. *Wonders and the Order of Nature*. New York: Zone Books, 2001.

Davis, Georgiann. *Contesting Intersex: The Dubious Diagnosis*. New York: New York University Press, 2015.

de Beauvoir, Simone. *The Second Sex*. New York: Vintage, 2012.

Deleuze, Gilles. *Foucault*. Minneapolis: University of Minnesota Press, 1988.

Deleuze, Gilles, and Félix Guattari. *Anti-Oedipus: Capitalism and Schizophrenia*. New York: Penguin, 2009.

———. *A Thousand Plateaus*. Minneapolis: University of Minnesota Press, 1989.

Dreger, Alice. *Hermaphrodites and the Medical Invention of Sex*. Cambridge MA: Harvard University Press, 1998.

Edelman, Lee. *No Future: Queer Theory and the Death Drive*. Durham NC: Duke University Press, 2004.

Fausto-Sterling, Anne. *Sexing the Body: Gender Politics and the Construction of Sexuality*. New York: Basic Books, 2000.

Feder, Ellen K. "Imperatives of Normality: From 'Intersex' to 'Disorders of Sexual Development.'" GLQ 15, no. 2 (2009): 225–49.

Foucault, Michel. *Abnormal: Lectures at the Collège de France, 1974–75*. New York: Picador, 2003.

———. "About the Beginnings of the Hermeneutics of the Self: Two Lectures at Dartmouth." *Political Theory* 21, no. 22 (1993): 198–227.

———. *The Birth of the Clinic: An Archaeology of Medical Perception*. New York: Vintage Press, 1994.

———. *Herculine Barbin (Being the Recently Discovered Memoirs of a Nineteenth Century French Hermaphrodite)*. New York: Vintage, 1980.

———. *The Hermeneutics of the Subject: Lectures at the Collège de France, 1981–82*. New York: Picador, 2005.

———. *The History of Sexuality*. Volume 1: An Introduction. New York: Vintage, 1990.

———. *The History of Sexuality*. Volume 2: *The Use of Pleasure*. New York: Vintage, 1990.

———. *The History of Sexuality*. Volume 3: *The Care of the Self*. New York: Vintage, 1988.

———. "On the Genealogy of Ethics: An Overview of a Work in Progress." In *Ethics, Subjectivity, and Truth*, Volume 1 of *The Essential Works of Michel Foucault*, edited Paul Rabinow, 340–72. New York: New Press, 1997.

———. *Society Must Be Defended: Lectures at the Collège de France, 1975–1976*. New York: Picador, 2003.

Garland-Thomson, Rosemarie. *Extraordinary Bodies*. New York: Columbia University Press, 1996.

Grosz, Elizabeth. "Bergson, Deleuze, and the Becoming of Unbecoming." *Parallax* 11, no. 2 (2005): 4–13.

Halberstam. J. Jack. *In a Queer Time and Place: Transgender Bodies, Subcultural Lives*. New York: New York University Press, 2005.

Haraway, Donna. *Modest_Witness@Second_Millennium: FemaleMan_Meets_Onco-Mouse: Feminism and Technoscience*. New York: Routledge, 1997.

———. "The Promises of Monsters: A Regenerative Politics for Inappropriate/d Others." In *Cultural Studies*, edited by Lawrence Grossberg, Cary Nelson, and Paula Treichler, 295–337. New York: Routledge, 1992.

Hardt, Michael. "Affective labor." *boundary 2* 26, no. 2 (1999): 89–100.

Hardt, Michael, and Antonio Negri. *Commonwealth*. Cambridge MA: Harvard University Press, 2009.

———. *Empire*. Cambridge MA: Harvard University Press, 2001.

———. *Multitude: War and Democracy in the Age of Empire*. New York: Penguin, 2005.

Holmes, Morgan. *Intersex: A Perilous Difference*. Cranbury NJ: Susquehanna University Press, 2008.

Jones, Ann, and Peter Stallybrass. "Fetishizing Gender: Constructing the Hermaphrodite in Renaissance Europe." In *Body Guards: The Cultural Politics of Gender Ambiguity*, edited by Julia Epstein and Kristina Straub, 80–111. New York: Routledge, 1991.

Karkazis, Katrina. *Fixing Sex: Intersex, Medical Authority, and Lived Experience*. Durham NC: Duke University Press, 2008.

Kessler, Suzanne. *Lessons from the Intersexed*. New Brunswick NJ: Rutgers University Press, 1998.

Klebs, T. A. E. *Handbuch der Pathologischen Anatomie*. Berling: A. Hirschwald, 1876.

Laqueur, Thomas. *Making Sex: Body and Gender from the Greeks to Freud*. Cambridge MA: Harvard University Press, 1990.

Lee, Peter A., Christopher P. Houk, S. Faisal Ahmed, Ieuan A. Hughes. "Consensus Statement on the Management of Intersex Disorders." *Pediatrics* 118, no. 2 (2006): 488–500.

Bibliography

Lorde, Audre. "A Litany for Survival." In *The Black Unicorn*, 31–33. New York: Norton, 1995.

Lugones, María. "Heterosexualism and the Colonial/Modern Gender System." *Hypatia* 22, no. 1 (2007): 186–209.

———. "Toward a Decolonial Feminism," *Hypatia* 25, no. 4 (2010): 745–59.

Lazzarato, Maurizio. "From Biopower to Biopolitics." *Pli: The Warwick Journal of Philosophy* 13, no. 8 (2002): 1–6.

Mak, Geertje. *Doubting Selves: Inscriptions, Bodies, and Selves in Nineteenth-Century Hermaphrodite Case Histories*. Manchester, UK: Manchester University Press, 2012.

Massumi, Brian. *Parables for the Virtual*. Durham NC: Duke University Press, 2002.

McClintock, Anne. *Imperial Leather: Race, Gender, and Sexuality in the Colonial Contest*. New York: Routledge, 1995.

McWhorter, Ladelle. *Bodies and Pleasures*. Bloomington: Indiana University Press, 1999.

Meyer, Richard. "Hard Targets: Male Bodies, Feminist Art, and the Force of Censorship in the 1970s." In *WACK!: Art and the Feminist Revolution*, edited by Cornelia H. Butler, 362–83. Los Angeles: The Museum of Contemporary Art, 2007.

Meyerowitz, Joanne. *How Sex Changed: A History of Transsexuality in the United States*. Cambridge MA: Harvard University Press, 2004.

Mittman, Asa Simon. "The Impact of Monsters and Monster Studies." In *The Ashgate Research Companion to Monsters and the Monstrous*, edited by Asa Simon Mittman and Peter Dendle, 1–16. Surrey, UK: Ashgate, 2013.

Money, John. *Biographies of Gender and Hermaphroditism in Paired Comparisons*. Amsterdam: Elsevier, 1991.

———. "Hermaphroditism." In *Encyclopedia of Sexual Behavior*, edited by Albert Ellis and Albert Abarbanel, 472–84. New York: Hawthorn, 1961.

———. "Psychology of Intersexes." *Urologia Internationalis* 19 (1965): 185–89.

Money, John, Joan G. Hampson, and John L. Hampson. "An Examination of Some Basic Sexual Concepts: The Evidence of Human Hermaphroditism." *Bulletin of the Johns Hopkins Hospital* 97, no. 4 (1955): 301–19.

Money, John, Reynolds Potter, and Clarice S. Stoll. "Sex Reannouncement in Hereditary Sex Deformity: Psychology and Sociology of Habitation." *Society, Science, and Medicine* 3 (1969): 207–16.

Moyer, Carrie. "United Society of Believers." *Cultural Politics* 3, no. 3 (2007): 381–92.

Muñoz, José Esteban. *Disidentifications*. Minneapolis: University of Minnesota Press, 1999.

Preciado, Paul. *Testo-Junkie: Sex, Drugs, and Biopolitics in the Pharmacopornographic Era*. New York: Feminist Press, 2013.

Proust, Françoise, and Penelope Deutscher. "The Line of Resistance." *Hypatia* 15, no. 4 (2000): 23–37.

Reis, Elizabeth. *Bodies in Doubt: An American History of Intersex.* Baltimore MD: Johns Hopkins University Press, 2012.

Repo, Jemima. "The Biopolitical Birth of Gender: Social Control, Hermaphroditism, and the New Sexual Apparatus." *Alternatives: Global, Local, Political* 38, no. 3 (2013): 228–44.

Rosario, Vernon A. "Quantum Sex: Intersex and the Molecular Deconstruction of Sex." *GLQ* 15, no. 2 (2009): 267–82.

Roth, Michael S. "Foucault's 'History of the Present.'" *History and Theory* 20, no. 1 (1981): 32–46.

Rubin, Gayle. "Thinking Sex: Notes for a Radical Theory of the Politics of Sexuality." In *Pleasure and Danger: Exploring Female Sexuality*, edited by Carole S. Vance, 267–93. London: Pandora, 1992.

Schapiro, Miriam, and Faith Wilding. "Cunts/Quilts/Consciousness." *Heresies* 24 (1989): 6–13.

Sedgwick, Eve Kosofsky. *Touching Feeling.* Durham NC: Duke University Press, 2002.

Serano, Julia. *Whipping Girl: A Transsexual Woman on Sexism and the Scapegoating of Femininity.* Emeryville CA: Seal Press, 2007.

Skidmore, Emily. "Constructing the 'Good Transsexual': Christine Jorgensen, Whiteness, and Heteronormativity in the Mid-Twentieth-Century Press." *Feminist Studies* 37, no. 2 (2011): 270–300.

Snorton, C. Riley, and Jin Haritaworn. "Trans Necropolitics: A Transnational Reflection on Violence, Death, and the Trans of Color Afterlife." in *The Transgender Studies Reader*, Volume 2, edited by Aren Aizura and Susan Stryker, 66–76. New York: Routledge, 2013.

Solomon-Godeau, Abigail. "The Woman Who Never Was: Self-Representation, Photography, and First-Wave Feminist Art." In *WACK!: Art and the Feminist Revolution*, edited by Cornelia H. Butler, 337–45. Los Angeles: Museum of Contemporary Art, 2007.

Spade, Dean. "Mutilating Gender." In *The Transgender Studies Reader*, edited by Susan Stryker and Stephen Whittle, 315–32. New York: Routledge, 2006.

——. *Normal Life: Administrative Violence, Critical Trans Politics, and the Limits of Law.* Boston: South End Press, 2011.

——. "Resisting Medicine, Remodeling Gender." *Berkeley Women's Law Journal* 15 (2003): 15–37.

Spivak, Gayatri Chakravorty. "Ethics and Politics in Tagore, Coetzee, and Certain Scenes of Teaching." *Diacritics* 32, no. 3–4 (2002): 17–30.

Bibliography

Steinbock, Eliza. "Generative Negatives: Del LaGrace Volcano's Herm Body Photographs." *TSQ* 1, no. 4 (2014): 539–51.

Stone, Sandy. "The Empire Strikes Back: A Posttranssexual Manifesto." In *Body Guards: The Cultural Politics of Gender Ambiguity*, edited by Julia Epstein and Kristina Straub, 280–304. New York: Routledge, 1991.

Stryker, Susan. "My Words to Victor Frankenstein above the Village of Chamounix: Performing Transgender Rage." *GLQ* 1, no. 3 (1994): 237–54.

Warner Marien, Mary. *Photography: A Cultural History*. London: Laurence King, 2002.

Whitman, Walt. *Complete Poems*. New York: Penguin, 2004.

Williams, Linda. *Hard Core: Power, Pleasure, and the Frenzy of the Visible*. Berkeley: University of California Press, 1989.

Young, Iris Marion. "Throwing Like a Girl." In *On Female Body Experience: "Throwing Like a Girl" and Other Essays*, 27–45. New York: Oxford University Press, 2005.

INDEX

Page numbers in italic indicate illustrations.

CPSIA information can be obtained
at www.ICGtesting.com
Printed in the USA
LVHW092306190219
608124LV00004B/22/P